## Advance Praise for *Driven*

*"Darwin with an MBA. In this seminal work, Lawrence and Nohria combine their world-leading knowledge of organizational behavior with a deep understanding of our evolved human nature. Both managers and theorists will learn from this wide-ranging opus sure to change the way we view the bipedal ape in the corner office."*

—Terry Burnham, coauthor, *Mean Genes*

*"This book provides a fundamental, controversial, and wonderful explanation of human nature. It provokes you to think more deeply and broadly about what drives people and their institutions."*

—Andrew H. Van de Ven, president,
Academy of Management, and professor, Carlson
School of Management, University of Minnesota

*"A stunning, pathbreaking view of the natural biological impulses underlying human behavior and guiding organizational systems. A succinct, pungent case for the coevolution of biology and culture in forming human nature. Tom Peters, move over."*

—William C. Frederick, author, *Values, Nature,
and Culture in the American Corporation*

## A WARREN BENNIS BOOK

This collection of books is devoted exclusively to new and exemplary contributions to management thought and practice. The books in this series are addressed to thoughtful leaders, executives, and managers of all organizations who are struggling with and committed to responsible change. My hope and goal is to spark new intellectual capital by sharing ideas positioned at an angle to conventional thought—in short, to publish books that disturb the present in the service of a better future.

## BOOKS IN THE WARREN BENNIS SIGNATURE SERIES

# DRIVEN

# DRIVEN

## How Human Nature Shapes Our Choices

Paul R. Lawrence
Nitin Nohria

Foreword by E. O. Wilson

JOSSEY-BASS
A Wiley Imprint
www.josseybass.com

Published by Jossey-Bass
A Wiley Imprint
989 Market Street, San Francisco, CA 94103-1741    www.josseybass.com

Jossey-Bass books and products are available through most bookstores. To contact Jossey-Bass directly call our Customer Care Department within the U.S. at 800-956-7739, outside the U.S. at 317-572-3986 or fax 317-572-4002.

Jossey-Bass also publishes its books in a variety of electronic formats. Some content that appears in print may not be available in electronic books.

**Library of Congress Cataloging-in-Publication Data**

Lawrence, Paul R.
   Driven : how human nature shapes our choices / Paul R.
Lawrence, Nitin Nohria ; foreword by E. O. Wilson.
      p. cm.
   "A Warren Bennis book."
   Includes bibliographical references and index.
   ISBN 0-7879-6385-2 (alk. paper)
   1. Motivation (Psychology) I. Nohria, Nitin, 1962- II. Title.
BF503 .L39 2002b
153.8-dc21                                                2002008889

FIRST EDITION
*PB Printing*            10 9 8 7 6 5 4 3 2 1

# Contents

## PART FOUR
## HUMAN NATURE AND SOCIETY

# Figures and Table

# EDITOR'S NOTE

As an editor and writer, I'm always on the lookout for a perfect book. This one, written by two distinguished Harvard Business School professors, two generations apart in age and centuries apart culturally, is as close as it gets to fitting that bill. I am equally thrilled and proud to have *Driven* in the Warren Bennis Signature Series—where we attempt to publish works at "an angle to conventional thought."

In this book, Paul Lawrence and Nitin Nohria provide a thorough, integrated, and complete four-factor framework of human nature based on a stunning synthesis of the biological and social sciences. I could stop now—but as the TV commercials say, there's "much, much more." Among other attributes, it is a totally original work, applying the truths of one domain, the highly sophisticated biological and neurological sciences, to another, the embryonic and needy organizational sciences. That is a breathtaking achievement. As the authors write in their Preface, they have used the "petri dish" of human organizations as an especially fecund venue to test their ideas.

There is one other huge reason that you, the reader, will soon, I hope, come to agree with my attribution of perfection. When you dig in and begin to understand the four-drive framework of human nature, I doubt that you will ever look at your organization, your work group, your world, your family in the same way. Or yourself, for that matter. I also doubt that you will cling to or be content with a simplified hegemony of one basic *Uber Alles* motive anymore; the sort of stuff we read in the pages of economic texts that venerate acquisition and self-interest exclusively or in the classic

Freudian writings that elevate the psychosexual drive to the exclusion of others, or certainly in the faux-heroic pages of Ayn Rand.

What Lawrence and Nohria are after, and to a great extent achieve, is a unified theory of human nature based on four basic drives. In a nutshell, they conclude that all humans have a persistent drive to acquire objects, experiences, money, and so on to improve their status relative to others. *Acquisition.* But add to that, three other equally important drives: the need to bond with others in long-term, caring, committed relationships. *Social Networks.* The need to learn and make sense of the world around them. *Inquiry.* And, finally, the need to defend one's loved ones and resources from harm. *Safety.* Getting. Loving. Learning. Defending.

The authors proceed to demonstrate the scientific sources for the four-drive theory, how the drives are deployed in everyday life, and how understanding them will illuminate the darkness of our everyday lives.

One last, parting shot about a "perfect book." The Nobel Laureate physicist James Franck once said that he always recognized a good idea because of the feeling of terror that seized him. You'll soon see what I mean.

*Santa Monica, California*                              WARREN BENNIS
*August 2001*

# FOREWORD

*D*riven offers a partial resolution between two conflicting trends in Western culture. The first trend is the close meshing of basic and applied science. Scientific discovery is enhanced when it yields practical results: science, like art, depends on patronage. The second tendency, opposed to the first, is the uneasiness felt when biology is brought close to accounts of the human condition, and especially when it promises real-world applications. In this pathbreaking book, Paul R. Lawrence and Nitin Nohria show one way to relax the tension. The deep study of human nature, they argue, does not justify Social Darwinism and gladiatorial commercial combat of the kind often portrayed in popular media. On the contrary, it offers formulas for a more harmonious and efficient conduct of human affairs. The approach suggested by Lawrence and Nohria is naturalistic, based on self-understanding and the cultivation of the strong cooperative instincts that have favored group survival for countless millennia.

Several features in *Driven* add to its persuasiveness. The authors steer clear of the noisy controversy that has befogged human sociobiology, or evolutionary psychology as it is often called nowadays. That logomachy has been more about political ideology than science, and is mercifully fading. Instead, Lawrence and Nohria guide the reader through key references in the discipline and present the concepts they themselves have found most convincing and useful. Further in their favor, they write with uncommon clarity.

The exposition in *Driven* is therefore suitable for a broad audience, and it is ideal for theorists and practitioners of business management. But the reverse is also true. What will come across immediately to sociobiologists who encounter this book is the rich and mostly untapped research material present in the history of corporations. They will also be stimulated by ideas of cultured evolution and organization still sequestered in studies of business management. It is true that the free-market economy is a Darwinian environment, but as Lawrence and Nohria stress, it is far more complex, gentler, and more interesting than widely stereotyped. To other behavioral scientists I recommend management case histories as a valuable database for future research.

Finally, the four-drive model will also be of interest to scholars because it has been conceived from an independent approach to the study of human nature. Its conception of broad instinctual categories can serve as a valuable reference point for future studies by both social scientists and biologists.

*Cambridge, Massachusetts*                         EDWARD O. WILSON
*August 2001*

# THE AUTHORS

PAUL R. LAWRENCE is Wallace Brett Donham Professor of Organizational Behavior Emeritus at Harvard Business School. He grew up in Michigan, where he did his undergraduate work in sociology and economics at Albion College. After serving in the Navy in WWII he finished his masters and doctoral training in organizational behavior at Harvard Business School. His research, published in twenty-four books and numerous articles, has dealt with the human aspects of management, organizational change, and organization design. His best-known titles (with coauthors) are *Organization and Environment, Renewing American Industry, Administering Changes,* and *Behind the Factory Walls: Decision Making in Soviet and U.S. Enterprises.*

NITIN NOHRIA is Richard P. Chapman Professor of Business Administration and chairman of the Organizational Behavior Unit at the Harvard Business School. Prior to joining the Harvard Business School faculty in July 1988, Nohria received his Ph.D. in management from the Sloan School of Management, Massachusetts Institute of Technology, and a B. Tech. in chemical engineering from the Indian Institute of Technology, Bombay. He specializes in leadership, corporate renewal, and organizational change, and is an active member of several advisory boards. Nohria is the author of over seventy-five articles and is coauthor or editor of seven books, including the award-winning *The Differentiated Network.*

*TO OUR PARENTS*
*Who started us on this journey*

# PREFACE

The sciences all offer their own windows on the world. In their search for the origins of human nature biologists rely on studies of various forms of animal behavior, psychologists on laboratory experiments, paleontologists on the fossil record, archaeologists on the remains of earlier human civilizations, anthropologists on the diversity in human cultures, and neuroscientists on the biochemistry and neural circuitry of the human brain. We, as long-time students of human behavior, have our own petri dish. It is the study of human behavior in work organizations. Given the extraordinary amount of time most people spend working in organizations of one kind or another and the wide range of behavior that can be observed within and across organizations, we believe the petri dish we have chosen offers a specially rich location to study human behavior.

In our earlier research, teaching, and consulting, we have mostly relied on models of human behavior proposed by various social scientists, but this book represents an effort to incorporate new knowledge about human evolution and the workings of the human mind that come from more biologically oriented scholars. This includes the work of evolutionary biologists, psychologists, anthropologists, and economists. We have also studied some of the work of neuroscientists, neurologists, archeologists, paleontologists, historians, philosophers, and linguists. In our search for a unified model of human nature we have focused on identifying findings across these fields that are consistent with each other and with our own up-close observations of human behavior, which span over seventy years of research in hundreds of organizations.

## The Roots of the Concept

As background to our endeavor it is useful to understand the historical tradition it builds upon.

Dean Wallace B. Donham initiated the study of human behavior at the Harvard Business School in the 1920s. He recruited Elton Mayo, a clinical psychologist, to lead the effort and secured the financial support of the Rockefeller Foundation. L. J. Henderson, a distinguished physiologist from the Harvard Medical School, soon joined Mayo in the work. Interestingly, some of the first studies in the field focused on studying the impact of various working conditions on the fatigue experienced by workers. In keeping with Henderson's medical background, the initial emphasis was on trying to understand the physiological underpinnings of fatigue such as disorientation caused by poor lighting or loss of vital body fluids due to hard manual labor and inhospitable factory working conditions. In addition to studying the effects of varying working conditions on fatigue in the laboratory, it was early on felt vital to study the phenomena in actual organizations where people were engaged in their real work.

The most notable product of the early research was a comprehensive field study conducted at AT&T's Western Electric Hawthorne Plant. The results of this research were primarily published in *Management and the Worker* by F. J. Roethlisberger and W. Dickson. The principal findings of this widely influential study were that the social needs of workers and managers had a powerful impact on their behavior at work, and that workers responded enthusiastically to an opportunity to contribute their thinking and learning to workplace issues. These researchers were seeking a more unified theory of human behavior and deliberately chose to search in the organizational context. The findings and theories of all the social sciences were applied in the study. This broad, multidisciplinary approach is reflected in the titles of Mayo's principal publications: *The Human Problems of an Industrial Civilization, The Social Problems of an Industrial Civilization,* and *The Political Problems of an Industrial Civilization.* This early body of literature established a tradition of doing multidisciplinary work on human behavior in a manner that aspired to be useful to the management of organizations, an action theory, if you will. The process of applying this growing body of knowledge was governed by the cautious medical dictum of "least harm."

The work in this tradition was pursued in the subsequent generation of scholars under the intellectual leadership of Fritz Roethlisberger and George Homans. As a member of the first group of doctoral students trained in this tradition, Paul Lawrence, the senior author of this book, was guided into the study of the basic literature of all of the social sciences. A sample of the titles of some of the books emerging from this tradition indicates the multi-disciplinary themes: *The Human Group, Behavior in a Selling Group, Industrial Jobs and the Worker, The Changing of Organizational Behavior Patterns,* and *Organization and Environment.*

## POTENTIAL AUDIENCE

Viewed in the context of the history of research on human behavior at the Harvard Business School, we appear to have come full circle. Mayo and Henderson's early efforts to understand human behavior tried to bridge knowledge in the medical and biological sciences with the social sciences. They were perhaps ahead of their time. Much less was known then about the biological underpinnings of human behavior. We think the time is now ripe to reinvigorate the quest for a unified theory of human behavior that is consilient across the natural and social sciences. This book represents what we think is a significant step in this direction. It is for anyone and everyone interested in finding out more about their own nature as humans and the ultimate motives behind the choices they and those around them make every day.

## WHAT THIS BOOK OFFERS

The first three chapters provide the essential story of the evolution of the human mind. How did the brain, the most distinctive feature of humans, evolve on a step-by-step basis? In particular, we start by exploring the mystery of the "Great Leap" in human development that occurred in a small pocket of hominids in Africa about a hundred thousand years ago.

The following four chapters, Part Two of the book, describe the four primary innate drives that we believe are hard-wired in the brains of all humans. These drives shape the choices we make. The first (Dl) is the drive to acquire objects and experiences that improve our status relative to others. The second (D2) is the drive to bond with others in long-term relationships of mutually caring commitment. The third (D3) is the drive to learn and make sense of the world and of ourselves. The fourth (D4) is the drive to defend ourselves, our loved ones, our beliefs, and resources from harm. In each case we try and answer such questions as these: What is the evidence for the existence of these particular drives? How could they have evolved? How do they play out in everyday current life?

In Part Three we deal with the obvious big questions that our four-drive theory generates. How do the four drives interact with human culture, with emotions, and with human skills? How can we account for all the diversity of human behavior—between cultures, between historical periods, between belief systems, and between individuals? How can civilizations arise with their complex social institutions and creative technical achievements?

Part Four, the two final chapters, addresses the issues of application and future prospects. First, we spell out the implications of the four-drive theory for organizational life, our own area of expertise, and an important example of the theory's application. Finally we look ahead at the possibilities of other applications. We hope that our work will inspire others to test the four-drive theory and use it to help build the road toward a greater unity of all knowledge.

## ACKNOWLEDGMENTS

Over the years that we have worked on this research project we have benefited greatly from the many scholars and friends who have studied various drafts of this work and helped us develop its strengths and avoid its pitfalls. The following people have read and provided insightful comments on one or more drafts of the work: Carliss Baldwin, James Baron, Max Bazerman, By Barnes, Michael Beer, Joseph Bower, Terry Burnham, Tiziana Casciaro, Allen Cohen, Tom DeLong, Lex Donaldson, Amy Edmundson, William Frederick, Stephen Freeman, Jack Gabarro, Sumantra Ghoshal, Ranjay Gulati, Richard Hackman, Morten Hansen, Monica Higgins, Linda Hill, Tarun Khanna, Rakesh Khurana, John Kotter, George Lodge, Hans Loeser, Jay Lorsch, Joshua Margolis, Nigel Nicholson, Charles O'Reilly, Lynn Paine, Donald Pfister, Steven Pinker, Joseph Platt, Jeff Polzer, Jo Proctor, Michael Raynor, Raaj Sah, Edgar Schein, Robert Simon, Jitendra Singh, Carl Sloane, Philip Stone, Renato Taguiri, David Thomas, Michael Tushman, Kathleen Valley, Andrew Van de Ven, Charalambos Vlachoutsicos, Debra Vidaver-Cohen, Ann Wardwell, and Rod White.

In addition, we wish especially to recognize the help of the following:

- Teresa Amabile, our director of the Division of Research at HBS.
- Kim Clark, our dean at HBS, who has not only provided us

with consistent administrative and financial support but also the steady encouragement of reading several drafts.

- Warren Bennis, the general editor of the Jossey-Bass series on Leadership, for his enthusiastic support of the merit of our work.
- Ike Williams, our agent, for his practical judgment.
- Susan Williams, our senior editor, and Rob Brandt, our associate editor at Jossey-Bass, for their wise guidance and hard work throughout the publication process.
- Joan McDonald and Eileen Hankins, who provided secretarial assistance and good humor with printing and copying numerous drafts of the book.
- Anne Lawrence, for all her splendid editing and her insightful comments.
- Ed Wilson and Ernst Mayr, the deans of evolutionary biology, who have generously guided our biological education.
- Martha and Monica, our wives, for their constant support and their amazing patience with our years of preoccupation with this project.

Especially because this book is pushing on the edges of knowledge in a diverse set of fields, it is by no means perfunctory for us to add that we take full responsibility for any errors and other shortcomings of the text.

*Boston, Massachusetts*                                     PAUL R. LAWRENCE
*July 2001*                                                 NITIN NOHRIA

# DRIVEN

# PART ONE

## BRIDGING GAPS

### SETTING THE STAGE FOR
### UNDERSTANDING HUMAN NATURE

# TOWARD A UNIFIED UNDERSTANDING OF HUMAN NATURE

*The proper study for mankind is man.*

—ALEXANDER POPE

I won't take no for an answer," Kirk told his doctor. "I'm fifty-four. I'm not ready to just pack it up and die. I'm a fighter. You're my last hope. . . . I don't give a tinker's damn about the product. In your world, what matters is new knowledge that can lead to curing a disease. For me, the product means nothing. It can be oil or platinum or software or widgets. For me, it's the delicious pleasure of seeing where to go before the crowd does; the challenge of making fast decisions; the fun of everyone trying to outsmart everyone else. It's all a shell game played for big money."

Kirk was a high-stakes investor whose body was riddled with cancer. His story forms the first chapter of Dr. Jerome Groopman's poignant *The Measure of Our Days,* which recounts stories of people living with terminal illness, the crucible that reveals the essence of each individual's basic human nature.[1]

Confronted with the overwhelmingly bad results of the tests, Kirk told Groopman, "Jerry, I'm a damn successful venture capital-ist. And I know what a lousy investment I am. But I'm willing to fight, to my last breath, and to try and make it. If you will help me,

I'll undergo anything. The worst side-effects. They can't be worse to me than being dead." So the most extreme chemotherapy procedures went ahead—four complete courses of interleukin-2 and vinblastine with progesterone. Kirk gradually regained his healthy form. It seemed a miracle. He had entered a complete remission, with no evidence of residual disease. Kirk's case became the talk of the hospital.

When Kirk and his wife, Cathy, were moving back to New York after two months of recuperation, however, he responded to the question of whether he was ready to return to real life with an unconvincing, "I guess so." Two weeks later on the phone Cathy told the doctor, "He won't read the newspapers. He used to devour them." Kirk added, "I don't think I am depressed, Jerry. It's just that the information in the papers doesn't seem important anymore."

Some months later in a routine exam Kirk reported a persistent pain in his back. Testing revealed that the cancer was back in a hopeless way. Groopman tells the story:

> I sat by the bedside and for a long time we were silent. I felt we were speaking telepathically, acknowledging to each other that we knew that we had tried and tried hard but now the end had come.
>
> "I'm sorry that magic didn't work longer," I finally offered.
>
> "It did more than anyone expected, Jerry. But you shouldn't feel sorry. There was no reason to live anyway. When I went into remission, I couldn't read the papers because my deals and trades seemed pointless. The remission meant nothing because it was too late to relive my life. I once asked for hell. Maybe God made this miracle to have me know what it will feel like."

"Have you thought about telling Cathy and the children what you've told me?" I gently suggested.

"Why? So they can hear what they already know? That I was a self-absorbed uncaring shit? That's really going to be a comforting deathbed interchange."

Kirk had chosen to live his life with a total focus (in the terms of this book) on his drive to acquire. He put up an enormous fight to defend that way of life—only to discover at the end that, in the absence of attention to his other drives, his life was meaningless. The tragedy was that his discovery came too late.

## No Single Answer

This book is about four innate drives—the drive to acquire, the drive to bond, the drive to learn, and the drive to defend—that we believe are central to the nature of all humans, the drives that play a vital role in all human choices. Using this four-drive theory as a lens, it becomes clear why Kirk's life felt meaningless, even though he got a miraculous second chance. When he realized that in pursuing his drive to acquire he had completely neglected the other equally human drives, his will to live left him.

Reflect a moment on your own life or the lives of others you are familiar with. We would predict that those who have found ways to satisfy all four drives (at least over time) will feel more fulfilled than those who have focused on some to the exclusion of others. Those who have neglected their drive to acquire are more likely to lack self-esteem and feel envious of those who have done better. Those who have neglected their drive to bond with others are apt to feel empty and disconnected from life. Those who have neglected their drive to learn and lived a life with little opportunity to pursue their own curiosities are more likely to feel stunted in their personal development. Those who have neglected their drive to defend or have been unable to do so are more likely to feel abused and victimized.

Human beings are driven to seek ways to fulfill all four drives because these drives are the product of the species' common evolutionary heritage. They have been selected over time because they increase evolutionary fitness, that is, the ability of our genes to survive and carry on the species. The independence of these drives is what forces people to think and to choose—because not all drives can be met at all times. In short, the four drives are what make people distinctly human—complex beings with complex motives and complex choices.

## Why Look for Drives?

The four-drive theory we advance in this book started with a simple question: What drives people as human beings? This age-old question has even greater significance today because humanity confronts great transitions that it must successfully navigate. The world is moving from an old industrial economy to a new information economy. Around the world, people are tearing down socialist and totalitarian nation states in favor of capitalist and democratic nation states. People are shedding traditional family structures in which men worked outside while women took care of the home and moving to greater equality in the distribution of work inside and outside the home. People are dismantling old hierarchical forms of work organization based on long-term employment relationships in favor of newer network forms of organization based on flexible, free agent–style employment relationships.

Indeed, it may not be an exaggeration to assert that every social institution on the micro-macro spectrum from the family to the nation state is in the midst of a significant transformation, presenting a special opportunity for humanity. It is now possible to reinvent the world so that the twenty-first century is the beginning of another golden era in human history—a period of growing economic prosperity, social harmony, discovery, and global peace, free from the scourge of poverty, alienation, dogma, and war. But capitalizing on this truly special opportunity is far from a simple matter.

We believe that one of the vital determinants of the ability to seize this opportunity is the extent to which the new social institutions are founded on a sound understanding of human nature. As Rousseau observed during the Enlightenment, institutions can only flourish if they are founded on a "social contract" that enables human beings to pursue their individual and collective interests to the fullest extent possible.[2] These social contracts are the building blocks of every social institution from the family to the business organization to the state. The viability and durability of social contracts depends on the extent to which they resonate with the enduring human condition and with contemporary technical possibilities.

## Acquisition Isn't Enough

The late twentieth century has seen the triumph of the neoclassical economist's view of human nature and a corresponding view of the ideal social contract. Drawing on the foundations laid down by Adam Smith, economists view human beings as selfish maximizers of their own self-interests. The ideal social contract between individuals is thus based on the principle of the division of labor and economic exchange, whereby each individual can be better off by trading goods and services with others. Markets that facilitate free economic exchange are therefore the institutions most conducive to human progress.

The triumph of this perspective is evident everywhere. At the level of the nation state, the ideal of the capitalist free market economy has won over socialist alternatives, prompting declarations of the end of economic and political history. Through institutions such as the World Trade Organization, the whole world is being joined into an integrated market promoting the free trade of goods and services within and across national boundaries.

At the level of the organization, the idea of a vertically integrated, hierarchical organization founded on long-term contracts between the organization and the individual is being supplanted by a vision of the firm as a network or nexus of contracts, held together by obligations that are no deeper than the economic value that each party attaches to the contract.

At the level of the family, the ideal of marriage as a union that must be preserved through thick and thin is being undermined by a view that marriage is an economic contract that sets out the expectations of the parties involved and can be readily annulled if either party does not feel it is getting its expected returns from the exchange.

It is hard to argue against the triumph of the economic perspective. It has, in most cases, been a clearly superior alternative. Socialist nations have been less prosperous than capitalist nations. Market-oriented firms have been more effective than bureaucratic firms. Rejecting traditional views of the family has certainly promoted gender equality at home and at work.

Yet the current triumphs of the economic perspective should not lure anyone into thinking that this view of human nature is entirely correct, or that institutions founded on the social contract of market exchange are necessarily the best of all imaginable alternatives. There have been, as well, some significant failures from totally embracing the economic view. Efforts to reform Russia by encouraging it to embrace a market economy through shock therapy have hardly been successful.

The dot-com mania has already shown that those firms that are no more than a nexus of contracts put together solely to pursue transient economic opportunities are unlikely to flourish when the going gets tough. The rising tide of the recent economic expansion has barely hidden the anxiety that lurks below the surface. Only a decade ago, the headlines in the business press were all about the alienation and economic anxiety that was being experienced by American workers and managers as they were being laid off from previously stable long-term employment relationships. Many dot-com free agents are beginning to think wistfully of the days when membership in an organization was also an obligation of loyalty and mutual commitment. Many business leaders are puzzling over what they can do to win back the loyalty and commitment of their employees.

The redefinition of the family has certainly improved gender equality. But it has also had some alarming unintended consequences such as negative birth rates in highly advanced countries, an increasing rate of divorce, an increasing rate of births to teenaged single mothers, and an increasing rate of child neglect.

By raising these concerns, our intention is not to turn the clock back and bring back old social institutions that were seriously flawed. Instead, our intention is to prevent people from becoming complacent, from feeling satisfied with current triumphs. We want to encourage the continued search for a better understanding of human nature that will allow human beings to invent superior social contracts that will create institutions more successful than the ones we have today.

## Lapses of Rational Self-Interest

We began our own work of coming up with a fresh synthesis regarding human nature by challenging one of the time-honored assumptions of economics: that people are rational maximizers of their own self-interest, with these interests best served by unrestricted markets.

We had long been uncomfortable with this view. It struck us that human motives begin as subconscious drives that are only later manifested as conscious emotions and influenced by rational calculations. And we had also seen much evidence that pure self-interest, while a powerful drive, could not account for all human behavior. We also believed that markets work best in a context of a broader social contract that keeps competition within fair bounds. We began to explore the idea that human behavior is motivated by a small set of innate, subconscious, brain-based drives—and we asked ourselves just what those drives might be. We thought long and hard about this question, testing our answers against our accumulated experience and all available clues in the scientific literature, generating and rejecting many possibilities.

Four ideas survived our testing process. We concluded that all people do have a persistent drive to acquire objects and experiences that improve their status relative to others. In other words, they are indeed motivated, in part, by self-interest as defined by economics. But human beings also have three other basic drives: to bond with others in long-term relationships of mutually caring commitment; to learn and make sense of the world and of themselves; and to defend themselves, their loved ones, their beliefs, and their resources from harm. All four of these primary drives have been established in the human brain as a result of Darwinian evolution, because the existence of these drives improves the odds that the genes of their individual carriers will pass into subsequent generations.

## Can Four Answers Be Better Than One?

This insight about the existence of four genetically based drives immediately generated a multitude of questions. Is there empirical evidence that these drives exist? How do these subconscious drives express themselves in everyday conscious life? Could the four drives have been established in the brain through evolution? If so, by what mechanism were they established? Would the existence of such drives be consistent with the latest findings of neuroscience and genetics? Is there evidence that these drives are universal? How would such drives mesh with acquired learning from our cultures and from science? Could a mere four drives underlie all the diversity of behavior we observe in the world? Might there be a fifth or sixth—or a twenty-first—that we were missing? The magnitude and scope of these questions were daunting, to say the least.

## A Case in Point: Post-Communist Russia

To understand better why we have undertaken the formidable task of answering these questions about human nature, we must focus briefly on the case of Russia at the time of the breakup of the Soviet Union. Paul Lawrence was part of a group of American and Russian scholars that conducted an intensive field study of Russian managerial decision making during the key years 1989 to 1991.[3] These years in the annals of Russian history rank in significance with the Bolshevik Revolution of 1917.

The Gorbachev era was ending. In the span of just a few years, Gorbachev and his allies had facilitated rapid, bloodless revolutions in the Soviet satellite countries of Eastern Europe and a rush of internal reforms known as glasnost and peristroika. The Communist party, with its tactics of rule by secret police and terror, had been totally discredited by its last-gasp effort to depose Gorbachev in a coup in 1990. Yeltsin, as the first elected president of Russia, had faced down the Army tanks and soon proceeded to dissolve the Soviet Union, thereby eliminating Gorbachev's role as premier. The Cold War that Khruschev had framed as an economic war in his famous "kitchen" debate with Nixon in 1959 was over.

Khruschev's boast that America would be buried had been proven false. The American political and economic system had emerged the clear victor.

The way seemed clear to establish a democratic, free-market system in Russia and to bring the second most powerful nation in the world into the international family of peaceful, democratic states. The removal of the ultimate threat to all humankind— nuclear warfare—seemed possible. With their own theories in total disarray, many top officials in the Russian government were eager to receive and use the advice of Western experts on how to implement political and economic reforms. With the State owning all the assets, the opportunity existed to redistribute them to the people in a way that could get the reformed, privatized economy off to a flying start. The historical situation offered the social sciences a unique opportunity for constructive influence over a vast portion of humanity.

Experts were, in fact, selected to advise Yeltsin and his senior officials. The experts did act with the best of intentions and to the best of their abilities. Their recommendations were based almost exclusively on the logic of neoclassical economics: that all humans were rational maximizers of their self-interest and that unrestricted markets could best coordinate their efforts. They urged the Russian government to manage the transition from a collectivist economy to a market economy by sudden shock therapy—in total confidence in the invisible hand of an unrestricted market. This was an application of economic theory on an unprecedented scale.

The Russians essentially acted on the experts' advice. The results were appalling. As of 2001, the production of goods and services has declined by 50 percent—and the end is not yet in sight. The waste of capital, not only economic but also social capital and human capital, has been immense. More than half the people are impoverished as against only 2 percent some ten years ago. Since

1990 the mortality rate of Russian males has shot up at a rate unprecedented in modern times. The political leadership has stumbled from crisis to crisis. Even the most recent presidential election was grossly distorted by the slanderous attacks on all opposition candidates by the media allied with the Yeltsin regime. The extent of the Russian reform disaster has been largely ignored in the West, even though it has been carefully reported.[4] The suffering of the Russian people has been enormous, and the risk of violent backlash cannot be ruled out.

Although the causes of this reform disaster are multiple, it is patently clear that the Russians could surely have used better advice from their foreign experts. The experts had achieved some success with the shock therapy approach in other countries, but Russia was a very different case. Better advice for Russia would have had to be based on a much broader, more unified understanding of human behavior than the experts had available to them. These comments are in no way intended to single out neoclassical economists for blame. We strongly doubt whether experts from any of the other fragmented social sciences could have done any better; they might well have done worse. The best theories in each of these social sciences would have been inadequate to the challenge—not so much wrong as incomplete and culture-bound. The economists were simply the unlucky ones chosen for the task. Furthermore, putting together a panel that combined experts from each of these fields would only have generated endless arguments with no coherent advice, making matters even worse. We speak from experience.

What the Russians really needed was a well-rounded, seasoned general practitioner for an entire human society, an expert, to use an old-fashioned term, in applied political economy. Such a person, of course, did not exist. To qualify as an expert in that field, one would have needed a unified theory of human behavior that met several extremely challenging criteria:

- It should be multilevel, that is, able to work back and forth among all levels of analysis from individual to societal.[5]
- It should be consistent with most of the findings of the various social science disciplines, as well as with human biology.
- It should be amenable to empirical testing.
- It should be action-oriented—that is, practical (teachable and usable)—and, therefore, as parsimonious as possible while still taking into account most of the principal features of human behavior
- It should be valid in different cultural settings.

## BUILDING A NEW THEORY

The Russian experience highlights the need for such a theory, but how could such a highly ambitious goal be approached? As we thought about the issue it became more and more obvious that nothing short of an up-to-date, scientifically developed theory of the universal innate features of human nature was needed. Such a theory would establish a solid base upon which a unified understanding of human behavior in all its diversity could then be built. We know a great deal about what makes humans different from one another. But what are the things that make them alike—the characteristics that are distinctly human? What are the specific features that make all humans different from their nearest interspecies cousins, the chimpanzees? The answer has to be found in evolutionary heritage. The common human gene pool contains so little variability around the world that it is estimated that everyone shares ancestors who diverged only some seventy to a hundred thousand years ago from a prior variety of hominids. This group of modern *Homo sapiens* may have been as small as four to ten thousand people.[6] Nothing less than the knowledge of what made this primeval group distinctly human would enable experts in the future to take up a challenge such as the Russian one with any solid confidence in their recommendations. Only then could anyone claim to have a broader theory of human nature upon which could be built a theory of human behavior that would truly make it possible to comprehend complex human phenomena and propose sensible action.

Our question about the fundamental nature of all humans is, of course, not a new one. It was one of the central questions pondered by Greek and Roman scholars and again by the philosophers of the Enlightenment. Darwin addressed this question in a revolutionary manner. But the social sciences have largely ignored, or possibly avoided, the question of the biological base of human nature since Darwin's time. This was abetted, no doubt, by the coincidence that, even as Darwin was publishing his major works, the study of human behavior was breaking away from biology and into the separate social science disciplines as we know them today. This breakup threw the disciplines into competition with each other. Also, the thought leaders of the various social sciences were properly appalled by the early misuse of Darwin's ideas by exponents of so-called Social Darwinism, eugenicists, and apologists for racial and gender discrimination. The response of the social sciences, essentially on moral grounds, has been to act as if Darwin's theory had nothing to do with their task of understanding human behavior. They came to believe that using terms like *human nature* or *innate* led automatically to racism. They stopped pursuing the goal of understanding the universals of human nature, probably for fear they would not like what they found—perhaps some beastly features that were better left hidden in the mists of time.

And certainly many of the evolutionary biologists did not help allay the fears of the social sciences by continuing to emphasize the negative aspects of human nature. The titles alone of some of their best-selling books on the subject were probably enough to repel most social scientists. For example, what response did the biologists expect to get from books with such titles as *The Ape Within Us, Selfish Genes,* and *Demonic Males,* to name just a few?[7]

The legitimate concerns of social scientists about the potential misuse of evolutionary biology created a kind of taboo on any examination of innate human nature. Even as recently as fifteen years ago, any serious discussion of the topic would have generated a wave of negative reaction. But today, based on an updated understanding of evolutionary theory and of human biology, it is clear that these concerns are unjustified. The differences between the so-called races are superficial, and the brainpower of women is fully equal to that of men. These well-established facts, which were not clear until fairly recently, mean that the question of human nature can now be addressed without fear of igniting false charges of racism and sexism.

Furthermore, we reasoned, the strange fact that the human nature question has been largely neglected by social scientists since Darwin's time might now work to our advantage. Over the last 140 years the separate behavioral sciences, alongside human biology, have been accumulating findings clearly relevant to the human nature question that have never been pulled together. Are pieces of the giant jigsaw puzzle available now that were not available to Darwin—pieces that have never been assembled? Might the intense specialization of the various disciplines—which has in many respects impeded the human nature inquiry—now be turned around to help generate a much stronger theory?

The history of science and human invention is replete with examples of important advances resulting from synthesizing previously fragmented ideas. One such process began in 1820 when a Dane, H. C. Oersted, discovered that a wire carrying an electric current was surrounded by a magnetic field. In 1825 an Englishman, W. Sturgeon, wound a live wire around an iron bar and created an electromagnet. In 1859 a German pianist and scientist,

H. von Helmholtz, discovered he could make piano strings vibrate by singing to them. Later a Frenchman, L. Scott, attached a thin stick to a membrane. When he spoke to the membrane, the other end of the stick would trace a record of his voice sounds on a piece of smoked glass. In 1874 a Scotsman from Canada, working in Cambridge, Massachusetts, put these scattered and diverse elements into one instrument. The instrument was the telephone and the man was Alexander Graham Bell. The only thing Bell contributed was a fresh synthesis—there was no new discovery.

The present state of the discussion among the multiple sciences of human behavior reminds us of the status of the telephone invention before Bell arrived on the scene. The various behavioral sciences—economics, psychology, sociology, anthropology, and political science—each view humans from their own particular perspectives, and, as a consequence, none can view the whole person with accuracy.

We believe the time is ripe to synthesize these different strands of thinking about human nature. This book is an effort to begin this synthesis, and to start bridging the gap between the latest findings from evolutionary biology and insights about human behavior derived from the social sciences. To the extent that we can do so, we propose to lay the foundation for a unified understanding of human nature and, in turn, human behavior.

## Who Are We to Forge Ahead?

Two Harvard Business School professors might seem like unlikely candidates to propose a new synthesis, a unified science of human nature. Yet we feel that we are ideally suited to the task. We are fundamentally interdisciplinary in our orientation, and we have spent our entire careers studying the way people behave in that most fascinating setting of human behavior, the workplace.

We have done our work at close range, observing real people take on tough problems in organizations of all kinds. In fact, we were attracted to working at the Harvard Business School because of its action orientation and its search for research findings that could contribute to solving real-life problems in organizations. We have studied problems not only in the business organizations of most major industries, but also in city governments, hospitals, universities, and large federal agencies. We have studied entrepreneurial start-ups as well as large multinationals in highly diverse cultures.

In the course of our education and our work we have acquired considerable training in all the human behavioral sciences—without tying ourselves exclusively to any one of them. That freedom has given us the license to roam throughout the disciplines, choosing the best they have to offer while avoiding their specialized tunnel vision.

Over the years we have dealt with fragmentation among the social sciences as an unchangeable fact of life. After all, it may have complicated our lives as researchers and teachers, but it was doing no great harm in the world beyond the academy. And yet, we were never fully comfortable with it. We came from a research tradition at the Harvard Business School that, from its inception in the 1920s, was committed to a multidisciplinary approach to understanding human behavior. The long-term goal of this tradition was always a unified theory of human behavior that could be applied to organizational issues in ways that could help practicing managers.

In approaching managers we talked, when needed, in hybrid terms such as socioeconomics, sociotechnology, social psychology, and cultural anthropology. However, the true integration of the disciplines always seemed a long way in the future. It took the shock of the Russian reform disaster to shake us out of this complaisant attitude and set us on the road toward a unified science of human nature.

We started by working to fill in our knowledge about the various relevant disciplines allied with human biology. We have spent a great deal of time learning about evolutionary biology, neuroscience, genetics, primatology, and archeology. And it is now our great hope—indeed, our belief—that this combination of experience, study, and contemplation has enabled us to generate deep new insights toward a unified science of human nature.

We became even more convinced of the potential value of our efforts following the publication in 1998 of E. O. Wilson's *Consilience: The Unity of Knowledge.* His book was a challenge to the entire scientific community to renew the search initiated by the Enlightenment thinkers: the search for consilience, or the unification of knowledge. For Wilson, the most important gap in knowledge was the one between the natural sciences—physics, chemistry, and biology—and the various social sciences. He believed it would also be the most difficult to overcome. "In the last several decades," he wrote, "the natural sciences have expanded to reach the borders of the social sciences and humanities. There the principle of consilient explanation guiding the advance must undergo its severest test."[8] Wilson argued that new findings about how the mind works—especially the relationship between innate features and acquired features—would hold the key to closing the gap. And he believed it was up to the social sciences to take the next steps.

Wilson's book also opened the door for us to locate intellectual compatriots. It turns out that in some social science disciplines, long-held assumptions are being challenged by small groups of scholars who draw on the insights of evolutionary biology. Evolutionary psychologists are pursuing new theories on the innate workings of the mind. Evolutionary anthropologists also are asking a radical question: What are the universal behavior patterns of humankind? And small comparable groups are forming in economics, sociology, and political science.

~

Having now studied the relevant work from these new splinter groups, we are encouraged that our thinking is on the right track. We have found that many of the pieces of the human nature puzzle exist, often thanks to the recent research of creative and gifted scholars. The evidence about shared human nature is being generated by a wide array of research methodologies, including the comparative study of brain-damaged people, the study of infant eye movements, the electronic scanning of brain activity, genetic testing, broad cultural surveys, archaeological explorations, laboratory experiments, and historical reconstructions. And we have become increasingly convinced that our insight about the fundamental drives of all humans can add an essential piece to the puzzle.

We propose that the dynamic interplay within the brain among just these four drives alongside the cognitive centers, in active adaptation to changing environments, can largely account for the vicissitudes of human experience, for both individuals and societies. We propose that the four drives exist as hard-wired mental modules in the brains of all modern humans as primary drives, not derived from one another. This means that fulfilling one drive does not fulfill any of the others. Sometimes the four drives act together in complementary ways; at other times they are in conflict with each other. The drives significantly influence but clearly do not totally determine particular behaviors.

Much evidence supports the arguments we make in this book. Still, our theory should be seen as a complex set of hypotheses that will require further testing. Also, in striving to cover such a wide scope of the scientific literature, we have no doubt made mistakes of commission and omission. Keeping those disclaimers in mind, we will consider our work a success if we open fresh pathways to the task of discovering a universal human nature, upon which a unified theory of human behavior can be constructed.

# 2

# HOW THE MODERN
# HUMAN MIND EVOLVED

*Humans are social animals endowed with reason.*

—ARISTOTLE

n 1970 one of the authors went on safari in Kenya and
Tanzania. Four scenes from that trip are indelibly etched in
memory. The first was a long talk with Jane Goodall at her
campsite. As a pioneer of the study of chimpanzees in their natural
habitat, she laid the foundation for modern knowledge of the
behavior of chimpanzees, the closest living relative of the species
that split from the primate line to start the multimillion-year evolution to modern humans.

The second was a stop at Olduvai Gorge, where Mary Leaky
pointed out the spot where she and her husband George Leaky had
discovered the 1.75 million-year-old skull of Zinjanthropus man.
These remains, along with subsequent hominid finds, have helped
scholars reconstruct the evolutionary steps leading to modern
*Homo sapiens.*

The third was an opportunity to visit a Masai village to get
a brief feel for the strength and sophistication of their hunter-
gatherer-herder way of life. Tribes such as this offer the best available approximation of the way of life of the biologically modern

humans who, as hunter-gatherers, moved out of Africa approximately seventy thousand years ago fully equipped to thrive in all parts of the globe.

The final scene was a dawn's-light view of huge clusters of herbivores—wildebeests, zebras, gazelles, giraffes, and many others—moving gracefully in a vast grassland. In their midst were two Masai warriors, spears over their shoulders, striding with total confidence across the huge plain. That scene epitomized the environment where modern human genes were formed and selected. It felt like Eden.

Darwin's work provided the fundamental breakthrough to an understanding of how humans evolved in such a setting. Since then, a number of different scientific specialties have contributed significant new elements to the story. At first, the additional new findings came slowly. Recently, they have been coming in a rush, and it is now possible to describe the evolutionary changes that created the modern human mind, making humans a unique species.

## DARWIN'S THEORY

Darwin's theory of organic evolution by natural selection is central to modern biology. Today it takes the form of the evolutionary synthesis that was worked out in steps from the 1920s forward among population geneticists, systematists, and other evolutionary biologists.[1] Darwin's key idea was that the algorithm of *Variety*, *Selection*, and *Retention* (V/S/R) could explain the indisputable fossil record of biological step-by-step evolution. In individuals, variety is generated by random mutations in the genes and in the random recombination of these units of heredity in the process of sexual reproduction, with 50 percent of the genes supplied by each parent. Selection is accomplished by the environment and by mate selection. The only genes that are passed on to a new generation are the genes of individuals who succeed in surviving to maturity, in securing a mate, and in raising offspring. Over time, genetic mutations and recombinations that enhance chances for genetic survival are retained in the population. Retention occurs, then, as the DNA records in the genes are passed from one generation to the next. Darwin's theory is that simple and that profound.

For all organisms, this blind, trial-and-error, V/S/R process has been going on since the first speck of biological matter came into existence. It goes on at the level of the molecule, of the cell, of the organs, and of the complete organism. The process may be slow, but it never rests. It is still going on at all these levels; it cannot be stopped. The overall theory is now accepted by essentially all biologists.

In fact, the theory became accepted by biologists even though its primary support, the fossil record, is indirect evidence. Scientists have regarded evolution as such a slow process that they would never be able to observe genetic change within a species and the start of a new species directly. Recently that has all changed. Evolution has been seen in action in quickly reproducing laboratory species such as fruit flies, and also in slower-reproducing wild species such as the Galapagos finches of Darwinian fame.

A comprehensive study of these finches, conducted over more than twenty years under the leadership of Peter and Rosemary Grant, has been beautifully presented in Jonathan Weiner's award-winning book, *The Beak of the Finch*.[2] The Grants tracked all the finches, each and every one of them, on an entire island over several generations with detailed records of their features, behavior, reproduction, and births and deaths, along with records of rainfall, food availability, and other characteristics of the environment. Their detailed data enabled them to track intergenerational changes related to variations in environmental conditions. For example, in 1984 the mean beak width of the *fortis* finch was 8.86

millimeters. The formula that the Grants had developed predicted that by 1987—given the reduced rainfall and seed availability of the intervening years—the mean width should have dropped to 8.74 millimeters. The actual mean width of *fortis* beaks on Daphne Island in 1987 was precisely 8.74 millimeters. And beak width is a trait that is faithfully passed on genetically from parents to offspring. Even in a span of only three years, narrower beaks had been selected, and the species as a whole had evolved. The Grants suspect they may even be watching the start of a new species on the island.

Biologists now accept that the human brain has evolved by the same evolutionary process as other organs of the human body. No doubt the human brain is the most complex mechanism ever created by evolution. But genetic evolution has demonstrated the ability, given enough time, to create amazingly complex mechanisms. Brains of other organisms—even those very much smaller than those of humans—show extraordinary complexity. Consider, for example, the echo-locator skill of bats in catching insects in flight in the dark, the celestial navigation ability of some migrating birds, or the dead-reckoning ability of Tunisian ants in returning straight to their nests after a day of foraging in the trackless desert.

As knowledge about humans' closest mammalian relatives grows, it's becoming clear that the various species' brains are not impossibly different in evolutionary terms. Chimpanzees, for example, have the beginnings of culture and social organization. They have limited use of a few simple tools. They can, with considerable effort, be taught to use sign language with over a hundred symbols to create simple sentences. Such basic emotions as fear, anger, and curiosity can be seen quite clearly in chimpanzees, as well as social bonding of limited duration. The mental gap between chimpanzees and humans, while large, is not impossibly large.

The brains of modern *Homo sapiens* contain a hundred billion neurons—each with up to a thousand dendrites and synapses to contact other neurons. Messages are conveyed from one nerve cell to another by electrochemical impulses that can fire forty times per second. It is estimated that the brain's structure is prescribed by at least 3,195 distinctive genes, 50 percent more than for any other human organ.

## The Brain as a Computational Mechanism

Scientists now understand the human brain as a complex computational or information-processing mechanism. This great insight is built on the idea that information and computation reside in patterns of data and in relations of logic that are independent of the physical medium that stores, carries, and processes them. In other words, patterns of data can be recorded and transmitted by many different media: by mechanical wheels, by electrical impulses and silicon chips, or by neurons and synapses. Brains do not work like desktop computers—each mechanism can handle information in ways the other cannot, but both process information.

The computational nature of the mind was first understood many years ago by Alan Turing, a mathematician; this insight was later advanced by computer scientists Alan Newell, Herbert Simon, and Marvin Minsky and philosophers Hillary Putnam and Jerry Fodor. Their collective work has enabled us to bridge the historic gap between our understanding of the physical features of the brain, with its billions of neurons, and our understanding of the psychological, subjective life of the mind as people experience it in everyday life. Stephen Pinker, in *How the Mind Works,* summarizes the argument as follows:

The computational theory of mind has quietly entrenched itself in neuroscience, the study of the physiology of the brain and nervous system. No corner of the field is untouched by the idea that information processing is the fundamental activity of the brain. The axon (the long output fiber) of a neuron is designed, down to the molecule, to propagate information with high fidelity across long separations. . . . When its electrical signal is transduced to a chemical one at the synapse (the junction between neurons), the physical format of the information changes while the information itself remains the same. . . . The tree of dendrites (input fibers) on each neuron appears to perform the basic logical and statistical operations underlying computation. Information-theoretic terms such as "signals," "codes," "representations," "transformations," and "processing" suffuse the language of neuroscience.[3]

## THE DEVELOPMENT OF THE MIND/BRAIN; CONCEPTION TO MATURITY

Genes launch the developmental process that forms the physical nervous system, part by part, during the fetal period and through the early years of life. Almost from the moment of fertilization, genetic and environmental influences interact as the brain systems develop. But much of this mental development is based on genetic coding shared by all normal human beings. As humans mature, various brain modules develop and begin to operate one at a time, based on coding laid down by the V/S/R process during the millions of years that hominids worked to survive in the grasslands of sub-Saharan Africa.

Microbiologists have mapped the effects of genes on the development of the brain in a wide variety of organisms. They have accumulated evidence of how the genes shape not only the physical features of the brain but also the features of behavior itself.[4] For example, Weiner cites research demonstrating that although fruit flies normally move toward light, they can be selected and bred to move away from light instead.

Darwin's V/S/R algorithm is remarkable in both its simplicity and its power. It works in the body at levels other than the genetic during the lifetime of each individual. The best-researched example of this is the immune system.[5] Confronted with the invasion of an unknown foreign molecule, the human immune system will produce, on a trial-and-error basis, thousands of antibodies that approximate a mirror image of the foreign body. This process of generating variety (V) continues until an antibody molecule is generated that can exactly fit onto the foreign molecule and kill it. This exact antibody is selected (S) and reproduced to attack the remaining foreign molecules. In only a short time period the immune system, when functioning properly, will have evolved an antibody to destroy a completely unknown foreign element, and the body will retain (R) this antibody to its death to repel any such invasion that may occur again.

Edelman has carefully developed the argument that the brain works by a similar V/S/R process at the level of neurons and clusters of neuron sets. The network of millions of neural sets is able to conduct mental experiments, that is, to imagine new concepts (V) that are tested for goodness of fit as representations of the external reality as perceived through the sense organs. Those representations selected (S) as superior matches are retained in long-term memory (R). This process allows humans to build up through experience a vast repertory of tested representations that are available for rapid pattern recognition and skillful responses—a process often called intuitive decision making. The mind is also constantly reprocessing and re-sorting these representations (especially during sleep) to achieve more internally consistent memories. In this way, he argues, each human builds individual understandings of the world and the self by the same Darwinian V/S/R process that accounts for the genetic heritage. Edelman further argues that the neural apparatus that enables this buildup of representations is put in place by the genes. This understanding of the brain as a physical system that processes information still leaves open, however, the question of how the gap between the most advanced primate brain and the human brain was navigated on a step-by-step basis. And what are the specific qualities of the human mind that make humans distinctly different from chimpanzees and earlier hominids?

## EVOLUTIONARY STEPS TOWARD THE HUMAN MIND

Both the archeological and comparative genetic records now support the estimate that the hominid line split off from the line that evolved into chimpanzees and pigmy chimpanzees (bonobos) between five and seven million years ago. The first upright hominid that has been identified as a separate species is *Ardipithecus ramidus* of Africa. This species, or another very similar to it, diversified into a variety of others, some of which coexisted from four to one million years ago. Two and half million years ago, *Homo rudolfensis* and its close relative *Homo habilis* appeared; the latter is the first hominid thought to have used a crude stone ax. *Homo erectus* first appeared around 1.7 million years ago. Much more is known about *H. erectus,* since this hominid migrated from Africa to most parts of the Eurasian continent, where it was known as Peking and Java Man. *H. erectus* continued to use a crude stone ax and probably acquired the use of fire. Archaic *Homo sapiens* first appeared around 500,000 years ago. The Neanderthals were a branch of archaic *H. sapiens* that lived in Europe up to around 30,000 years ago.

The fossil evidence indicates that the human skull was growing in size to three times that of the chimpanzee during this entire time period, but, curiously, there seems to have been very little development in human technology. Crude stone axes were still the only tools—or at least, no others have been found. This situation has been summarized by Ridley, "The evidence from the tools, far from suggesting continuous human ingenuity, speaks of monumental and tedious conservatism. The first stone tools, the Oldowan technology of *Homo habilis,* which appeared about 2.5 million years ago in Ethiopia, were very simple indeed: roughly chipped rocks. They barely improved at all over the next million years. They were then replaced by the Acheulian technology of *Homo erectus,* which consisted of hand axes and teardrop-shaped stone devices. Again, nothing happened for a million years and more."[6]

A major shift toward civilization, generated by some much more sophisticated humans, occurred about 75,000 to 100,000 years ago. Evidence discovered in a cave in the eastern part of the Congo, dating from this period, included finely crafted bone implements—daggers, shafts, and barbed points—together with grindstones brought from miles away. From this time onward there was a dramatic change in the archeological record, which has come to be known as the Upper Paleolithic transition or the Great Leap Forward.

Pinker has summarized this dramatic change:

Calling it a revolution is no exaggeration. All other hominids come out of the comic strip B.C., but the Upper Paleolithic people were the Flintstones. . . . The toolkit [of the Cro-Magnon] included fine blades, needles, awls, many kinds of axes and scrapers, spear points, spear throwers, bows and arrows, fishhooks, engravers, flutes, maybe even calendars. They built shelters, and they slaughtered large animals by the thousands. They decorated everything in sight—tools, cave walls, their bodies—and carved knick-knacks in the shapes of animals and naked women, which archeologists euphemistically call "fertility symbols." They were us. . . . [This] first human revolution was not a cascade of changes set off by a few key inventions. Ingenuity itself was the invention, manifested in hundreds of innovations tens of thousands of miles and years apart.[7]

In short, about seventy-five thousand years ago, a sophisticated human culture, with evidence of religion, art, and complex technology, evolved relatively suddenly. What had happened to the human brain that can account for this Great Leap?

This situation has posed a major puzzle for biologists. As Wilson notes, "Natural selection, in short, does not anticipate future needs. But this principle, while explaining so much so well, presents a difficulty. If the principle is universally true, how did natural selection prepare the mind for civilization before civilization existed? That is the great mystery of human evolution: how to account for calculus and Mozart."[8]

## THE GAGE EPISODE

Rather strangely, an event that has provided one of the strongest clues to understanding the Great Leap happened at about the same time that Darwin was writing up his theory. A railroad construction foreman named Phineas P. Gage had a serious accident that not only dramatically changed his life but also triggered a chain of research that is still forcing a reevaluation of the workings of the human mind.

Gage was bright, hard working, and highly respected by his crew and his superiors at the railroad. One day, however, he inadvertently began tamping a hole full of blasting powder before his helper could pour in the sand they used as insulation. The meter-long iron tamping bar struck fire in the rock, and an explosion drove the bar upward into his face. It entered at his left cheek and exited through the back of his head, and landed more than a hundred feet away. But Gage could still speak afterwards; he sat up in a cart for a three-quarter mile ride to a hotel. The local doctor reported later, "I can safely say that neither at that time nor on any subsequent occasion, save once, did I consider him to be other than perfectly rational." Unfortunately, although Gage's physical recovery was complete—he could touch, hear, and see (with his remaining eye); he was not paralyzed of limb or tongue, and had no noticeable difficulty with speech or language—he was never again able to hold a regular job.

Nor was he ever again able to maintain a friendship. So radical was the change that he was hardly recognizable as the same man. The problem was not lack of physical ability or mental skill; it was that he no longer acted with a sense of purpose. He drifted from one brief job to the next, winding up in San Francisco—drinking and brawling in questionable haunts. He died of a massive seizure thirteen years after the explosion.

But Gage's influence did not end with his death. His brain injury and its impact on his life stirred significant scientific interest at the time, and it has ever since. Only in the last decade, with the help of Gage's skull and the original tamping rod (preserved at the Harvard Medical School), a complex computer simulation has determined the exact brain areas that were destroyed. Antonio Damasio writes, "Gage's story hinted at an amazing fact: Somehow, there were systems in the human brain . . . concerned specifically with unique human properties, among them the ability to anticipate the future and plan accordingly within a complex social environment; the sense of responsibility toward the self and other; and the ability to orchestrate one's survival deliberately, at the command of one's free will."[9] Gage's story has helped focus scientific attention on the unique aspects of the human mind that were first displayed as the Great Leap. Now, some 150 years and several theories later, much has been learned that has profound implications for the understanding of human life.

## THE MIND/BRAIN AS A REPRESENTATIONAL MECHANISM

One of the theories about the origin of the unique aspects of the human mind builds directly on the brain's increase in size. As noted, modern humans have brains approximately three times the size of those of their nearest primate cousins, the chimpanzees. Much of this extra capacity is undoubtedly committed to humans' exceedingly powerful memory.

Merlin Donald, a psychologist, has drawn upon the literature of many disciplines to reconstruct the stages of development of human memory.[10] He describes these stages as different kinds of representational systems that have evolved as the brain has evolved its increased capacity.

Starting with *Homo erectus,* Donald describes the pre-language, *episodic* stage of representation that seems to be shared with the large apes and some other mammals and birds. This memory, in effect, records scenes—rather like snapshots of the surrounding world, pictures that flash into the mind's eye and are stored for future reference. This type of memory enables squirrels, for example, to retrieve acorns they have stored some months before. Episodic memory is probably guided by genetically established filters that unconsciously select for recording those scenes that have survival value. Neuroscientists report that this screening for long-term memory is done in humans by the hippocampus, one module in the limbic center of the brain. Human memory capacity is great, but it is, after all, not infinite. As Herbert Simon pointed out, human brains are bounded and human minds need to be selective about all the potential things they could be saving in memory.

Donald's second representational system is the *mimetic.* This system makes it possible to make a mental copy of behavior observed in others so as to mimic it. This may seem like a simple trick for the mind to perform, but in fact it is exceedingly complex. Contrary to the old expression ("monkey see, monkey do"), monkeys do not readily mimic the behavior of other monkeys or of humans. At least for now, animal behavior scholars have not yet discovered such an ability in monkeys and believe it exists in only a limited way in the great apes. Human are, of course, very good at it. Human infants, as early as forty minutes after birth, can stick out their tongues and move their heads from side to side to reenact the behavior of adults. This innate capacity greatly speeds up the process of our learning many useful things from others.

The third representational system that Donald believes evolved in archaic *Homo sapiens* species is the *mythic.* This representational capacity evolved alongside the evolution of language. Its name refers to the storytelling capacity of humans. Stories are basic to human memory processes. The mind establishes a story line, with the memory of one event triggering the memory of the next. Early humans passed on knowledge from one generation to another primarily through storytelling. This created the shared memory of the tribe and not just of the individual. It greatly enlarged the human capacity to retain and share useful knowledge.

Finally, with the invention of written language, humans developed the first powerful memory system external to the human brain, which Donald labels the *theoretic* representational system. This final form of memory is not a physical adaptation in the brain like the others, but a purely cultural adaptation. He argues that theoretic representation, although used by the Egyptian and Eurasian civilizations, first fully flowered with Greek civilization with its extensive use of writing. This last system may have led to some real-location of brain capacity from long-term memory to working memory and other uses. After all, why try to store so much information internally when books are readily available—and now computer hard drives and the Internet?

Donald presents evidence that all four of these representational systems are active in modern human minds.[11] People use them all. As representations form in the mind from messages received from the sense organs, they are mentally tested for relative accuracy, usefulness, and fit with prior knowledge. Since the world contains an infinite amount of empirical information, humans must selectively process information and compress it into knowledge, concepts, and cognitive systems that fit into their physically limited brains. A more useful representation is one that can account for empirical evidence more accurately and compactly. Evidence suggests that people are genetically programmed to give priority to establishing representations of some kinds of information over other kinds that are less useful. It's much easier to remember the hazard that caused a big fall than the one that caused a minor stumble.

Although remarkable memory capacity is part of the story of the unique features of the human mind, it alone cannot account for the relative suddenness of the Great Leap, since memory capacity must have accumulated slowly and gradually over millions of years as hominid brains grew larger.

## THE DEVELOPMENT OF LANGUAGE

A second theory about the basis of the Great Leap has been argued most comprehensibly by Jared Diamond, a physiologist, in *The Third Chimpanzee*.[12] Diamond has drawn on all the relevant disciplines in assembling his argument. He has documented the full array of artifacts that have been found at Cro-Magnon and other similar sites, dating from forty thousand years ago.

> Standardized bone and antler tools appeared for the first time. So did unequivocal compound tools of several parts tied or glued together, such as spear points set in shafts or ax heads fitted onto wooden handles. Tools fall into many distinct categories whose function is often obvious, such as needles, awls, mortars and pestles, fishhooks, net sinkers and rope. The rope (used in nets or snares) accounts for the frequent bones of foxes, weasels, and rabbits at Cro-Magnon sites. Sophisticated weapons for safely killing dangerous large animals at a distance now appear—weapons such as barbed harpoons, darts, spear throwers, and bows and arrows.

Diamond acknowledges that there is yet no consensus on the key factors that produced the Great Leap. After reviewing the evidence he concludes, "I can think of only one plausible answer: the anatomical basis for spoken complex language. The answer seems to involve the structure of the larynx, tongue, and associated muscles that give us fine control over spoken sounds." These vocal structures involve a few small bones but mostly soft tissues that quickly disappear. This makes it difficult to date the origin of human language. Some evidence, however, suggests that some of the required throat bones were present in Neanderthals. This weakens Diamond's argument for language as the critical ingredient, since he has himself pointed out the sharp contrast between the crude tools of the Neanderthals and the complex tools of their contemporaries, the Cro-Magnon.

Terrence Deacon has recently offered even stronger evidence for a much earlier origin of hominid language. In *The Symbolic*

*Species: The Co-evolution of Language and the Brain*,[13] he argues that hominids developed the unique features of their language skills around two million years ago—long before the Great Leap. He presents a strong case that the feature of human communication that distinguishes it from communication in other species is the use of symbols to represent objects in the environment. Moving to this higher level of abstraction facilitated the social life of hominids and served, by mutual reinforcement, to gradually increase the size of the working memory (prefrontal) area of the human brain where multiple ideas can be reviewed together. Symbolization created pressure for more working memory—and an enlarged working memory enabled more symbolization. Of all areas of the growing hominid brain, the prefrontal area has grown the fastest.

~

In summary, there can be no doubt that spoken language gave a significant boost to the capacity of early hominids to engage in complex and coordinated social behavior, such as tool making and hunting or gathering in groups. However, the evidence assembled by Deacon indicates that spoken language in some form was developed by hominids some one to two million years before the emergence of modern *Homo sapiens* only some hundred thousand years ago. And the Great Leap roughly coincides with the appearance of modern *Homo sapiens.* So language alone seems inadequate to account for the timing and magnitude of the Great Leap; it cannot by itself account for the emergence of the observed burst in inventiveness and social institutions. We realized we had to look further for clues about what happened to the human mind to cause the Leap. This led us to explore recent discoveries about both the richness of genetically provided skill sets, of which language is only one, and of the role of drives in human minds.

# 3

# INNATE DRIVES AND SKILLS

*All that is comes from the mind; it is based on the mind, it is fashioned by the mind.*

—THE PALI CANON

One of the newest developments in the study of how the mind works is the avalanche of information about genetically encoded skill sets. For example, scientists now understand that human minds are preconditioned at birth to learn language. The human brain has evolved into a mechanism that can genetically carry some elements of language from one generation to the next.[1] This genetic base for language is what enables children to learn to talk in grammatically patterned sentences so quickly, and then to add on those elements of language such as vocabulary that are culturally created.

This example of the human brain's genetic skill set for language is but one example of such skill sets. Pinker has hypothesized that a more complete inventory of such skill sets will include at least those listed here:[2]

- Intuitive mechanics: how objects can be manipulated.
- Intuitive biology: how plants and animals work.
- Numbers: basic concepts of quantity.

- Orientation: mental maps for large territories.
- Habitat selections: the kind of territory best for humans to live in.
- Danger: understanding major hazards—snakes, heights, and so on.
- Food: what is good to eat.
- Contamination: intuitions about contagion and disease.
- Body monitoring: current status of bodily well-being.
- Intuitive psychology: predicting other people's behavior.
- A mental Rolodex file: a database on important individuals.
- Self-concept: a sense of the individual as a separate actor in the world.
- Justice: sense of rights, obligations, and so on.
- Kinship: intuitive recognition of kinship relationships.
- Mating: an inbuilt preference for certain types of potential mate.

This list shakes up many conventional assumptions about human behavior. Is Pinker serious about a genetically available Rolodex file about important individuals in your life? He is very serious. Consider the number of people whose voices you can recognize over the phone after they have spoken about five words, any words. That recognition instantly opens up a mental file on the speaker, allowing you to jump right into a sophisticated conversation. While the specific information about each of these people has, of course, been learned through long association, the mental mechanism that makes it work is preloaded, Pinker argues, as an innate skill. He has assembled evidence from many sources to build a reasonable, even though preliminary, case for each of these skill sets.

Language capacity is his first, and best-documented, example. To cite just one piece of evidence, tribes in the highlands of New Guinea, who have been separated from other human contact for up to forty thousand years, use the same symbolic structure and grammatical constructions as all other humans across the globe. This strongly suggests that all humans share a common genetic basis of language.

More recently, Gary Marcus and his team of psychologists at New York University have found that seven-month-old infants pay more attention to sentences with unfamiliar structures than to sentences with familiar structures. This means that they can recognize sentence structures, generalize about the abstract, almost algebraic rules they involve, and display curiosity about shifts in these rules. The babies recognize these formal rules well before they can understand what words mean or how to say them. The infants demonstrate a well-stocked, innate intellectual tool kit for learning human speech. "This is a universal property of the human mind. . . . Babies' minds are built to look for such rules—even without being told."[3]

Pinker has assembled somewhat similar evidence for the existence of skill modules under each of the categories in the list. For example, consider the skill set for habitat selection. Until recently in evolutionary time, human forebears were hunter-gatherers who needed to move on to new living sites whenever local plant and animal resources gave out. Picking the right next site was a vital life-or-death issue. It would not be surprising, therefore, if humans developed an innate skill set for this selection process. The human genetic homeland is the African savanna—grasslands dotted with clumps of trees. When biologist George Orians and several collaborators conducted experiments of human habitat preferences, they showed American children and adults slides of landscapes and asked which ones they would prefer to visit or live in. The children preferred savannas, even though they had never been to one. The adults expressed an equal preference for savannas and for deciduous and coniferous forests—similar to much of the American landscape. Neither group liked the idea of living in or visiting deserts or rain forests. In a second stage of the study, Orians asked professional gardeners, photographers, and painters what kinds of landscapes people find beautiful. Their answers described the features of a savanna: semi-open space, even ground cover, views to the horizon, large trees, water, changes in elevation, and multiple paths leading out. This clearly describes in some detail the kind of setting that would in all likelihood have been ideal for a group of hunter-gatherers.

The Darwinian mechanism that may have speeded up the process of evolving these skill sets was first spelled out by an American psychologist, James Mark Baldwin, a century ago.[4] He pointed out that any new behavior learned by humans that permitted them to persist in a new ecological niche would create selection pressure for any genetically carried features that would aid survival in the new niche. In this way culturally acquired adaptations would in time be indirectly reinforced by natural selection. For example, think of the hunter-forager bands that first migrated north in Eurasia to the edges of the Ice Age glaciers. The use of animal furs for clothing and shelters could have been among the learned behaviors that enabled this shift into the new, colder niche. Once there, given that having blue eyes improves survival chances in this region of snow and ice, this trait would now be favored by natural selection. Thus the presence of a cultural adaptation—the use of fur—favored certain genetic adaptations, such as blue eyes.

Building on this logic, Pinker points out, "Humans analyze the world using intuitive theories of objects, forces, paths, places, manners, states, substances, hidden biochemical essences, and, for other animals and people, beliefs and desires." He adds, "All people, right from the cradle, engage in a kind of scientific thinking."[5]

He hastens to point out that the existence of these skill sets should in no way undermine the conventional belief that humans are very skilled at learning new things as life proceeds. The innate skill sets simply provide a head start on learning all the things that are important for achieving human goals. "Talking about innate modules is not meant to minimize learning but to explain it. . . . Both scientists and children have to make sense of the world, and children are curious investigators striving to turn their observations into valid generalizations."[6]

Pinker is a member of a group known as evolutionary psychologists, probably the most rapidly growing group in contemporary psychology. They are quickly generating a stream of new discoveries about mental skill sets (they also term them "psychological mechanisms") that are both universal and genetically programmed. The latest findings of this new field have been assembled by David Buss in *Evolutionary Psychology: The New Science of the Mind.*[7] Did the accumulated development of mental skill sets trigger the Great Leap? Neither Pinker nor Buss makes that claim, but their description of skill sets certainly suggests it. But the development of innate skill sets, like that of memory and language, must have been a gradual process that, while necessary for the Great Leap, would not have been sufficient. However, new work has pushed Pinker's argument one step closer to a sufficient cause.

## The Intermingling of Skill Sets

Steven Mithen, an archeologist who has focused his work on the contribution of skill sets to the Leap, supports Pinker's case that the mind of archaic *H. sapiens* gradually became programmed with different types of specialized skill sets.[8] But he goes on to emphasize that these skill sets or modules were separated—literally disconnected from one another in the mind.

He postulates that various isolated skill modules were preceded in evolution by a rather primitive general problem-solving ability that could deal only in a slow and laborious way with novel situations. He points to evidence in chimpanzees that the earliest specialized module in primates was the one for social skills. He believes that much later the language skills of hominids were developed as a part of this module. After social skills, he argues that hominids evolved a set of skills for dealing with the natural environment and also a set of technical skills.

The capstone of his argument is that at some critical point these separated modules were connected directly to one another in working memory, so that, for the first time, humans could use all their skills simultaneously to address compound problems. In making his argument Mithen draws not only on the work of the evolutionary psychologists but also on his thorough knowledge of the latest findings of his own discipline, archeology. He concludes, quite persuasively, that it was the *intermingling* of genetically based skill sets that enabled the Great Leap. Such a change in mental wiring need not have taken terribly long in evolutionary time. He suggests that the combination of genetically based environmental skills (hunting, gathering, and so on), technical skills (tool making and the like), and social skills (coordination of hunting parties) were greatly facilitated by the bridging made possible by the use of language. For example, bridging between social skills and natural environmental skills led humans to anthropomorphize animals so that they could for the first time visualize the motives behind animal behavior and better predict their actions. This in turn could have enabled humans to combine their technical tool-making skills with their improved skills in predicting animal life, greatly upgrading their hunting skills.

The evidence Mithen assembles leaves little doubt that at some point some such interconnecting of skills did take place in the human brain, and that this was an important, even critical step toward achieving the dramatic developments of the Great Leap. Furthermore, Mithen's hypothesis gains support from the recent work of neuroscientists with their powerful new techniques for scanning the brain in action.

## THE CONTRIBUTION OF BRAIN SCANNING

The several methods for electronically scanning the brain are rapidly making it possible to determine what parts of the brain are engaged in what kinds of mental work. This is making it possible to find out, for instance, where signals coming into the brain from the various sense organs are processed; where the motor centers are located; and where in the brain the different skill sets such as language reside. On the basis of work of this kind, a team of neuroscientists at McMaster University headed by Sandra Witelson generated headline news recently with an announcement of their new findings. They had discovered that Albert Einstein's inferior parietal lobe—the part of the brain that is now known to process mathematical concepts, three-dimensional images, and spatial relationships—was significantly larger than normal. This certainly does sound like the skill set with which Einstein was specially gifted.

Scanning research on the frontal cortex of the brain is of particular interest here. Scientists have known for some time that the frontal cortex behind the forehead—and especially the prefrontal cortex—is the most recently developed major part of the brain. It now seems clear from the work of neuroscientists that it is this part of the brain that houses the critical capacity to *combine* the various skill sets that have evolved over time in different parts of the human brain.

The work of combining the action possibilities of several skill sets probably occurs in the dorsolateral prefrontal cortex, where—to quote from Rita Carter's new compendium on neuroscience findings—"Things are held 'in mind' and manipulated to form plans and concepts. This area also seems to choose to do one thing rather than another."[9] She goes on, "The orbito-frontal cortex seems, then, to be the area of the brain that bestows a quality we may refer to as free will." More generally, it is this prefrontal cortex part of the brain "that is given over to man's most impressive achievements—juggling with concepts; planning and predicting the future; selecting thoughts and perceptions for attending and ignoring others; binding perceptions into a unified whole; and, most important, endowing those perceptions with meaning."[10]

This all sounds as if neuroscientists have found the center of human consciousness—and that is exactly what they say they have found. But how does brain scanning technology make such conclusions possible? Consider the following example. A person's head is placed in a scanning device. When all is quiet, the researcher offers some simple instructions, say, to lift up the right index finger. The machine lights up to report which part of the brain becomes active to perform this task—in this case, the auditory processing and motor centers. The next request is to choose any single finger on either hand and lift it up. Now for the first time the prefrontal cortex also lights up—there is a choice to be made about which finger. Proceeding from one such question to another, the researchers map the functions of the various parts of the brain, and their conclusions are what permit the kinds of statements quoted earlier. Thus we can say that the dorsolateral prefrontal cortex, also known as the working memory, carries out the combining of skill sets that Mithen hypothesized.

## ADDING FOUR-DRIVE
## THEORY TO THE PUZZLE

We have one more theory—our own four-drive theory—to put forward, which we believe is necessary to fully account for the puzzles of the modern human mind. This takes us back to Phineas

Gage and the role that the limbic center of the brain plays in the mystery of the Great Leap. Armed with contemporary knowledge of the brain, it's much clearer why Gage's injury made such a dramatic change in his character. Much of the latest work on this subject is by Antonio Damasio, including his new work on the Gage case itself. Damasio is a neurologist who has specialized in providing medical care to people suffering from significant brain damage. He describes one of his early patients, who was very similar to Gage in terms of the type of brain damage and the associated behavior change:

> I had before my eyes the coolest, least emotional, intelligent human being one might imagine, and yet his practical reason was so impaired that it produced, in the wanderings of daily life, a succession of mistakes, a perpetual violation of what would be considered socially appropriate and personally advantageous.
>
> He had had an entirely healthy mind until a neurological disease ravaged a specific sector of his brain and had, from one day to the next, caused this profound defect in decision making. The instruments usually considered necessary and sufficient for rational behavior were intact in him. He had the requisite knowledge, attention and memory: his language was flawless; he could perform calculations; he could tackle the logic of an abstract problem. There was only one significant accompaniment to his decision-making failure: a marked alteration of the ability to experience feelings. Flawed reason and impaired feelings stood out together as the consequences of a specific brain lesion, and this correlation suggested to me that feeling was an integral component of the machinery of reason.[11]

Damasio goes on to say, "Two decades of clinical and experimental work with a large number of neurological patients have allowed me to replicate this observation many times, and to turn a clue into a testable hypothesis." Damasio's hypothesis involves the way the limbic brain center and the prefrontal cortex work together in decision making. The limbic center is a cluster of brain modules located in the lower central brain.[12] He argues that as neural messages are routed from the sense organs through the limbic centers of the brain they are evaluated, picking up what he calls "markers" that indicate whether the representation is registering as beneficial or harmful in terms of basic human purposes or drives. As Damasio put it, "Since many decisions have an impact on an organism's future, it is plausible that some criteria are rooted . . . in the organism's biological drives (its reasons, so to speak). Biological drives can be expressed [as feelings] and used as a marker . . . in a field of representations held active by working memory." "A drive . . . originates in the brain core, permeates other levels of the nervous system, . . . and emerges as either feelings or non-conscious biases to guide decision making."[13]

Damasio concludes that the affective signals originating in the limbic brain center are an essential part of the reasoning and decision-making process, providing two essential ingredients to the work of the prefrontal cortex, the seat of consciousness. Reasoning does not work without affective signals to provide goals, intentions, purposes, and ultimate motives. It is the role of affective signals to provide consistency and continuity to human behavior, the element of commitment. That is, feelings provide the quality of integrity to the self that was so lacking in Gage and in the similar patients that Damasio examined.

Second, affective signals serve to speed up the choice process by rapidly eliminating unpromising options that will not serve human purposes. Without affective signals' reducing the number of potential actions to be evaluated, decision making would be much too slow to be practical. These signals sort the multitude of potential options available for action to a much smaller set that an individual can then take the time to review in a rational analytical process. The basic drives that produce the affective signals would have developed in evolution to steer, to activate, and to speed up the decision process and thus enable survival.

Human drives are located in the limbic region of the brain. This part of the brain has, until recently, been referred to as the most primitive part of the brain, the home of the most primitive impulses. Now, following Damasio's lead, neuroscientists are finding out much more about it and its central, sophisticated role in the entire functioning of the modern mind. It turns out that the limbic center, the seat of subconscious drives, is very closely wired to the prefrontal cortex, the seat of consciousness, meaning, and choice. It is this connection that Gage apparently lost. When an incoming perception is routed through the limbic center it is coded for strength of relevance to basic human drives. This coding, Damasio's "marker," is sent to the prefrontal cortex where it can be evaluated and juggled along with relevant long-term memories and skill sets. Possible lines of responsive action are imagined; these can be shunted back and forth to the limbic center for further evaluation in terms of basic drives. The prefrontal cortex then makes a conscious choice that is enacted through the motor centers of the brain.

The biological drives that Damasio refers to have been discussed using other labels by many other leading students of the mind from a variety of disciplines. The range of terms they employ is informative: ultimate motives (Barkow, Cosmides, and Tooby—among the founders of evolutionary psychology),[14] primary values (Durham—a pioneer of evolutionary anthropology),[15] goals (Pinker), epigenetic rules (Lumsden and Wilson),[16] and value centers (Edelman). Wilson states, "Without the stimulus and guid-ance of emotion, rational thought slows and disintegrates."[17] Pinker pulls this whole line of analysis of the brain's functioning together: "Intelligence is the pursuit of goals in the face of obsta-cles. . . . The emotions are mechanisms that set the brain's highest-level goals. . . . Emotion triggers the cascade of subgoals and sub-subgoals that we call thinking and acting."[18]

None of these scholars, however, have ventured to name or describe the biological drives that they see as essential to human reasoning and decision making. Wilson has said that he believes it is up to the social sciences to undertake this task, arguing that the social sciences have been remiss in their reluctance to come to terms with Darwin's theory of evolution. His call for the unification of knowledge specifically targets this issue. There has, in fact, been no sustained scientific attention to the issue of drives among social scientists since the pioneering work of Sigmund Freud opened up the field of subconscious drives to scientific investigation nearly a century ago. Except for the work of a few psychologists such as McDougal and Thorndike, Freud's work was then largely neglected except for its application to psychotherapy. This neglect may have occurred because the modern methods of neuroscience were not available to test the early hypotheses and the resulting prolifer-ation of proposed subconscious drives rendered the whole idea meaningless.

The four drives that we propose in this book constitute our response to Wilson's challenge. As stated in Chapter One, the drives we hypothesize are the drive to acquire (D1), the drive to bond (D2), the drive to learn (D3), and the drive to defend (D4). These four subconscious drives are located in the brain's limbic center. Mental drives of this type have an exceedingly long history. As soon as multicelled animals had the start of a central nervous system, some of these creatures would have evolved primitive mental systems that steered them toward essential resources and away from hazards. Creatures with such mechanisms would be able to pass on more genes to future generations than those without. Over time these drives became more sophisticated but they retained their original function of initiating goal-directed behavior; they provided the urge to action, the intentionality and purpose behind all behavior.

One way to test for the evolution of such subconscious drives is to ask a simple question: Which species of animal would be more likely to survive—one whose central nervous system has evolved modules that drive behavior toward essential resources, or one without such mental drive modules? The answer is, of course, obvious, and it is backed up by the evidence that all animals with a central nervous system exhibit signs of having drives. And there is no reason not to believe that humans, with the most complex central nervous system, could have evolved drives with unique forms and complexities.

We believe that each of the four specific drives we propose is primary, that is, independent from all the others in the sense that fulfilling one does not fulfill the others. We argue that, in combination with one another, these four drives have provided humans with a significant increase in *inclusive fitness,* to use the term of evolutionary biologists. These four drives, while not necessarily the only human drives, are the ones that are central to a unified understanding of modern human life. They provide the ultimate motives—the *what* of human behavior—even as other parts of the human mind, such as skill sets and memory, provide the *how.*

More specifically, we hypothesize that the four drives, explicated in detail in the next four chapters, have been genetically evolved in humans to act as a set of decision guides. These drives serve to energize and partially steer human reasoning and decision making (cognition), perceiving (the senses), remembering (representation) and acting (skill sets and motor centers) in individuals. A growing body of evidence from complexity theory suggests that even a few such fundamental drives, in dynamic interaction with each other and with other parts of the brain, can generate the very complex behavior that characterizes everyday life.[19]

Biologists since Darwin have made an implicit and unchallenged assumption that humans' most basic drives were genetically frozen millions of years ago. We follow both Wilson and Pinker in believing that this is an erroneous assumption. New knowledge about the working of the mind supports the idea that all parts of the brain continued to evolve over the many years that hominids were developing into modern humans. We will offer and support the hypothesis that the basic drives of humans have been subject to relatively recent genetic change. Further, we will argue that shortly prior to the Upper Paleolithic, a critical reconfiguration of these basic drives occurred that provided the final element necessary to account for the Great Leap. This was a reconfiguration within the limbic center of the brain that transformed a very smart hominid into a human being, modern *Homo sapiens.* This genetically based reconfiguration, somewhat ironically, served to place cultural change rather than genetic change at the forefront of further human development.

The review of Wilson's *Consilience* in the *Economist* commented that Wilson's examples of how genetic rules (*drives,* in our terms) were reflected in human behavior, such as color perception and the incest taboo, were somewhat trivial and did not go to the heart of the distinctive features of being human. With the exposition of our four-drive theory, this valid point can now be addressed.

It is our hypothesis that in archaic *Homo sapiens,* the drives to acquire and defend were the primary, ultimate drives; the drives to bond and to learn were secondary or derivative drives. We propose that during the critical developmental period that triggered the Great Leap, the brain evolved in three related and mutually reinforcing ways. First, the drives to bond and to learn were extended and reconfigured to become primary alongside the drives to acquire and defend. Second, clusters of multiple skill sets became interconnected in the prefrontal cortex as Mithen has proposed. Third, humans, under the press of fulfilling all four drives, evolved a new integrating skill set that enabled them to develop complex social contracts, not only with other individuals but with groups and with their tribal entity conceptualized as a totality. This social contracting skill enabled humans to integrate individual action with collective action toward the fulfilling of all four primary drives. In combination, these three steps created the uniquely adaptive capacities humans have demonstrated ever since. We believe that without these changes in the brain the remarkable developments that followed in human history could not have taken place. To put it in other words, a population made up of Gages, without the basic four drives independently at work through their tight connection to the integrative work performed in the prefrontal cortex, could not have created human civilizations. These developments, we propose, were the final changes that triggered the Great Leap.

As noted in Chapter One, it seems likely that at some point the ancestral human population dwindled to as few as four to ten thousand—small enough to maintain and propagate the genetic changes that enabled the Great Leap. It was from this group that humans with biologically modern brains multiplied and dispersed within and from Africa in sophisticated, fairly egalitarian hunter-gatherer bands of at least 100 to 150 people. These bands were, in all likelihood, equipped with several types of wood, stone, bone, and fiber tools, with shelters, clothing, fire, and perhaps domesticated dogs. To have created such artifacts each such band would probably have been, in effect, a complete well-developed, tightly bonded organization. Each band would probably have had a decision-making or governance system with a simple chain of command, some division of labor, a set of behavioral ground rules (norms) with associated incentives (rewards and punishments), and a belief system that addressed the meaning of human existence with associated myths and rituals (religion). Each band would probably have developed a patterned relationship with adjacent bands, characterized by trading and raiding. Such a social organization in combination with their technology would have given these bands a massive advantage in overall fitness over any variety of archaic *Homo sapiens*.

~

Our hypothesis about the four drives, the interconnected skill sets, and the social contracting skill will be supported by a wide variety of evidence drawn from a number of disciplines. Each of these mental elements will be considered in detail, along with the mechanism by which they could have evolved. Still, it is a compound hypothesis that will require much more testing by other scholars from the relevant disciplines who can bring to bear their specialized methods and understandings. If supported by subsequent testing, our hypothesis will have significant implications for many aspects of practical everyday affairs.

The first of the four drives we will consider is the drive to acquire. Even though this drive is probably one of the oldest, it remains one of the key pieces to the puzzle of human nature.

# PART TWO

## THE FOUR DRIVES
## BEHIND HUMAN CHOICES

# 4

# THE DRIVE TO ACQUIRE (D1)

*It comes with us from the womb and never leaves us 'til we go
into the grave.*

—ADAM SMITH

Two landmark studies of the health of British civil servants
starkly reveal the impact of the oldest and most basic
human drive—the drive to acquire. The work has come to
be known as the Whitehall studies, named after the district in
London where many government offices are located.[1]

What makes the British Civil Service such a remarkable example of bureaucracy is that almost everything depends on your rank
and position. What you earn, the perks you enjoy, the quality of the
teacups you drink from, all are strictly ordered according to a hierarchy of employment grades. There is little variance within grade,
and sharp distinctions, both material and symbolic, across grades.

In both Whitehall studies, the researchers attempted to determine the relationship between the health of civil servants and their
relative position in the Civil Service hierarchy. The first study was
conducted between 1967 and 1969 and involved eighteen thousand males between the ages of forty and sixty-nine. Risk of death
from coronary heart disease and other causes proved to be inversely
related to employment grade for male civil servants aged between

forty and sixty-four. Put simply, the higher one's rank in the Civil Service, the lower the risk of death at any given age. And the differences were not trivial. The lowest-ranked civil servants were more than three times more likely to die from heart disease than their highest-ranked colleagues.

In the second set of Whitehall studies, two decades after the first, the sample consisted of over ten thousand male and female civil servants aged between thirty-five and fifty-five. Again, the researchers found a strikingly similar relationship between the risk of death at any given age and position in the status hierarchy. Furthermore, they found that not only the death rate, but the rate at which civil servants experienced long illnesses (defined as an absence of more than a week that was supported by a required doctor's certificate) was also inversely related to employment grade. For instance, relative to their highest-ranking female colleagues, women in the lowest employment grade were four times more likely to have been ill for extended periods.

As Robert Frank notes, "What is striking is that this gap in mortality and morbidity between the highest and lowest employment grades did not shrink at all despite two decades of economic growth between the studies."[2] In absolute terms, the lowest grades had become wealthier and had access to more modern medicine, yet the gap in their health relative to their higher-ranked colleagues persisted. What makes this finding even more striking is that even the lowest-ranked British civil servants cannot be considered poor or ignorant in an absolute sense, and hence these factors cannot explain their relatively poorer health. Nor can access to medical care be the cause, because they all had access to the British National Health Service, which although not the best health care system in the world is certainly better than most.

The exact mechanism by which relative position influences health is not fully understood. Some argue that it is due to the increased stress associated with low relative positions. Because stress compromises the human immune system, low relative position may lead to higher mortality and morbidity. Others suggest that it may not be low status but rather the loss in autonomy and control that is associated with lower-ranking jobs.

Given the striking relationship between relative status and well-being, the ubiquity of social stratification in all societies is hardly surprising. Nor is the widespread existence of employment systems based on fine gradations of rank, offering salaries and benefits tied to mobility through these ranks. We have encountered such employment systems in virtually all kinds of organizations we have studied throughout the world. As bureaucratic and cumbersome as these systems might appear, they are consonant with the fact that in a world of limited resources, humans who achieve relative success in acquiring have both literally and figuratively better survival prospects.

## A War of All Against All?

The Whitehall studies support the Hobbesian view of human nature as a war of all against all. To survive and prosper you have to do better than others. In a world of scarce resources, survival depends on constantly striving to outdo your fellow human beings.

Thus one of the innate drives located in the minds of all humans is the drive to acquire. This we define as a drive to seek, take, control, and retain objects and personal experiences humans value. In the course of evolution humans have been selected naturally for this drive by survival pressures, based primarily on the basic needs for food, fluid, shelter, and sexual consummation. Humans identify themselves with acquired objects and pleasurable experiences and feel a sense of ownership in this regard. Given the general scarcity of desired objects and experiences, this drive draws humans into competition with other humans. It is usually—but not always—a zero-sum game.

In human history objects of value were acquired in the first instance by gathering, scavenging, hunting, and fishing, and later by transforming natural objects into more valued forms such as stone tools. Secondarily, they were acquired by exchange, and also by the use of force and stealing.

People are driven to acquire both regular and positional goods, a distinction drawn by Robert Frank that also parallels Plato's distinction between the erotic and thymotic parts of the human soul.[3] *Eros* or regular goods include material objects such as food, clothes, and housing, as well as pleasurable activities such as eating, drinking, entertainment, and sex. *Thymos* is the demand for positional goods that confer status or recognition in a social hierarchy. Of course, this distinction is often inseparable in practice. You can want a Ferrari because you want a fast car and the exhilarating experience of speed as well as the status it confers on you. The conflation of eros and thymos is also evident in Veblen's discussion of so-called inferior goods—items, like paintings by Picasso, that in contrast to most economic goods increase in demand as their price increases, because the value of the good lies not in its intrinsic worth (though the owner may certainly enjoy the aesthetic pleasure of viewing a great painting) but in its conspicuous display of social status.[4]

Despite these complications, it is important to recognize that people have a drive to acquire both material and positional goods because neither is entirely reducible to the other. As the last generation in Thomas Mann's epic novel *Buddenbrooks* so painfully discovered, you can't eat status.[5] The precious family silver and fine artifacts—symbols of the Buddenbrook family status—eventually had to be sold when material survival was at stake. At the same time, as the *nouveau riche* have time and again discovered, acquiring material goods does not immediately confer social status. Even though they have all the material goods in the world, the newly rich are still driven by the desire for social status. The drive to acquire is thus rarely satisfied. You can always want more and you can always seek ever-greater status distinctions.

We have often been asked if the drive to acquire is ultimately derived from what Freud called the sex drive.[6] Is the acquisitive drive all about increasing sex appeal? In Chapter Nine, we more fully discuss the role of sex, via the mechanism of mate selection, in shaping all four drives. At this stage, let us simply highlight a few main points that establish that the drive to acquire cannot be reduced to or deduced from the need to have sex. Drawing on E. O. Wilson's insightful discussion of sex in human nature, we must start by recognizing that sex is not designed primarily for reproduction.[7] If multiplication of the human species were the only objective, it would be better off with asexual reproduction. Bacteria, fungi, and numerous other creatures have evolved far more efficient ways to multiply than the human method of sexual reproduction.

The main advantage of sexual reproduction is that sex creates genetic diversity in succeeding generations—and diversity promotes adaptability. Of course, diversity can theoretically be obtained by a sexual system based on one sex or a hundred. The reason a two-sex system prevails in the animal world is that it permits the most efficient division of labor. The female specializes in producing eggs, and the male in producing sperm. The difference between these two kinds of sex cells is often extreme. In the case of humans, the egg is eighty-five thousand times larger than the sperm. Moreover, a woman can produce only about four hundred eggs in her life, of which at best twenty can be fertilized and converted with significant additional investment of time and energy to surviving children. In contrast, a man releases about 100 million sperm each time he ejaculates. Females thus have a greater stake in each sex act. A woman must make sure that a man is willing to invest more in the care of her children than the few seconds it takes for him to impregnate her.

While men and women might equally seek sexual pleasure, women are unlikely to select men solely on the basis of their drive to acquire. No doubt, men who display a drive to acquire material and positional goods will be desirable. Yet a man's sex appeal will hinge not only on his drive to acquire but also on his ability to form long-term bonds, because the woman needs his commitment to help raise her children. This is why human females do not have the sharply defined period of *estrus*—of being "in heat" and both ready to breed and interested in doing so—that characterizes most mammals. Humans' sexual responsiveness is diffused evenly over time, encouraging frequent sexual intercourse, rather than insemination during peak heat. This ongoing sexual intimacy serves to fulfill the drive to bond as well as the drive to acquire. As E. O. Wilson concludes, "Love and sex do indeed go together."[8]

The drive to acquire cannot be seen as being derived from sexual desires. Nor can sexual desires be seen as exclusively a manifestation of the drive to acquire.

## REASON AND DRIVES: ECONOMICS VERSUS EVOLUTION

In a world of scarce resources, the undisputed importance of pursuing acquisitive desires in competition against others has led to the popularity and near-dominance of economic models of human nature. The classical economic view, first articulated by Adam Smith, was that human behavior was best understood as individuals' maximizing their self-interest in competition with others. Of course, the idea of human nature as a war of all against all had been advanced earlier by Hobbes. The difference between the two was that Smith did not see this self-interested struggle among individuals as leading to chaos, whereas Hobbes did. Smith argued that the market mechanism could readily harmonize self-interested competitive behavior, whereas Hobbes thought that only a monarch or a state with absolute power could control the war of all against all.

Recently, a group of economists influenced by the modern evolutionary perspective have suggested that the classical model developed by Adam Smith and others may be incomplete. In this view, advanced by Robert Frank among others, the pursuit of self-interest is undoubtedly an important and fundamental aspect of human behavior. But, by itself, it fails to explain the full range of human behavior. This perspective has come to be known as evolutionary economics.[9]

One major difference between the evolutionary and classical economic views of human behavior is the role of rational analysis in human choices. The evolutionary perspective suggests that, though rationality is certainly an important influence on choice, people are routinely influenced by more innate drives. These drives, which are the product of evolution, are occasionally at odds with rational self-interest. Yet they persist because they enhanced the survival prospects or inclusive fitness of early human ancestors.

Take the case of the most basic human need—food. Most people have a craving to acquire and eat foods that are sweet and high in fat content. It is hard to resist chocolate and potato chips, even though most people rationally understand that unrestrained consumption of such food products increases the risk of such deadly diseases as heart attacks. Despite this knowledge, which would predict that most rational, self-interest-maximizing individuals would exercise restraint in their eating habits, one in three Americans is clinically obese—that is, overweight to an extent that significantly reduces life expectancy. Americans, and increasingly people in other parts of the world, also spend billions of dollars on mostly futile weight loss programs, products, and fads. All this when all it would take would be a simple "no" every time the dessert trolley wheeled past!

Such behavior, Robert Frank notes, may appear unintelligible from the standpoint of orthodox economic models, but is not surprising at all in view of the environmental circumstances under which natural selection molded human appetites.[10]

The principal threat during the Pleistocene period during which humans evolved was not heart disease but starvation. When famine was a real and common threat, the greatest survival prospects belonged to individuals who ate and stored as much fat as possible when food was plentiful. Individuals who had a greater taste and hence a stronger desire for calorie-rich foods would work harder and endure greater risks to hunt for and acquire these foods, thereby building up stores of fat that increased their survival prospects during famines. Such individuals passed on these genes and traits to their progeny, who as a result were more likely to survive. Over time, this process of selection led to a heightened drive to acquire rich foods in the population as a whole.

Even though famine is no longer a common threat to personal survival, people are still prisoners of appetites that were vital to the survival of their Pleistocene-era ancestors.

Would it not have been better for early humans to have evolved cognitive flexibility, to be able to choose to store fats during lean times and to exercise restraint in times of plenty? As desirable as such cognitive flexibility might appear, Frank argues that powerful drives that manifest in consciousness as emotions and commit their holders to certain courses of action may actually be preferable.[11] Drives may indeed assist rather than hinder the ability to make choices. This is because in many situations time is of the essence, and the brain—as fast and agile as it is in humans—can only process information so fast. Inborn drives and emotional reactions to stimuli help the brain by focusing attention and providing rough-and-ready ways to tell what counts.

## Drives and Survival

Drives that produce strong emotions serve the further function of providing an impetus to take action when the stakes are high. Many a Pleistocene human may have been paralyzed by the rational calculus of computing the economic risks and benefits of pursuing food in extremely hostile conditions. Faced with the possibility of death, only those with an instinctive propensity to take risks to acquire food would have survived. As Frank puts it, "Under these circumstances, it is important that a person not only know that he needs food, but that he cares, lest he be unwilling to risk what needs to be done."[12]

This is not to say that reason and rationality play no role in choice. The ability of the human species to make purposeful, rational calculations is certainly a major source of competitive advantage against other animal species. But reason is closely intertwined with the emotions generated by underlying drives. More often than not, choices reflect reason and emotion, rather than simply one or the other.[13]

Consider again the case of food. Notwithstanding the common desire for fat and sugary foods, many people are able to refrain from eating such foods because they reason that being fat is not in the interest of long-term health. In these situations, reason has certainly played a role, but Frank suggests that it is an indirect one. The rational calculation informs the limbic center of the brain that eating will have adverse consequences. This prospect triggers unpleasant feelings that compete directly with the impulse to eat. What drives behavior is a contest among the emotions, not the rational calculation alone. Whether the immediate craving or the fear of long-term problems wins out will determine the outcome of the battle of the bulge.

It turns out that not only does the magnitude of a prospective gain or loss matter, so does its timing. When choosing between rewards that are available at the same time, people always prefer the one that leads to a large gain. Thus the choice between one reward of $100 and another of $120, if both are available at the same time, is a no-brainer. Everybody picks the $120. But if the rewards are available at different times, behavior is often at odds with that predicted by rational choice models. Consider, for instance, the choice between a reward of $100 available in twenty-eight days and a reward of $120 available in thirty-one days. Most subjects given these choices in an experiment behave rationally and choose the $120 reward. They are able to make the calculation that, barring hyperinflationary circumstances, it is better to postpone gratification for three days. But if the same subjects are given the choice between $100 today and $120 three days from now, they are much more likely to choose the $100 today. Given their first choice, this behavior is clearly irrational. Why should these subjects not delay their gratification as they had done earlier? After all, the difference in the timing of the rewards is the same in both situations.

The evolutionary psychologist's explanation is that when both rewards are far away, the cognitive faculties aren't competing against the inherited drive to seek immediate gratification by acquisition. The rational choice wins out. But when the cash is available right away, the instinctive emotional tug of the first choice is too vivid and powerful for many subjects to ignore. Drives win over rational calculation, and they choose the $100 reward. This explains why most people are susceptible to impulse shopping, and can't resist acquiring things that they later regret. Impulse purchases get made every day because the drive to acquire is part of the human evolutionary heritage.

The drive for immediate gratification or acquisition may partly explain the short-term thinking that seems to plague managers of business organizations. It's easy to think of instances when managers have chosen a course of action that leads to immediate returns rather than a strategy that would produce greater returns in the long term. This has been observed, for example, in the field of organization change. Managers are more inclined to take short-term measures to improve firm performance—such as downsizing, or acquiring or divesting companies—than they are to undertake longer-term adaptive actions, such as investing in changing the culture of their firm.[14]

## THE DARK SIDE OF THE DRIVE TO ACQUIRE—THERE'S NEVER ENOUGH

The drive to acquire is not just immediate and inbuilt. It is insatiable. Most people think that if they won the lottery or received that coveted promotion, they would be happy for life. Rarely is that true. As intense as the feelings of pleasure and happiness might be when the event occurs, these feelings diminish rapidly, and people end up being about as happy as they were before. Their desire to acquire returns in full force.[15]

"How much is enough?" ask Terry Burnham and Jay Phelan.[16] Their answer: "When it comes from our genes, the answer is 'as much as possible.' Evolution is a competitive game in which victory comes not from achieving some fixed number of points but by simply outscoring the competition. We are descended from the humans who had the most children, not from those with 'enough' children."

A more benign but equally powerful example of the insatiable drive to acquire goods that improve relative status is the current boom in spending for luxury goods documented by Robert Frank.

In *Luxury Fever,* he documents the ever-escalating competition for status-defining goods, be it Phillipe Patek watches or ever-larger sport utility vehicles. This drive for more is at the heart of the widening disparity between the rich and the poor in America and other countries.[17]

A more troubling manifestation of the drive to acquire is various forms of addiction—to drugs, alcohol, gambling, and other vices. The pleasurable emotions that accompany the consumption of such goods are so compelling that people are driven to seek more—spellbound, as it were, incapable of stopping the longer-term harm that such behavior is bound to cause. In his study of addictions, Jon Elster notes that "addicts have two strong desires: the desire to consume and the desire to stop consuming. In the struggle for self-control, now the one, now the other desire, seems to be gaining the upper hand."[18] Alas, "emotions and cravings might sometimes be so strong as to short-circuit rational choice, or even choice altogether. At their strongest, these urges seem to have an overpowering quality that leaves little room for comparison and choice."[19]

## RELATIVE STATUS BEATS ABSOLUTE WELL-BEING

Experimental research provides ample evidence to support the relative nature of the desire to acquire. When subjects are given the choice of living in two worlds, in which prices are the same, but in one they earn $90,000 and their neighbors earn $100,000 versus another in which they earn $110,000 but their neighbors earn $200,000, they are more likely to choose the former situation. Such behavior is at odds with standard utility-maximizing models of human behavior—in absolute terms subjects would be better off earning $110,000 instead of $90,000. But as the experiments suggest, what humans care about more is their relative status.

Anyone who has raised more than one child or been responsible for managing employees who view themselves as peers will readily recognize this result from real-world experience. Try giving one child (or for that matter one employee) a 20 percent raise in allowance or pay when you have given the other one a 30 percent raise. Though the target of this experiment is clearly better off than before (and even if the target was expecting only 10 percent), you are more than likely going to have to deal with some degree of disgruntlement. "But why did I get less?" is the inevitable question. The desire to avoid having to answer this question may explain why in most companies there is less wage dispersion than the compensation system might allow. Given the choice, most managers would rather give everyone similar bonuses or pay increases than deal with the discontentment caused by sharp differentials.

Nobel Laureate Amartya Sen, who has studied famines, argues that the drive to improve relative status makes sense because even in the most severe famines, there is always some food.[20] The ones who are likely to get it are the people of higher relative status.

Given the certainty of being outranked by someone, Robert Frank asks, why don't people have inner voices that urge them to do their best rather than maximize rank? "A relentless focus on relative position seems more like a recipe for unhappiness than a useful motivational tool."[21] Alas, from an evolutionary perspective, Frank argues, the "purpose of human motivation is not to make us happy but to make us more likely to succeed against the competition."[22] To bolster his case that "concerns about relative position are indeed part of the evolved circuitry of the human brain and not just a cultural artifact,"[23] Frank points to some biochemical evidence that supports this view. He discusses studies by Michael McGuire and his collaborators at UCLA that show that relative position in local primate groups appears to affect, and be affected by, concentration levels of the neurotransmitter serotonin, which regulates moods and behavior. What these studies show is that dominant males in vervet monkey groups have significantly higher serotonin levels. Moreover, changes in their relative status lead to changes in their serotonin levels in the expected direction. Monkeys whose status elevates show higher serotonin levels and those whose status declines show lower serotonin levels. Within limits, serotonin levels are known to be directly related to feelings of well-being. High serotonin levels lead to positive emotions whereas low serotonin levels are associated with a variety of negative emotions including irritability, mania, and depression.

Though the research on humans is much more limited, there is some evidence consistent with the possibility that serotonin levels are related to status rankings. For instance, McGuire and his colleagues have found elevated serotonin levels in the leaders of college fraternities and athletic teams. As tentative as this evidence is, it is a finding that is consistent with research from other traditions that suggests that people are driven to acquire and achieve more than their fellow human beings. Serotonin and other chemical pathways that produce sensations of well-being or depression can be thought of as carrots and sticks that are built into the brain to keep each individual constantly striving—because from an evolutionary perspective, this drive enhances survival prospects.

## POSITIVE AND NEGATIVE CONSEQUENCES OF THE DRIVE TO ACQUIRE

Ambition and envy, two of the most powerful human passions, both stem from our drive to acquire more than others.[24] Ambition is the positive manifestation of this drive. It is the passion, the will and determination to do better, to achieve more, to rise in the status hierarchies that are ubiquitous in all fields of human endeavor. Our evolutionary heritage not only goads us to achieve more for ourselves, it warns us to beware the success of others. Envy is thus the negative manifestation of the drive to acquire. It arises when others get ahead of us. We react enviously and in the extreme we can even act to undermine or sabotage the other person's success.

The drive to improve relative ranking can have productive or deleterious consequences. Leaders of business organizations have long tried to harness this drive to get the most out of their employees. Most corporate mission statements rally their employees to the cause of becoming the leading company in their industry. One of the best-known examples is the former motto of Avis, the second-largest U.S. car rental company: Being number two, "We try harder." When stoked in this way, the drive to improve relative standing can be quite productive.

But the same drive can also lead to cutthroat competition. It's easy to think of cases when human beings have been driven to acquire things they prize by hook or by crook. This acquisitive drive can have disastrous consequences.

One of the earliest examples is the devastation wreaked by early humans on the ecology of the planet, sometimes known as the Pleistocene overkill. Ridley provides a distressing summary of how the rise in human populations in many ecological niches led to the extinction of other species.[25] In North America, for instance, 73 percent of the large mammal population—including grand bison, wild horse, short-faced bear, mammoth, mastodon, saber-toothed cat, giant ground sloth, and wild camel—were quickly eradicated as human populations grew. In South America, 80 percent of the large-mammal genera were soon extinct. Similar accounts of ecological devastation can be found in all other parts of the world. In a battle for relative gain, human ancestors showed little restraint. They were forced to kill today rather than wait for tomorrow for fear that if they waited, their prey would be killed by their competitors. Modern humans may be somewhat more restrained, but the ecological damage fueled by the drive to improve relative well-being continues. The difficulties surrounding the implementation of the Kyoto accord that called for reducing greenhouse gas emissions reflect our continuing inability to restrain ourselves when we think others might get ahead, even though the consequences might be collective disaster—in this instance, widespread global warming.

The drive to acquire more relative to others is probably at the root of the many atrocities human beings have conducted against each other. Wars, slavery, exploitation, discrimination are all at least partly the result of the drive to improve and maintain rank relative to others. Many people see these events as evidence of the existence of an innate aggressive drive in humans.[26] We believe, however, that it is more accurate to describe aggressive action as only one of several means to the end of acquisition. These behaviors do not occur with the frequency one expects in a universal primary drive.

## COMPETITION AND COOPERATION

Relative ranking is a zero-sum game. As you move up in any ranking hierarchy, be it in sports, the corporate ladder, the Forbes list of wealthiest people, or in the collection of rare paintings and artifacts, someone else moves down. The drive to acquire thus naturally leads to competition.

Yet the drive to acquire can also lead to cooperation. This was Adam Smith's great insight. He was the first to see that the selfish drive to increase individual well-being did not necessarily have to lead to a war of all against all, because of the benefits each participant can derive from a social division of labor. Smith recognized that each individual benefited from specialization and subsequent trade or exchange with others who were similarly specialized. The benefits of the division of labor and trade have been most clearly spelled out in Ricardo's theory of comparative advantage. Imagine two Pleistocene hunter-gatherer tribes. One of them is superior to the other at both hunting and fishing. But the superior tribe is slightly better at hunting than it is at fishing and the inferior tribe, though terrible at hunting game, is not as bad at catching fish. According to Ricardo, both tribes are better off if the former specializes in hunting game and the latter in catching fish, so long as they can agree on the right price to exchange game for fish. Even if the first tribe wants to promote its relative status, it should specialize and trade because that will be better for its members. Not surprisingly, the drive to acquire goes hand in hand with what Adam Smith called the propensity to barter, truck, and exchange. As Ridley observes, "because of the division of labor, my selfish ambition to profit from trading with you and yours from trading with me can both be satisfied."[27]

Thus we have evidence from the earliest times of human beings engaging in various forms of economic exchange. In this regard we would hypothesize that humans have an innate skill set for defining what is owned by them as distinct from what is owned by others, and how such objects can be traded. The cultural institutions of property rights, currencies such as money that enable exchange beyond barter, and marketplaces that enable buyers and sellers to discover each other, have greatly facilitated satisfying the drive to acquire.

## THE DRIVE TO ACQUIRE AND THE SENSE OF FAIRNESS

Not all exchanges predicted by a self-interest maximization model occur. Moreover, some of the exchanges that do occur are inconsistent with models of self-interest. These departures from the self-interest model suggest that as powerful as the drive to acquire is, it is far from a complete model of human behavior.

One of the most persistent ways in which individuals deviate from the prediction of the self-interest model is in rejecting exchanges they perceive as unfair. A good example is what is known as the "ultimatum bargaining game." In this experiment, John, one of the subjects, is given $10 to share with Jane, the other subject. If the offer is accepted, both get to keep the money. Otherwise they both lose it. The rational thing for John to do would be to offer Jane a paltry sum like $1, though in principle it could be one cent. For Jane, the rational thing is to accept the offer because she is better off so long as the offer is greater than zero. Yet in ultimatum bargaining games, most subjects in Jane's position refuse an offer they perceive as unfair. On average, Jane accepted the offer when she was offered 40 percent of the reward. In over 20 percent of the cases, those in Jane's position in the experiment refused to accept a non-zero offer.

Such concerns of fairness are common in all forms of exchange—from bazaars in Morocco to investment banking deals on Wall Street. Yet they have no place in a world in which human beings are purely motivated by self-interest.

The behavior of those in John's position in the ultimatum bargaining game is equally at odds with the self-interest model. Most individuals in John's situation offered a fifty-fifty split. Less than 10 percent offered less than 10 percent of the reward. The generosity of those in John's role in the ultimatum bargaining game also reflects concerns about fairness.

Indeed, acts of selfless generosity or altruism abound in human affairs. As often as we are disgusted by the shameful pursuit of self-interest by immoral means, we are heartened to learn about the moral valor of people who go so far as to put themselves in harm's way to help others. Beyond these acts of selfless valor, we observe in everyday behavior generosity that is at odds with self-interest. As Frank observes, "We trudge through snowstorms to cast our ballots, even when we are certain they will make no difference. We leave tips in restaurants in distant cities we will never visit again. We make anonymous contributions to private charities. We often refrain from cheating even when we are sure cheating would not be detected."[28] The list can be extended indefinitely.

How do we explain these behaviors that violate the single-minded pursuit of self-interest? Economists such as Gary Becker have tried to incorporate such behaviors into traditional utility-maximizing models by arguing that people derive nonpecuniary benefits from such acts.[29] They argue that these actions can be seen as investments in reputation that have benefits in the long run, that they are undertaken with the expectation of reciprocity in the future, that the utility function can also include the utilities of others we care about, and so on. In this line of reasoning, altruism is simply seen as a calculated action that confers some gain, however distant or indirect that gain might be.

~

As appealing as the parsimony of explaining all human behavior as stemming from the single-minded pursuit of self-interest might be, it is important to remember that this view was considered suspect even by the founding fathers of modern economics. Adam Smith viewed moral sentiments such as benevolence (the highest virtue) to be just as central to understanding human behavior as the pursuit of self-interest. Even Alfred Marshall, the man historians view as responsible for giving economics a distinct identity separate from moral and political philosophy, recognized that " human beings are capable of unselfish service," and thus "the supreme aim of the economist is to discover how this latent social asset can be developed more quickly and turned to account more wisely."[30]

In the next chapter, we will show the lasting wisdom of these founding fathers of economics in recognizing the limitations of arguments that attempt to reduce all human behaviors to a single drive. We will show that it is more accurate to view such moral sentiments or acts of fairness, generosity, compassion, and caring as stemming from another basic human drive—the drive to bond—which exists independent of, but works in conjunction with, the drive to acquire.

# 5

# THE DRIVE TO BOND (D2)

*That we derive sorrow from the sorrow of others . . . is by no means confined to the virtuous and humane. . . . The greatest ruffian, the most hardened violator of the laws of society, is not altogether without it.*

—ADAM SMITH

*I believe that love cannot be bought, except with love.*

—JOHN STEINBECK

In the heart of Dorchester, a lower-income neighborhood in Boston, a Catholic priest has initiated a simple way to try building a close-knit community from a highly fragmented one.[1] After church every Sunday he began passing a hat and urging people, whether Catholic or not, to put their name in and later draw out another person's name. He asked the " partners" randomly selected in this way to find a time to sit down and talk with each other for thirty to forty-five minutes over a cup of coffee or tea, and suggested that they tell one another something of their life story and about the things that weighed most heavily on their shoulders. That was all there was to it.

This one-on-one community-building campaign has generated hundreds of conversations. It has made friends of strangers and allies of people who thought they had nothing in common. The priest comments, "We were siting on a gold mine all the time and now we have struck gold."

"You walk down the street, and now you know people," says an elderly Irishwoman, who has become friendly with the Cape Verdean, Haitian, Vietnamese neighbors she'd found too strange to speak to after her Irish neighbors moved away. "They have the same problems, the same worries you have. You just didn't know it before."

A sixty-year-old Panamanian has started to feel at home, saying, "I've started realizing we want the same things, we have the same values." A teacher from Boston Latin School reports, "Initially I was very skeptical, because it seemed like kid's stuff— putting names in a hat and all. But it's an amazing thing that's happened. I've met individuals who quietly live very heroic lives." An Italian lifelong resident said she finally feels vindicated for staying through so many changes. "The wonderful thing is that it feels like the old neighborhood. It was pretty lonesome for a while." Now several committees have formed that are taking the initiative to do something about some of the problems they have in the area that they have found they share.

If this story brings a warm glow to your heart, you are experiencing emotions stemming from your own bonding drive. And so were the citizens of Dorchester.

~

Our mission in this chapter is to present a convincing case that humans, all humans, share an innate drive to bond—and that this drive is a primary one, a drive that is independent of and not derived from the need to acquire. We argue that humans have an innate drive to form social relationships and develop mutual caring commitments with other humans that, in fact, is fulfilled only when the attachment is mutual. Early hominids without an innate drive to bond were less likely to get their genes into the next generation than those with such a drive. Female hominids without such genes were less likely to behave so that their children survived to adulthood. Male hominids without such genes were also less likely to be selected by females as mates—good husbands and fathers. And very clearly hominid infants of either gender had to have such a drive because any infant that was unsuccessful in achieving a bond with one or more caring, loving adults was very short-lived. Groups of individuals who were bonded to one another had a better chance of surviving environmental threats than groups that were not. For all these reasons individuals with the genes for bonding had a relative advantage over those without such genes. Nor are the rewards of bonding readily interchangeable with the rewards stemming from the drive to acquire. Where is the marketplace where one can exchange a lifelong friendship for a monetary sum?

## CONVENTIONAL WISDOM AND SOCIAL BONDING

With the celebration of individualism, it may not seem easy to accept the existence of a bonding drive. After all, ever since Adam Smith observed that the bakers and the shoemakers of the world were not going to all their trouble just to be nice to their customers, most economists have argued that self-interest explains not some but all of human behavior. This basic belief has become well established in conventional wisdom in spite of the fact that Smith's own writings dealt extensively with innate social drives and morals as a major factor in human behavior. Following the passage that opens this chapter, he continues, "How selfish soever man may be supposed, there are evidently some principles in his nature, which interest him in the fortune of others, and render their happiness necessary to him, though he derives nothing from it except the pleasure of seeing it."[2] Albert Hirschman, in *Passions and the*

*Interests,* traces in great detail the train of ideas on this subject from Aristotle to Adam Smith and well beyond.[3] He explains how the study of human "passions" evolved into the subject of "interests" (in the plural) and, finally, how this evolved into defining "self-interest" in the singular, almost entirely in terms of rational economic self-interest, as is commonly done today.

It is further ironic that the argument for economic determinism has received more support in the last 150 years from Darwin's theory than from Smith's—and the irony is that it is all based on a massive misunderstanding of Darwin's theory. Most people, if asked to summarize Darwin's theory, would respond by saying, "Survival of the fittest"—a phrase that Darwin never used. If pushed further, most would elaborate that the *fittest* means the strongest, toughest individual—not the one who best "fits in" with and adapts to the surroundings, as Darwin intended. Today, however, it is clear to biologists that evolution is simply not a theory about the survival of the ruthless. As Bateson, a leading British biologist, recently explained it: "Such a conclusion does not follow from an acceptance of Darwinism. It is a travesty of what biologists have observed and what most now believe."[4]

## Evidence for the Drive to Bond

The bonding drive is associated with terms like love, caring, trust, empathy, compassion, belonging, friendship, fairness, loyalty, respect, partnership, and alliance. This drive draws humans into cooperation with others. It has the potential of being a non-zero-sum game, with all parties being winners.

Sociologists and psychologists have studied many obvious manifestations of this drive in modern life. Consider, for example, such phenomena as the bonding between mother and child, the strength of family ties, and the universal presence in all known cultures of some kind of a moral code regarding social relations. Consider, too, acts of loyalty of individuals to various kinds of collectives (sometimes to the point of death), the power of collective symbols, and the power and persistence of social structures, social networks, and embedded relationships.

Sociologists and psychologists have seen social behavior as stemming primarily from the emotions, but they have resisted seeing these emotions as based on an innate drive. A notable exception is the position taken by Roy Baumeister and Mark Leary in their *Psychological Bulletin* article, "The Need to Belong: Desire for Interpersonal Attachments as a Fundamental Human Motivation."[5]

This article does a remarkable job of reviewing the social and psychological literature to determine whether it supports the existence of a fundamental, innate drive to bond with other individuals. Baumeister and Leary define the "need to belong" as "a pervasive drive to form and maintain at least a minimum quantity of lasting, positive and significant interpersonal relationships."[6] We use the term *bond* rather than their *belong* advisedly, because the former clarifies the mutuality of the commitment, the "sticking together" that is essential for its survival power. We will draw extensively upon this article to summarize the evidence for bonding.

Baumeister and Leary test the bonding drive with six rigorous questions.

- *Is there evidence that bonding is a fundamental motive—that it forms relatively easily and operates in a wide variety of settings?* After reviewing extensive evidence drawn from many studies, they conclude, "People seem widely and strongly inclined to form social relationships quite easily without any special circumstances or ulterior motives. Group allegiance seems to arise spontaneously and readily, without needing evidence of material advantage. People invest a great deal of time and effort in fostering supportive relationships with others. External threat seems to increase the tendency to form strong bonds."

- *Is there evidence that people have strong negative emotions associated with breaking social bonds?* They conclude, "The weight of the evidence does favor the conclusion that people strongly and generally resist the dissolution of relationships and social bonds. Moreover, this resistance appears to go well beyond rational considerations of practical or material advantage."

This conclusion will be readily supported by anyone who knows someone who has been laid off from a firm such as IBM, once well known for its tradition of loyalty toward its employees. When these bonds are severed, people report experiencing a deep sense of betrayal. They are shocked and angry. As one ex-IBM employee we interviewed after a layoff put it: "It was worse than discovering that your wife was cheating on you and getting divorced. I felt violated." Interestingly, studies of life inside companies that have downsized found that rather than feeling happy, survivors suffer from acute feelings of guilt, owing to sympathy for those who have been laid off. Managers entrusted with the task of conducting layoffs also report feeling burnt out by the process.

- *Is there evidence that people devote considerable cognitive processing to interpersonal interactions and relationships?* Again the answer is a clear yes. The tendency to ruminate on bonded relationships is captured in the age-old daisy game: "She loves me—she loves me not—she. . . ." This agonizing question is not just restricted to young lovers; it is manifest in different guises in all types of relationships including families, neighbors, and coworkers.

- *Do stable conditions of bonding produce an abundance of positive affect and do chronic deprivation of bonding produce an abundance of negative affect?* Baumeister and Leary conclude, "Many of the strongest emotions people experience, both positive and negative, are linked to belongingness. Evidence suggests a general conclusion that being accepted, included, or welcomed leads to a variety of positive emotions (e.g., happiness, elation, contentment, and calm), whereas being rejected, excluded, or ignored leads to potent negative feelings (e.g., anxiety, depression, grief, jealousy, and loneliness)."

- *Do people without stable, strong bonds with others suffer any adverse or pathological consequences?* They conclude, "Deprivation of stable, good relationships has been linked to a large array of aversive and pathological consequences. People who lack belongingness suffer higher levels of mental and physical illness and are relatively highly prone to a broad range of behavioral problems, ranging from traffic accidents to criminality to suicide."

- *Is there evidence that the bonding drive is universal, innate, and independent—not derivative of other motives?* Baumeister and Leary state that this proposition is difficult to verify because empirical criteria for testing such a hypothesis are not widely recognized. They approach it by examining how well the empirical evidence conforms to evolutionary arguments. They state their conclusions with scientific caution, "Several patterns seem consistent with evolutionary reasoning. It remains plausible (but unproved) that the need to belong is part of the human biological inheritance. If so, the case for universality and nonderivativeness would by strong. At present, it seems fair to accept these hypotheses as tentative working assumptions while waiting for further evidence." We will return to this issue later in this chapter.

In the course of their article Baumeister and Leary cite no less than 296 references to buttress their argument. They close their article by saying, "The desire for interpersonal attachment may well be one of the most far-reaching and integrative constructs currently available to understand human nature."[7]

## EVOLUTION AND INDEPENDENCE OF THE DRIVE TO BOND

It is now generally accepted among biologists that bonding could have evolved in humans by the two basic genetic processes, natural selection and mate selection. Darwin himself believed that some animals, including humans, had social instincts that could steer them toward altruistic behavior. He was, however, somewhat vague about the mechanism for accomplishing this. He was certainly handicapped by not knowing about genes and how they work. Some of Darwin's statements on the subject in *The Descent of Man* are informative. "Every one will admit that man is a social being. We see this in his dislike of solitude and in his wish for society beyond that of his own family. Solitary confinement is one of the severest punishments which can be inflicted."[8] Later, "The feeling of pleasure from society is probably an extension of the parental or filial affections, since the social instinct seems to be developed by the young remaining for a long time with their parents; and this extension may be attributed in part to habit, but chiefly to natural selection."[9]

At another point Darwin made a comment about "social instincts" that later led to significant controversy. In this passage, he stated, "With strictly social animals, natural selection sometimes acts on the individual, through the preservation of variations which are beneficial to the community. A community which includes a large number of [such] individuals increases in number, and is victorious over other less favored ones; even though each separate member gains no advantage over the others of the same community."[10] Decades later one school of biologists built on this comment and put forward the idea of "group selection"—the argument that genes could orient behavior toward the good of the group and even of the whole species.

Subsequent biological theorists argued that group selection was impossible, because the survival of genes was totally dependent upon the survival to successful reproduction of *individual* carriers. Further, any carrier with a genetic disposition to be nice to others would be, in time, wiped out by the selfish free-riders in the population. For a time this seemed to rule out genetically based bonding. This argument came to dominate thinking in the field.

Now, however, many biologists have come to accept the proposition that social bonding is a trait that could have evolved. We will quote just two leading biologists on this current issue. Bateson, in "The Biological Evolution of Cooperation and Trust," states that "cooperative behavior has evolved because those who did it were more likely to survive as individuals and reproduce than those who did not."[11] The innate nature of bonding and group life has been further carefully studied by Fran deWaal in *Good Natured: The Origins of Right and Wrong in Humans and Other Animals*. To quote him, "If group life is based on a social contract, it is drawn up and signed not by individual parties, but by Mother Nature. And she signs only if fitness increases through association with others, that is, if sociable individuals leave more progeny than do solitary individuals. We are seeing how social tendencies came into existence—via a genetic calculus rather than a rational choice. One cannot decide to become what one already is."[12]

There are now two theories on the evolutionary process that led to social bonding. Both offer viable explanations; possibly the two worked hand in hand, coevolving to bring it about. The first of these has been best developed by Elliot Sober, an evolutionary philosopher, and David Sloan Wilson, an evolutionary biologist, in

*Unto Others: The Evolution and Psychology of Unselfish Behavior.*[13] In essence they demonstrate how the free-rider problem has not been a barrier to the evolution of bonding. In their view, social bonding is selected in a multilevel process. Once any social bonding genes get started by any variety-generating process, such genes will, in the first instance, create a disadvantage for their individual carriers, but since their group as a whole will benefit, their group will reinforce the group-oriented behavior. For instance, an expert hunter who shares the meat could well have more offspring than others. Such practices that promote reproductive success have been widely reported in contemporary hunter-gatherer groups both to reinforce pro-group behavior and sanction anti-group behavior.

The kind of bonding that Sober and Wilson discuss is usually called *reciprocal altruism* or *long-term contracting*. Robert Trivers first developed the idea, on a suggestion from George Williams. Trivers states,

> It seems likely that during our recent evolutionary history, there has been strong selection on our ancestors to develop a variety of reciprocal interactions. I base this conclusion in part on the strong emotional system that underlies our relationships with friends, colleagues, acquaintances, and so on. Humans routinely help each other in times of danger. We routinely share food; we help the sick, the wounded, and the very young. We routinely share our tools, and we share our knowledge in a very complex way. During the Pleistocene, and probably before, a hominid species would have met the preconditions for the evolution of reciprocal altruism; for example, long lifespan, low dispersal rate, life in small, mutually dependent and stable social groups, and a long period of parental care leading to extensive contacts with close relatives over many years.[14]

Trivers goes on to explain how certain very human emotions can be derived from this bonding drive. Liking is the emotion that initiates and maintains the process. It indicates a willingness to offer a favor to another who seems willing, in time, to offer one back. Anger protects a person whose niceness has left vulnerable to being cheated. Gratitude calibrates the desire to reciprocate according to the benefits of the original act. Guilt can rack a cheater who is in danger of being found out. Shame is the emotion evoked by public disclosure of cheating.

This is how E. O. Wilson summarizes the argument: "For [non-human] mammals, social life is a contrivance to enhance personal survival and reproductive success. As a consequence, societies of non-human mammalian species are far less organized than the insect societies. They depend on a combination of dominance hierarchies, rapidly shifting alliances and blood ties. Human beings have loosened this constraint and improved social organization by extending kinship-like ties to others through long-term contracts. Contract formation is more than a cultural universal. It is a human trait as characteristic of our species as language and abstract thought, having been constructed from both instinct and high intelligence."[15]

An alternative explanation of the evolution of bonding is best explained by Geoffrey Miller.[16] His account of how humans developed both social bonding and bigger brains goes as follows. The most demanding selection pressure on archaic *Homo sapiens* was created by other members of the species. They competed with one another not only for food and other resources but also for mates. As food and shelter became less of a problem for the survival of their genes into the next generation, the pressure centered on securing mates. Humans have evolved, unlike other primates, to be uniquely choosy about mates. A female chimp is keen to mate with many different males in the troop. A female gorilla is happy to mate with the head male in her troop. Both chimp and gorilla males will mate with any females in heat that they can find. The mating pattern among humans is distinctly different. Given the large brain that humans evolved, they are born in a less developed condition than their primate cousins and require intensive care for a much longer period. Given the bodily commitment that women have to carrying, birthing, and nursing infants, they, or at least their genes, had a big stake in selecting mates who would be supportive fathers and successful food providers. So women would have tended to select husbands who showed promise in this regard, using such indicators as intelligence, wealth, and credible promises of faithfulness. Monogamy evolved to become the mating pattern, with some exceptions, among humans. Meanwhile the genes in men would have tended to bias their selection toward females who appeared young and healthy, who were, on average, going to have more children. Any genes that turned up that delayed the maturation process in females and thereby made them look younger (and as a by-product have bigger brains) would have improved the odds for successful mating.

Some thousands of generations of mate selections, female and male, with these criteria at work could account for the gradual increase in brain size and eventually for the creation of an independent bonding drive. After all, the most convincing promise of lasting care and fidelity is one that is based on the sincere bond of love, not on the short-term motive of sexual pleasure.[17]

Once the bonding drive became established by either or both of these processes, it was greatly reinforced by its by-product, the great burst in productivity it enabled in material terms. The tribe that carried bonding genes could easily outproduce and outfight one that consisted of egocentric individuals with no solid and lasting basis for trusting each other. The bonding drive provided the glue that first made larger organizations like tribes possible.

The extension of the bonding drive beyond the nuclear family unit has enabled humans to undertake all manner of complex tasks that require teamwork. The drive to bond has enabled humans to develop, over millennia, the highly complex and productive interdependencies, specialized division of labor, and elaborate trading systems that we rely on in modern economies for our everyday essentials. The pay-offs of bonding have given humans a tremendous increase in productivity and in their relative fitness in comparison to nonhuman animals. They help us understand the puzzle of the Great Leap, the burst of complex social organizations associated with the Upper Paleolithic period that we discussed in Chapters Two and Three.

In addition to this work on bonding developed by evolutionary biologists, studies by social scientists, mostly psychologists, have also demonstrated the potency and independence of the bonding drive. We will cite three studies as examples; each uses different subjects and different methods.

Robert Hays involved one hundred newly arrived undergraduates as volunteers in a longitudinal study of friendship development.[18] This is one of the very few detailed studies about the way friendships develop in natural settings. All the participants kept detailed records of their evolving friendships with same-sex others over a period of twelve weeks, with a follow-up some three months later. Not surprisingly, these students spent a significant amount of time with their closest friends. Hays asked the students to report on the benefits of these friendships (for example, "we have a lot of fun together," "I feel comfortable talking to 0 about my personal problems") and their costs (for example, "I don't have as much privacy as I'd like due to my relationship with 0," and "being with 0 is at times emotionally aggravating").

Their answers are of special interest as regards the independence of the bonding drive from the acquiring drive. As

hypothesized, the ratings of the benefits received from the relationship were highly correlated with friendship intensity. More
important, the benefits-*plus*-costs score was more highly correlated
with friendship intensity than the benefits-*minus*-costs score.
Providing benefits for a friend at some cost to oneself seems to
enhance the relationship more than it detracts from it.

At the end of Chapter Four we reported on a simple laboratory
experiment called the ultimatum game. In a variation on this game,
the principals in an experiment were given a free choice (without
others knowing) of keeping all of the $10 at stake or of sharing
some of the money with an unknown other person. Contrary to
self-interest theory, a number of people shared some of the money.
Even more shared money when they were shown a snapshot of the
other person before they acted. Here we see the drive to bond
moving into action against the clear-cut best economic interest of
the decision maker.[19]

Finally, we would cite the kind of "thought experiment" that is
used by philosophers to test rival propositions. If one accepts the
well-supported premise that bonded relationships have been historically essential for human success in mating and survival, then
the test for the independence of Drive 2 from Drive 1 would be
stated as follows. Would survival pressures favor the individual who
is biologically equipped with a strong drive to bond (as well as with
the other drives), or the individual who is biologically equipped
with a strong drive to acquire and who also has a cognitive capacity to learn that the surest route to personal acquisitions, including
a sex partner, is at times to form opportunistic alliances with
others? We argue that this would be no contest—the first individual could bring an inbred sincerity to the bonding process and
would, therefore, have a superior chance to form essential bonds
and to pass genes to the next generation. Having a totally opportunistic spouse or ally is not an attractive proposition for anyone

who has an option to select a sincere one. And even though this is only a thought experiment, we feel it offers a strong argument for the independence of the bonding drive from the acquiring drive.

## BONDING IN RELATION TO ACQUIRING

Bonding is fundamentally different from acquiring, since it can only be fulfilled with another human who is acting voluntarily. It cannot be forced by threats of violence or withdrawal of essential resources. The bond must be mutual and have some degree of commitment; only then is the drive fulfilled. To use an expression from everyday life, bonding means *sticking together.* Fulfilling the drive to acquire, even to the level of abundance, does not fulfill the drive to bond. As the song says, "Money can't buy you love." And as the ad proclaims, "Some things are priceless—MasterCard can get you everything else." Of course, what makes it possible to fulfill this drive at all is that other humans share it. While bonding can be seen in other mammals, it is only in humans that it has moved well beyond bonding with close relatives (kin selection) and short-term reciprocity to long-term reciprocity and, in some circumstances, to communal sharing.

It is important to emphasize that every human relationship contains a mix of both competitive (D1) and cooperative (D2) elements. It is possible, of course, that any given paired relationship can be dominated by competition at one time or in one context, and by collaboration at another. Relationships in entire cultures can also be dominated by a long-lasting emphasis on either competitive or cooperative relations generated by such factors as key historical turning events, core technology, and cultural inertia. Robert Putnam traces in rich detail how the culture of southern Italy for over a thousand years has operated primarily on ground rules of all-against-all competition, characterized by distrust and power plays.[20] By contrast, the culture of middle and northern Italy has persistently emphasized ground rules of social bonding and trust. These cultural differences, Putnam argues, have had dramatic consequences for these regions' political and economic organizations. Southern Italy has experienced persistent poverty and considerable violence, while the rest of Italy has the opposite record.[21]

Everyone can remember situations when the drive to acquire came into clear-cut conflict with the drive to bond. Literature is full of the drama of such conflicted situations. Will you squeal (notice the negative term) on a friend for a substantial monetary reward? Will you lay off long-term employees to keep from going into the red? The questions could go on and on. People experience these situations as real dilemmas, as being caught between a rock and a hard place, precisely because they have two independent drives (to acquire and to bond) that tug in different directions. They are forced by this genetic heritage to use their rational powers to search for action plans that will at least minimize the hardest features of these trade-offs.

There are other situations in which the drives to acquire and to bond work together, to complement rather than conflict with each other. A prime example is team sports, where players bond together in teams that compete with other teams to acquire fame and fortune. And well-bonded teams can often beat teams consisting of individual stars who are not well bonded. The popularity of team sports throughout human history may well be explained by the unique opportunity that these situations provide to satisfy both the drive to acquire and the drive to bond.

The tension that can arise between the drive to acquire and the drive to bond can, hopefully, clarify another classic philosophical question—free will versus determinism. These two genetic drives, we argue, develop in different modules of the brain and can at times be pushing in different directions. Yet no one can go both ways at once. Such conflict at the level of subconscious drives forces the issue into the cognitive brain centers. On such occasions there is no option but to consciously and deliberately choose which way to go. You are forced to weigh the pros and cons and try to make the decision whose multiple consequences are least onerous for both drives.

This description of the human condition fits with the philosophy of Isaiah Berlin. In "Two Concepts of Liberty," Berlin offers a view of humans as being forced by their very nature to choose between often incompatible and incommensurate goals.[22] Another writer who has also addressed the issue of bonding and its linkage to the drive to acquire is Gerald Cory, who focuses on the dynamic interplay between the two drives.[23] He posits that the key to bridging between the two drives is often the alternation of attention, first to one drive and later to the other.

## The Forming of Social Bonds

What can science tell us about how social bonds are formed? The bonding process seems to begin with eye contact, smiling, touching, and talking, then go on to sharing food and drink and exchanging token gifts. It then evolves as a process of synchronized exposures of vulnerability, exposures of intimate feelings, personal secrets, and aspirations, which progresses in an alternating, one-step-at-a-time manner as tests of escalating trust.[24] There is no generalized bond between all people, but rather finite bonds between discrete individuals and between individuals and discrete organizations. These bonds are developed over time, one at a time. Baumeister and Leary hypothesized that the intensity of the drive to bond begins to lessen after some significant number of bonds become well established. This undoubtedly varies across individuals, with some people preferring a few intense relationships and others preferring a larger number of less intense ones, or at least a different mix. Much more needs to be learned about the satiation process in bonding and individual differences in this regard.

Darwin himself is the source of some evidence of the universal nature of the process of bonding between humans. Wright quotes Darwin on his early contacts with Fuegian Indians. "After we had presented them with some scarlet cloth, which they immediately tied round their necks, they became good friends. This was shown by the old man patting our breasts, and making a chuckling kind of noise, as people do when feeding chickens. I walked with the old man, and this demonstration of friendship was repeated several times; it was concluded by three hard slaps, which were given me on the breast and back at the same time. He then bared his bosom for me to return the compliment, which being done, he seemed highly pleased."[25] Captain James Cook's journal records his many first encounters with the people of remote islands and repeats similar stories of such events.

There is strong evidence that bonding does not have to be taught to infants. Wilson reports on some of these studies.

Experiments have shown that within ten minutes after birth, infants fixate more on normal facial designs drawn on posters than on abnormal designs. Psychologists and anthropologists have discovered substantial degrees of similar programmed development in the use of smiling across cultures. The expression is first displayed by infants between the ages of two and four months. It invariably attracts an abundance of affection from attending adults. Environment has little influence on the maturation of smiling. The infants of the !Kung, a hunter-gatherer people of South Africa's Kalahari desert, are nurtured under very different conditions from those in America and Europe. Yet their smile is identical in form to that of American and

European infants, appears at the same time, and serves the same social function. Smiling also appears on schedule in deaf-blind children and even in thalidomide-deformed children who are not only deaf and blind but also crippled so badly they cannot touch their own faces.[26]

The most conspicuous example of bonding among humans is the ceremony of marriage—which is observed in some form by all cultures as a public declaration of lasting commitment by both parties.[27] Bonding can, of course, take place in modern times in a range of degrees of closeness and duration. There is no inherent reason why bonding cannot take place between any two human beings no matter how different or distant. As the Irish saying goes, "The world for me has no strangers, only friends I haven't met." Of course, distance and differences in language, appearance, and culture do make it more difficult to bond. But in this regard, humans are different from many other social animals—they are not innately constrained to bond only within kinship or other limited groups. The Dorchester story at the beginning of the chapter provides clear evidence of this fact.

## Bonding and Morality

It is reasonable to hypothesize that basic moral codes are a skill set that have emerged genetically as a means for satisfying our drive to bond.

James Q. Wilson, a political scientist, writes, "We suggest that these [moral] principles have their source in the parent-child relationship, wherein a concern for fair shares, fair play, and fair judgments arises out of the desire to bond with others. All three principles are rational in a social and evolutionary sense, in that they are useful in minimizing conflict and enhancing cooperation.

At some stage in the evolution of mankind—probably a quite early one—cooperative behavior became adaptive. Groups that could readily band together to forage, hunt, and defend against predators were more likely to survive than were solitary individuals."[28]

It is not a big step from bonding to the practical rule that the key to bonding is to treat the other person, most of the time, as that person wants to be treated. This is a variation of the Golden Rule that would have evolved in the service of the drive to bond. From this start, humans probably evolved such basic rules as help, not harm; keep, not break, promises; seek fair, not cheating, deals; respect, not steal or destroy, the property of the bonded other. These basic moral ground rules are taught in some form by all the major religions. They are the ground rules that children seem to understand at an early age.[29] The bonding drive and its associated moral skill set provide children with a significant head start toward learning the more elaborate and varied norms and values of the unique society to which they are born.

The most common punishment for violating social norms is, appropriately and powerfully, social ostracism, the silent treatment, and, at the extreme, solitary confinement or even exile. Ostracism as a social norm enforcer is both powerful and low in cost. Even an infant almost instantly cries out in distress when an adult responds to a welcoming smile with a frozen stare. Another type of low-cost enforcer is "bad words." Societies tend to save their most negative terms for social defectors. Words associated with violations of bonded relationships include *betrayal, double-cross, traitor,* and *treason.* The personal feelings associated with such accusations are intense shame and guilt. Anticipation of these powerful negative feelings helps reinforce the bonding commitment. Ask any school child if America has ever had a traitor. Benedict Arnold will be the quick answer. Is there anything worse? He was and remains the lowest form of humanity, a traitor to his country.

These basic moral sensibilities appear in all children at such an early age that it seems they are for all humans an inbred skill set, akin to the native ability to learn language. This skill set is called human conscience. This explanation of morality is echoed by deWaal: "This common benevolence [mutual caring] nourishes and guides all human morality. Aid to others in need would never be internalized as a duty without the fellow-feeling that drives people to take an interest in one another. Moral sentiments came first; moral principles, second."[30]

Edward Wilson echoes this point. He states, "Orthodox social theory holds that morality is largely a convention of obligation and duty constructed from mode and custom. The alternative view, favored by Westermarck in his writings on ethics, is that moral concepts are derived from innate emotions. The evidence now leans strongly to Westermarck."[31]

This way of thinking about morality obviates the persistent concern of philosophers about what they term the *naturalistic fallacy*, that is, the logical impossibility of deriving an *ought* (such as moral principles) from an *is* (such as the bonding drive). In this way of thinking, "ought" becomes simply a logical means to a human purpose. This point has been made by the philosopher Colin McGinn. Building on Chomsky's argument about the innate aspects of language, McGinn points out that humans acquire ethical knowledge with very little explicit instruction, without great intellectual labor, and the end result is remarkably uniform across cultures, despite their other obvious differences.[32]

This way of thinking about morals also moves beyond the conventional wisdom of the scientific community that science cannot—or, at least, should not—have anything to do with morals, ethics, and values. It clarifies that norms and morals are such a central and pervasive aspect of human life that we badly need a scientific way of understanding them. Establishing that morals are rooted in genes can give people respect for their past and more confidence in their future.

This way of understanding human morals moves well beyond the very limited type of morals that have been observed in chimpanzees and some other primates. In *The Moral Animal,* Robert Wright does an excellent job of pulling together and analyzing observations of this type. With the important exception of the strong and lasting bond between mother and child and the implicit morals of these relationships, chimpanzee alliances seem to be purely temporary expediencies. This seems true even though chimps do at times seem to be expressing anger at alliance violations. This is to be expected when relationships are based only on the self-interest (D1) of the parties. These studies also reveal the prevalence of deception and trickery among these primates. For example, chimps have been observed going to great trouble to appear to hide food when they have actually already hidden the food in another place. Since humans have a drive to acquire as well as to bond, such deception and such opportunistic relationships obviously also occur among humans—but to a much lesser extent. Wright's analysis of chimpanzee behavior suggests that they lack, for all intents and purposes, genetically based moral tendencies other than mother-infant bonding. If this were also true of humans, then culture would have to provide a very substantial moral code to compensate. The moral codes built into human genes, by contrast, can be much more enduring and trustworthy. We, as humans, can be thankful that our strong bonding drives generate the need for basic moral skills as a means of fulfilling the drive. This combination contributes in a significant way to making humans unique.[33]

As a final argument supporting morals as an innate skill set, we return to Darwin. He comments,

The following proposition seems to me in a high degree probable—namely, that any animal whatever, endowed with well-marked social instincts . . . would inevitably acquire a moral sense or conscience, as soon as its intellectual powers had become as well, or nearly as well developed, as in man. For, firstly, the social instincts lead an animal to take pleasure in the society of its fellows, to feel certain amount of sympathy with them, and to perform various services for them. . . . Secondly, as soon as the mental faculties had become highly developed, images of all past actions and motives would be incessantly passing through the brain of each individual; and that feeling of dissatisfaction, or even misery, which invariably result as often as it was perceived that the enduring and always present social instinct had yielded to some other instinct, at the time stronger, but [not] enduring in its nature.[34]

It is especially interesting that he attached a footnote to this thought about morals that takes strong exception to the position of John Stuart Mill, the dominant economist of the day and one of the founding fathers of neoclassical economics.

Mr. J. S. Mill speaks, in his celebrated work, "Utilitarianism," [1864, pp. 45, 46] of the social feelings as a "powerful natural sentiment." He also remarks, "if, as in my own belief, the moral feelings are not innate, but acquired, they are not for that reason less natural." It is with hesitation that I venture to differ at all from so profound a thinker, but [since] it can hardly be disputed that the social feelings are instinctive or innate, [his belief] that the moral sense is acquired by each individual during his lifetime is at least extremely improbable. The ignoring of all transmitted mental qualities will, as it seems to me, be hereafter judged as a most serious blemish in the works of Mr. Mill.

This is the only place in all of Darwin's writings where we have observed this gentle man making such a pointed criticism of a scholarly colleague.

So on this subject of social instincts and derived morals Darwin is very clear. To our argument that morals evolved as a skill set that enabled successful bonding, he added a very important point—that a strong memory of the past and an imagination about the future would not only be necessary for the emergence of morals, but would make them inevitable.

## Bonding and Organizational Life

While Baumeister and Leary focus their work on bonds between individuals, they also cite evidence that humans carry over their bonding drive to their affiliations with groups and other collective entities. This fits with the fact that humans, after all, consistently anthropomorphize social institutions. People talk constantly about organizations having purposes and missions, as keeping or breaking promises, as hiring and firing, as being trustworthy or not. This way of thinking seems to come naturally to humans and helps them choose collectives to bond with or to avoid. People identify with and invest their time and effort in "their" organizations, in the same way they identify with their bonded friends. This is a mistake in a logical sense—but not in a social sense. Because organizations are made up of humans, they can be thought of in human terms with few, if any, serious errors. Organizations do display persistent behavior patterns that in individuals reflect personality traits. Even the law defines corporations as individual actors.

We can, therefore, say that bonding between humans starts with a one-to-one pairing, moves on to the nuclear family and thence to the primary face-to-face group, is extended to social networks and then to social networks that are interlocked and clustered into all kinds of collective entities, organizations, and associations. The step-by-step process by which the pairings between humans are built into complex social institutions has been carefully spelled out by the philosopher John Searle.[35] Humans go to great trouble to symbolize collectives and to develop rituals of membership. Humans are also disposed to bond with leaders of organizations as symbols of entire organizations.

The intrinsic tendency for humans to identify and bond with organizations to which they belong has been highlighted by Herbert Simon, a Nobel Prize winner in economics. A purely self-interested view of human behavior leads most economists, he notes, to highlight the shirking that occurs on the job. The fact that workers exert less effort than their maximum, economists argue, affirms the self-interested view of human behavior. No doubt, workers do often exert less than their full effort, Simon avers. But the more important question, Simon notes, is, Why do they exert any more effort than the minimum that can be monitored and enforced? He reminds us that one of the oldest and most devastating forms of worker protest is work-to-rule. Starting from this minimal standard, Simon observes, what is far more impressive is not how much shirking there is but how much extra effort people in fact contribute to the success of the organizations to which they belong. Simon suggests that this effort can only be explained if humans are intrinsically "docile" or derive value from sociability or membership in social organizations. Though he uses the term *docility*, Simon's argument strongly supports our view that a more complete model of human behavior would include the drive to bond in addition to the more self-interested drive to acquire.[36]

The bonding of individuals to organizational collectives is an ancient and strong pattern in human history. Humans are notorious joiners. Organizational affiliations are among the most important and valued aspects of life. As explored in Chapter Three, in the earlier stages of human history the pattern was the formation of hunting-gathering troops based on a set of interlocking bonded relationships. These were based on an in-group that lived and worked together, shared many resources, and together defended against predators. Other troops, the "strangers over the hill," were an out-group with whom one's own group did trading and, at times, raiding or fighting for scarce resources.

With today's global transport and communication systems, bonding can now take place between and among widespread sets of individuals. This can happen between units of multinational organizations and between leaders of different nations. Think also of the number of people across the world that seem to have bonded with Princess Diana. Through television and magazines, people experienced and responded to her compassion and empathy for others. Some see this as evidence of the superficiality of modern life. But it can also be seen as evidence that humans are capable, with the help of modern communication technologies, of developing positive bonds that stretch across distance and differences and even create a worldwide sense of community.

## THE DARK SIDE OF THE DRIVE TO BOND

We believe that the dark side of the drive to bond is genocide. This, on the face of it, seems ridiculous. How can the drive to bond in mutual aid with others lead to the killing of whole peoples, whole ethnic groups? The most famous lawgiver in the Judeo-Christian tradition, Moses, provides a clear example. He brought the Ten Commandments down from the mountaintop. Those rules, we submit, have met the test of time because they are rules that best ensure that humans can achieve lasting bonds with others. It is also noteworthy that Moses applied these rules only to his fellow tribesmen, the Israelites. The Biblical record shows that Moses had other rules for non-Israelites. The Biblical passage in Numbers 31 recounts the outcome: "And they warred against the Midianites, as the LORD commanded Moses; and they slew all the males. And the children of Israel took all the women of Midian captives, and their little ones, and took the spoil of all their cattle, and all their flocks, and all their goods. And they burnt all their cities wherein they dwelt." The Israelites had not gone through the bonding process with the Midianites. The Midianites were thus something less than truly human, beyond the rules for bonding of the Ten Commandments. And the nastiest part of Moses' message was still to come. When he learned that his soldiers had spared all the women and children, he was furious with them. He said, "Now therefore kill every male among the little ones, and kill every woman that hath known man by lying with him. But all the women children, that have not known a man by lying with him, keep alive for yourselves." Surely, this was genocide. And it was committed under orders from the great lawgiver.

We hasten to say that we do not in any way mean to single out the Israelites with this charge—especially since they have so often been the victims of genocide. Similar events seem to be a part of the history of every society that has gained a clear advantage over another people. Think of the Europeans' treatment of the American Indians. Think of the victims of the Nazis, the Mongols, the Turks, and the African slave traders. The list can go on and on, including the Serbians, the Tutsi, and the Hutu in current times. Jared Diamond has compiled a list of twenty-six major episodes of genocide from 1900 to 1990, with none involving less than ten thousand victims and two—the Nazi Holocaust and the Stalinist purges—involving on the order of ten million victims.[37] How is such a staggering problem as genocide related to bonding?

One of the simplest but most far-reaching skill sets that seems to be innate in humans in support of the drive to bond is the skill of making a distinction between "us" and "them." In the technical language of biology, this skill is known as the *dyadic instinct,* the proneness to use two-part classifications in treating socially important arrays. In American slang, it is known as the distinction between goodies and baddies. As Wilson reports, "Societies everywhere break people into in-group versus out-group. They fortify the boundaries of each division with taboo and ritual. To change from one division to the other requires initiation ceremonies, weddings, blessings, ordinations, and other rites of passage that mark every culture."[38] This innate skill helps people bond not just with other individuals but also with collectives of all kinds. It has enabled humans to undertake large tasks such as building temples and roads. It also enables them to assemble an army with soldierly bonds and attack people identified as the "enemy other." It enables genocide.

This represents a very dark side of human nature. Genocide has been a major stain on all human history. But in this case, unlike the D1 problem of environmental destruction, we feel there are somewhat more grounds for optimism—built into the drive to bond itself. We believe there is no evidence that humans require an "enemy other" to facilitate bonding with another individual or an entire group. We see no innate barrier to bonding with any and all other human beings and human groups. It does seem true that it is fairly easy to strengthen the bonds of any given group by rallying the group against an outsider. But it is by no means the only way to strengthen the bonds and, as we now know, using this method usually causes many more problems than it solves. The problem also arises from a skill set, the dyadic instinct, not from the basic drive itself. It should therefore be more subject to rational control.

We can see when leaders resort to the "enemy other" argument to rally the troops, and we know just how dangerous it is. Hitler was a master of the technique; Milosevich, a flagrant contemporary example. NATO's military response to Milosevich was clearly an attempt to break new ground in searching for an effective way for the international community to respond to genocide. Clearly, NATO's military approach was far from perfect, but what were the alternatives? In time, might it not be possible to nip the call for ethnic cleansing in the bud and set up enforceable international laws to help control such behavior? Could society make such verbal hate crimes an exception to the general support of free speech? Our understanding of genocide is still very limited, and even understanding is only the first step toward its control.

~

The existence in humans of a fundamental, innate drive to bond has been demonstrated in multiple ways. We have traced the intellectual history of this idea, from its treatment by Adam Smith through Darwin and on to its relative neglect in the twentieth century. We have reviewed the evidence from a wide variety of social science studies of its potency, universality, and innate character. Indeed, some branches of economics have also begun to recognize the importance of the drive to bond. These are giving more attention to the subject of human capital and innovation, and very recently, to social capital—the social bonds in a multi-organizational community. Agency theory is recognizing the force of the human desire for loyalty, love, and honor as well as material objects. Transaction cost economics is exploring trust as an important element in lowering transaction costs.

We have explored how bonding applies to organizations and larger collectives, such as firms and nation states, as well as to individuals. We have given special attention to how it could have evolved by natural selection and mate selection over human history. We have seen how it is independent of the drive to acquire, even as it interacts with D1 in both compatible and incompatible ways in modern life. We have seen how it has led to the development of a genetic skill set of basic moral rules.

In the next chapter we will explore the case for the next drive, the drive to learn.

# 6

# THE DRIVE TO LEARN (D3)

*Curiosity is one of the permanent and certain characteristics of a vigorous mind.*

—SAMUEL JOHNSON

*The natural thirst that is never quenched is the thirst for knowledge.*

—DANTE ALIGHIERI

The study of human infant behavior took a significant step forward when researchers learned they could discern a great deal about babies' mental activity by carefully recording their eye movements with high-speed videocameras. This methodology is completely benign. It causes no stress for the tiny children—they seem to treat it like a game. But it reveals a great deal. These studies of eye movements can demonstrate the abilities of infants so newly born that these abilities cannot possibility have been learned. They must be innate.

One such study is especially relevant to the theme of this chapter. Psychologist Karen Wynn worked with five-month-old infants to test for the existence of an innate capacity to deal with numbers.[1] The experimenter set up an object, such as a ball, in front of an infant and then moved a screen in front of the object. Then the screen would be removed to reveal the hidden object. If one ball had been covered by the screen, and one ball was revealed when the screen was removed, infants took a brief look at the single ball and then turned away to look elsewhere. They seemed to be bored. If, however, when the screen was removed it revealed two balls, the infants would do a double take and continue to examine the situation.

In further experiments, infants demonstrated consistent ability to make distinctions of this kind between expected and unexpected outcomes both for adding balls behind the screen and for subtracting balls. For instance, if two balls were covered by the screen and one was conspicuously removed, then the screen was removed to reveal two balls, the infants took a lively interest. Over many repetitions, infants consistently achieved a low error rate in discerning expected from unexpected numbers.

These studies have clearly demonstrated that infants have an innate ability to understand the abstract relationships between simple numbers. It is a remarkable finding. From our perspective this work serves a more general, even more important purpose. It demonstrates a drive to learn in infants and, beyond that, provides significant clues as to how the drive operates. The nature of human learning has been the subject of scientific study from at least the days of the Greek philosophers; now, these simple infant studies are helping pull together our knowledge of the learning process. This is the subject of this chapter.

We will focus on two questions. How do human minds work as learning machines? Is the drive to learn innate and primary, independent of the drives to acquire and to bond? As in the chapter on bonding, our answers fly in the face of conventional wisdom.

## CONVENTIONAL WISDOM AND THE DRIVE TO LEARN

With some exceptions, the social sciences generally teach two basic points about learning. One is that the newborn mind is similar to a capacious but empty sponge. Although empty of content, it comes equipped to soak up an enormous amount of information delivered by parents, peers, schools, churches, media, and so on—in short, modern culture in all its complexity. The second point is that the child's motivation for absorbing this knowledge is self-interest—in our terms, its innate drive to acquire objects and experiences that have value. We hope largely to displace both of these ideas. In support of this view, we will draw on arguments and evidence provided by dissenters in the various social science disciplines. But first, we need to define and roughly describe what we mean by a drive to learn.

## DEFINING THE DRIVE TO LEARN

Humans have an innate drive to satisfy their curiosity, to know, to comprehend, to believe, to appreciate, to develop understandings or representations of their environment and of themselves through a reflective process: the drive to learn. Humans carrying genes behind this drive have been selected for this drive to activate and energize the use of their amazing (though bounded) brains—the brains that without doubt give the species its distinctive advantage over other earthly creatures. The drive to learn is expressed in consciousness by an emotion variously labeled inquisitiveness, wonder, and curiosity. It pushes humans to collect information, examine their environment, make observations, and sustain an ongoing internal and external dialogue about explanatory ideas and theories. People puzzle over causes and effects. They want to know how things work. This drive is satisfied by a feeling of understanding, a feeling that things make sense.[2] It is energized by mankind's insatiable curiosity.[3] The theories of the world and of the self that the mind builds up will later, as a separate step, often be essential in guiding efforts to satisfy the drives to acquire, to bond, and to defend—and thereby, in combination, enabling survival of the holder's genes.

Knowledge, since it can be given to another without any loss of knowledge by the giver, has the great advantage that it can be disseminated on a relatively cost-free basis, in a non-zero-sum game.

One important piece of evidence supporting the existence of the drive to learn is the universality of religion. Anthropologists have not found a single culture that does not have a creation story and an afterlife story. People seem to need these beliefs to fill a gap in their overall representational systems, whether or not they have any direct relevance to the other three drives. The universality of art is also evidence of the drive to learn. No culture has been found that has not expressed in artistic form, through paintings, songs, and stories, its essential nature. For another example, consider the attraction that puzzles and intellectual games of all varieties have for humans. And why do children ask so many questions without knowing whether the answers will ever be of any use to them in terms of other drives? Children can also be seen testing answers to see if they are consistent with what else they know. Even newborns, when they are well fed and well loved, can be seen exploring their environment with their eyes and their hands.

Humans seem to have a predisposition to be open and curious about new theories, but it also seems true that they do not abandon old theories until convinced the new ones are better—that is, more useful, compact, and accurate. One can say accordingly that every human is an informal scientist, and that the species has been evolving a collective body of knowledge at least since the basic structure of the human brain emerged. Science, as a specialized focus of activity in modern times, is only an extension of this universal human characteristic.

Many obvious manifestations of this predisposition have been studied by the fields of cognitive, developmental, and evolutionary psychology, and by neurobiology. These scientists, however, have not for the most part pulled their observations together around a single basic drive. Antonio Damasio, whom we drew upon in Chapter Three, is one of the exceptions. He states, "It is as if we are possessed by a passion for reason, a drive that originates in the brain core, permeates other levels of the nervous system, and emerges as either feelings or unconscious biases to guide decision making. Reason, from the practical to the theoretical, is probably constructed on this inherent drive by a process which resembles the mastering of a skill or craft. Remove the drive, and you will not acquire the mastery. But having the drive does not automatically make you a master."[4]

Another important exception is psychologist George Loewenstein, who has comprehensively integrated human knowledge about the curious phenomenon of curiosity. We will rely extensively on his study of the emotion of curiosity as the engine of learning.

## EVIDENCE OF THE DRIVE TO LEARN VIA CURIOSITY

Loewenstein's seminal 1994 paper, "The Psychology of Curiosity: A Review and Reinterpretation," opens by reviewing the traditional understanding of curiosity. Aristotle saw curiosity as a desire for information that leads humans to study science for intrinsic reasons and "not for any utilitarian end."[5] Cicero referred to curiosity as an "innate love of learning and of knowledge . . . without the lure of any profit."[6] These early thinkers acknowledged that information was also desired for extrinsic reasons, but they drew a sharp distinction between such extrinsically motivated desire for information and curiosity, which they viewed as a "passion for learning." St. Augustine commented that curiosity was a "certain vain and curious longing for knowledge."[7] Bentham referred to the "appetite of curiosity."[8] Kant referred to an "appetite for knowledge."[9]

As a pioneer of the entire field of psychology, William James made some insightful comments on curiosity that prefigured how the topic was considered for most of the twentieth century. He viewed curiosity as an emotion that was closely associated with fear. He described animals making a fearful and tentative approach toward an object that seemed to be arousing intense curiosity. He proposed that "scientific curiosity" arose from "an inconsistency or a gap in . . . knowledge, just as the musical brain responds to a discord in what it hears."[10] The early behaviorists, such as McDougall, Thorndike, and Dashiell, followed James in seeing curiosity as a drive.

Loewenstein describes how later in the century psychologists tended to break the "passion" of curiosity into different segments and, in general, subsume it under the need for information to pursue rational self-interested objectives. Pavlov, for example, talked about the "exploratory behavior" of dogs that turned toward any unusual sight or sound without any indication of drive qualities. Freud saw curiosity as sublimated infantile sexual exploration.

In the 1950s the work of Berlyne signaled a wave of renewed interest in curiosity. Berlyne believed that the curiosity drive was aroused by external incongruities such as complexity, novelty, and surprise. At about the same time and independently, Piaget, the child psychologist, and Hebb, an experimental psychologist, came to similar conclusions from different starting points. They concluded that curiosity reflected a natural human tendency to make sense of the world that is activated by violated expectations. And this all brings us back to James and his notion of inconsistency—a gap in knowledge.

Loewenstein terms his synthesis of this line of research (supported by some of his own laboratory experiments) *information-gap* theory. In summary, the theory proposes that individuals start with what they previously know (or think they know) on a given topic. When they encounter an external observation that is perceived to be inconsistent with what is known, a gap is generated that is immediately experienced as an unpleasant sensation that they feel driven to remove. This sensation occurs whether or not they ran into the observation by chance or whether they sought it out to relieve boredom. The gap motivates individuals to seek an insight that reconciles the new observation by reordering their previous knowledge in a way that accommodates the new observation. At this point, a new piece of knowledge is lodged in the memory of the individuals involved. If this new piece of knowledge is incorporated in a story around the campfire or in a best-selling book it might enter the collective store of human knowledge. More likely, it will die with the original creator and have to be reinvented over and over again.

This account of curiosity and learning is totally consistent with the explanation of how the brain works that was proposed by Edelman and described in Chapter Two. In this view, the brain is seen as a computational mechanism that can compare new perceptions with the existing ones. Faced with inconsistency, the brain generates or *imagines* a set of possible resolutions (Variety) until it finds one that restores consistency (Selection), which is then preserved in long-term memory (Retention). In short, Edelman's theory proposes that the brain uses the Darwinian V/S/R algorithm at the level of neurons and neuron sets. Of course, not all inconsistencies can be easily resolved, and frustration may persist until the mind's attention shifts to something else.

This explanation of the learning process throws light on how specializations in certain kinds of knowledge emerge. It has been found by laboratory experiments that the more complete a subject's knowledge of a given subject, the more likely the subject is to recognize an inconsistent new observation and to become curious about the resulting gap. So such persons are drawn to add to their understanding of the subject, thus becoming more specialized. The early events that started this specialized learning chain reaction may well have been random, but, once started, learning proceeds in a systematic way. It is also possible that differences in the mix and strength of innate skill sets bias the developing individual toward further learning on a given track that offers a comparative advantage. In other words, people with a stronger innate skill set for numbers are more likely to specialize in mathematics.

Not all objectively inconsistent observations lead to learning. If the gap between what is known and what is observed is very small, the inconsistency will not seem big enough to bother with, and the previous knowledge will proceed unaltered. On the other hand, if the gap is very large—that is, new observation is greatly different from what is previously known—the inconsistency may go unobserved. If the gap is deemed impossible to close, to worry about it would after all be a waste of precious time. If the gap is large and still observed, it may be seen as threatening and repressed. So the brain seems to be able to select the gaps to which it will attend. Only when faced with medium-sized gaps that seem manageable will curiosity become intense. Only then will someone experience an intellectual itch that must be scratched. You experience the pleasure of relief only when you discover or create a way to reconcile your new observation with what you already knew to be true.

This feedback and learning process moves on all through life whenever an individual is not too preoccupied with acquiring, bonding, and defending. Over time, understandings developed in this manner accumulate as a complex set of beliefs about the world and the self. They are stored in memory for future reference. They help enable the survival of the genes and are thus reinforced in subsequent generations. Figure 6.1 expresses these ideas in graphic form.

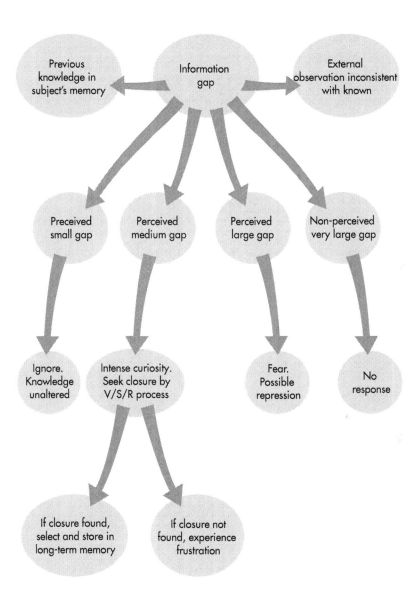

Figure 6.1. Information-Gap Learning.

This account of learning is consistent with the accounts that have been proposed by other disciplines and other schools of thought. For instance, it echoes the Gestalt theory of the 1920s, which argued that the mind seeks closure around "wholes" that "make sense." It also mirrors the line of research associated with Festinger that posits a human need to reduce *cognitive dissonance*.[11]

## EVIDENCE OF THE
## INDEPENDENCE OF THE LEARNING DRIVE

Curiosity, as a mechanism for learning, must have evolved over the millions of years of hominid development. Many other kinds of animals exhibit learning behavior, but in no other animal is it nearly as strong and flexible a drive. This is undoubtedly related to the fact that no other mammal's brain is such a significant percentage of its body weight. Terrence Deacon, whom we discussed in Chapter Two in regard to hominid development of language and the use of symbols, has assembled evidence of the independence of the learning drive. He cites the pleasure humans take in making their representations of the external world comply with symbolic rules. He writes, "Consider the intensity with which contemporary humans pursue mysteries, scientific discoveries, puzzles, and humor, and the elation that a solution provides. The apocryphal story of Archimedes running naked through the street yelling 'Eureka!' captures this experience well. The positive emotions associated with such insights implicate more than just a cognitive act."[12]

One important test of the independence of this drive from D1 (acquiring) is a thought experiment similar to the test we posed for the bonding drive. Think of an individual whose genes persistently impelled closing the information gap between known representations and any new observation that seemed to contradict the known. Would such an individual have a survival advantage over an individual who had a drive to acquire and reasoned that some knowledge of the outside world might help? Again, it would be no contest. The former would win hands down.

The experiment with newborns described at the beginning of this chapter also provides strong support for both the existence of the drive to learn and the information-gap mechanism by which it works. Infants demonstrate a drive to close the gap between their innate knowledge of numbers and their observations of what appears from behind the screen. The infants' drive to learn is manifested in their curiosity about the unexpected. It is analogous to the tension caused by the magician's trick that everyone is eager to uncover and reveal. This is how learning works, even scientific learning.

## Conditioned Learning

At this point we need to clearly distinguish the kind of learning we have been discussing from the kind of learning that has long been studied by psychologists and other social scientists—the kind known as conditioned learning, operant conditioning, or conditioned reflexes. This line of inquiry was first initiated by Pavlov, the Russian who studied dogs. He proved that when a bell was struck regularly along with the presentation of desirable food, dogs would start to salivate. Then, when the bell was struck without the food, the dogs also salivated—ergo, conditioned learning. This line of research was later carried on by such scientists as John Watson and B. F. Skinner. Animals can learn in this way to have their drive to acquire food activated, as evidenced by the saliva, in response to some arbitrary signal such as the bell. This has also been demonstrated in limited ways with human subjects. These signals and their associated rewards seem to be recorded in the memory circuits of the limbic system. It may well be that these are the memories that generate the emotional markers on the incoming sense-organ messages as they move through the limbic area into the working memory area of the brain. This description of the establishment of limbic memories and their role in learning is speculative. In any event, the process of establishing such conditional memories is quite different from the representational matching process that is activated by novelty and inconsistencies that we have been describing as the dominant mode of learning in humans. As the old saying goes, some people can learn from reading things in books or from their observations of everyday life, but some learn only from pissing on an electric fence.

## Learning and Building Collective Knowledge

As the learning process progresses over the life cycle, individuals accumulate their own increasingly comprehensive and coherent worldviews, as well as a complex set of beliefs about themselves that has been called a self-concept or self-identity. These self-beliefs provide the basis of self-esteem as a unique human being. The importance of ideas about the self has been developed by Charles Cooley, a pioneer of sociology; by Donald Snygg, a leading social psychologist; and by Carl Rogers, a creative psychotherapist. They all emphasized the role of social interaction in the process of building one's identity.

Given the drive to bond, it is to be expected that people will want to share their proudly earned views of the world with their bonded friends and allies. Everyone believes their insights will be helpful so they offer them freely. In the process, these interpretations of the world enter the collective domain of knowledge. The resulting collective theories are, in turn, passed on from generation to generation as part of culture. Such ideas are subject to change over time by the testing of natural selection. If they do not prove useful to others, they will soon be forgotten. These are the same survival tests and the same process of variety, selection, and retention that Darwin used to explain the evolution of species via genes.

These ideas about the natural selection of knowledge by cultures and environments have been carefully spelled out by evolutionary philosophers such as Dennett and by anthropologists such as Durham.[13] Population ecology scholars have studied this evolutionary process at the organizational level.[14] Hence collective representations have evolved, in spite of periods of regression, toward more useful ones. This process is often slow, as shown, for example, by the length of time it is taking to have Darwin's theory of evolution displace the human creation story of various religions.

Darwin himself made a brief statement about an innate drive to learn. "The belief in unseen or spiritual agencies . . . seems to be universal. . . . Nor is it difficult to comprehend how it arose. As soon as the important faculties of the imagination, wonder, and curiosity, together with some power of reasoning, had become partially developed, man would naturally crave to understand what was passing around him, and would have vaguely speculated on his own existence."[15]

Such speculation is the basic reason why the practice of religion is a human universal. No human group has been discovered that does not have a set of religious beliefs. This fact, by itself, is strong evidence of the existence of an independent drive to learn, to make sense of the world. Other mammals show no evidence of having a religion. While they certainly display curiosity, they have no strong, independent drive to learn and no capacity to employ abstract symbolization. Given their mental capacity, it is inevitable that humans would turn to the supernatural to find answers to compelling questions for which they have no natural answers.

Science, on the other hand, has a very different role to play in society, even though it is also clearly energized by the same drive to learn and understand. It has undertaken the specialized role of pursuing natural explanations of all phenomena. Scientists operate on the belief that all phenomena can eventually be understood with natural, materialistic explanations. Science also carries out its role by a very different method than is used by religion. Science operates on the basis of testing hypotheses against empirical data; religion operates on the basis of received faith. This difference in method is what places science in continuing conflict with religion. There has been increased interest in finding ways to address this conflict. However, these efforts are as yet preliminary and remain controversial.[16]

Predictability can be seen as an outcome of this drive for explanatory theories. As the learning drive is met, humans develop the ability to anticipate with some accuracy the events in the world around them and the likely consequences of their own actions.[17] Humans create "memories of the future" as they play out in their minds various scenarios of causal linkages that they store as a repertory of possible responses to unfolding events. These scenarios enable them to create and sustain access to desired objects and experiences and stable relations with other people. Reasonable success in making predictions supports—in fact is essential to—humans' efforts to fulfill their drives to acquire and to bond. But, given inevitable uncertainty about the choices that other humans will in fact make, predictions will always fall well short of perfection.

Learning can take place at the organizational level as well as the individual level.[18] The drive to learn plays a major role in the life of every organization. As new members join an organization, they are gradually socialized and indoctrinated with the collective knowledge of the ongoing organization. New members also add their prior beliefs to the pool of knowledge as they convince others of the usefulness of the beliefs they bring in. Representational schemes carried in the minds of organizational members are, along with existing bonded relationships, a primary source of the glue and inertia found in organizations. Organizational members conduct ongoing discussions about their organization's features and the viability of their strategies for adapting successfully to their environment. If these consensual theories of action are not making reasonably accurate predictions, the organization will probably not survive, and neither will its members' theories. As an extreme case, consider the short-lived theories of the Heavens Gate cult in Rancho Santa Fe, which incorrectly predicted the end of the world with the arrival of Haley's comet. Many less dramatic examples from the world of business of mistaken theories come readily to mind—think of the stock market value of dot-coms with market share but no revenue. The mental representations people create may well be felt to be meaningful if they are internally consistent, but they will not aid human survival or organizational survival, and will not themselves survive, if they are not reasonably accurate representations of the objective environment.

Scholars of the history of broad sets of ideologies are also tracking this behavior from an evolutionary perspective.[19] Scholars of cognition and knowledge such as Plotkin are making significant strides in understanding how and when humans switch from one theory to another, more accurate one.[20] This field of study is known as evolutionary epistemology.

Knowledge can potentially flow with only minimal cost, since it can be passed on without any loss of knowledge to its initial creator. This low-cost movement is to be expected when knowledge flows through a bonded network. In many cases, however, individuals will want to retain knowledge so as to acquire something tangible in exchange for what they regard as their intellectual property. Knowledge can, therefore, be expected to flow with difficulty through competitive relationships where patent laws and proprietary secrets are only the official barriers and where distrust and fear of opportunism are the more basic ones.

In this regard it should be emphasized that each of the drives has its own distinctive game or exchange dynamics, which strengthen the theoretical reasons for making distinctions among the four drives. The drive to acquire is usually a win-lose game because of the scarcity of resources involved. The drive to bond is usually a win-win game to insiders because of its potential for enhancing benefits to both parties through teamwork, specialization, and exchange of goods. The drive to learn has the potential to be nearly cost-free to the giver of knowledge and a win for the receiver—but this is certainly not always realized.

Although accounts of the scientific process tend to emphasize the cognitive aspect, the emotional or motivational aspects are also frequently cited. Herbert Simon commented that through scientific inquiry, "scientists are relieved of the itch of curiosity that constantly torments them."[21] Ernst Mach wrote that "the first questions are formed upon the intention of the inquirer by practical considerations; the subsequent ones are not. An irresistible attraction draws him to these; a nobler interest which far transcends the mere needs of life."[22]

## Learning and Symbolization

In the course of humans' development as a species, knowledge was probably initially spread from person to person by the process of imitation, copying based on the most obvious or proximate causes of desirable and undesirable outcomes. Later, with the development of language, humans could speed up the spread of knowledge by word of mouth, through stories and myths. Only later, by searching for underlying or more nearly ultimate causes of events, did humans acquire theoretical or systematic scientific knowledge.

Building such knowledge required the special human talent for symbolization at higher levels of abstraction.

Terrence Deacon has spelled out this linkage with great care.[23] He compares humans' skills of language and symbolization with those of the most gifted pigmy chimpanzee ever studied, the amazing Kanzi. Researchers were trying to teach Kanzi's mother to link symbols to objects—without much success—while the infant Kanzi played around the language lab where he'd been born. They paid little attention to him until he spontaneously began to display some remarkable language ability. Without any formal training, he demonstrated his understanding of a considerable number of spoken words by pointing to the proper referent object. Even more amazingly, he could demonstrate his understanding of simple directive sentences by carrying out the directives—even if they did not make much sense. When, for example, he was told to "put the soap on the apple" he would quickly do it. In this instance, he demonstrated an ability to understand the relationship between each one of the six word symbols in the sentence.

Kanzi seems to be the only nonhuman mammal to have not only understood object-symbol links but also the more difficult task of understanding symbol-to-symbol relations in a properly structured sentence. Deacon explains the difficulty of this step, and points to the very unusual circumstances in which it occurred. It happened because Kanzi was exposed to language at the right time—very, very young—and in the right way—through repeated, ritualized presentation of object-symbol linkages in a language lab.

Deacon uses the one-of-a-kind Kanzi example to highlight the fact that *all* humans quickly demonstrate the Kanzi-level of symbol skill. He then goes on to explain the even more difficult language skill that only humans possess. Humans, unlike other mammals, can readily see the pattern among a set of symbols and move to a higher level of abstraction by creating a symbol for the perceived pattern.

This is the step we call concept creation or *reasoning*. This innate skill set is probably located in our prefrontal cortex, and it is clearly a means humans have evolved to fulfill the drive to learn. Deacon believes that reasoning is the critical skill set that distinguishes humans from all other primates. Once this ability took hold in humans, the species could continuously build its collective knowledge base, employing ever-higher levels of abstraction.

## THE LEARNING DRIVE AND INNATE SKILL SETS

Over the millions of years of hominid evolution, the emerging drive to learn undoubtedly fostered the evolution of additional innate skill sets. Consider, for example, these skills: manipulating tools, creating all kinds of mechanical devices, muscular coordination or athletic ability, painting, dancing, creating and performing music. The universality of these skills among the world's diverse cultures supports the idea that they are innate and primarily a means of fulfilling the learning drive and secondarily a means of fulfilling the other drives. Any one of these skills is of great importance in human history. Much more research is needed to develop more solid knowledge about such innate skill sets.

As knowledge about the learning process grows it can be put to excellent use in facilitating formal education. For example, it has been learned that people grasp probability theory quickly if it is embedded in a human story, but they find it difficult to learn when taught as an abstract principle. With knowledge of the existence of such a story-based skill, teachers can more readily teach probability theory. Again, the existence of such innate skill sets in no way diminishes the importance of acquired learning—their existence simply provide humans with an innate starter kit for further learning in discrete areas.

Psychologists have postulated a variety of human motives and needs that can well be considered derivative of the drive to learn. Consider the following needs: competence (White), growth (Maslow), achievement (McCelland), mastery (Deci), creativity (Amabile), and efficacy (Bandura).[24] The same is true of the need of humans to enhance and sustain their dignity and self-esteem, as described by Rogers.[25] Drive 3 is quite clearly the basis of the *intrinsic* rewards of many types of work that have been studied by Hertzberg.[26] Alongside the other basic drives, it draws humans into adapting to changing circumstances and bettering the condition of their lives. While all these motives have a certain face validity, none of the psychologists have seen these motives as innate or described the mental mechanism by which they work. The drive to learn, as a key part of four-drive theory, pulls this motivation literature together and anchors it on biological human nature.

The importance of creating working conditions that have the potential for satisfying the intrinsic human drive to learn has long been recognized in research on job design. As we will discuss at greater length in Chapter Eleven, it is the frustration of this drive that makes assembly line jobs so alienating. As Charlie Chaplin pointed out in the movie *Modern Times,* humans are not adequately motivated simply by the higher pay these jobs often offer. They cannot check their drive to learn at the door when they enter the workplace. The inability to satisfy their drive to learn at work will frustrate them. If they find no outlet to exercise this drive at work, they are apt to turn their energies to finding inventive ways to frustrate management intentions.

Jobs are clearly more satisfying if they provide an opportunity to fulfill the drive to learn. This insight is at the heart of the success of the Quality Movement, which encourages problem solving by workers to improve quality and productivity. As Jack Welch, the much admired CEO of General Electric, put it, "When workers were given a real opportunity to contribute their ideas about how to improve productivity, what we found was that they didn't have just a small number of ideas. Almost 100% of the ideas we have implemented that have led to the enormous productivity gains we have seen have come from our workers."[27] In the same interview, he said, "Sometimes people ask me if there are any limits to productivity. Have we not squeezed out every ounce of savings that are possible? I tell them: Productivity improvements are limitless. There is no limit to human ingenuity. Every day someone finds a better way of doing things." This drive to learn is at the root of much human progress. Of course, it also enables people to satisfy their drive to acquire more efficiently. But as most detailed case studies of great innovations show, the drive that led to these breakthroughs was not so much an economic or acquiring drive but an innate drive to solve what appeared to be challenging problems. Put simply, the drive to learn is a fundamental aspect of human behavior that is independent of other drives.

## The Dark Side of the Drive to Learn

When it comes to the dark side of the drive to learn, we believe the hazard is the capacity to believe plausible but inaccurate stories, the tendency to go on mind journeys of unchecked fantasy, the attraction of novelty for its own sake, and the general susceptibility to incomplete ideologies. The record shows that humans are often gullible. With some regularity, people sign on with cult leaders who are truly weird. The Middle Ages saw some mass events of this kind, such as the Children's Crusade. This tendency of humans to get hooked on ideologies is a major contingency that can generate significant variability among cultures.

Once a plausible ideology becomes established in the minds of a community of people, it is very difficult to dislodge. Research has been done on the tenacity of the belief systems within groups that predict the time of the end of the world—even after the predicted day goes by without the event occurring. The hostile response of the Catholic Church to the findings of Galileo is another famous historical example. This phenomenon is also evident in business. The Xerox PARC labs invented many of the major ideas of the computer revolution, but the orthodoxy of headquarters stopped the firm from capitalizing on almost all of these ideas.

There are even today some small schools of thought in the social sciences that push sensible ideas about the social construction of reality to the nonsensical extreme idea that there is no reality beyond our perceptions. Forgoing the effort to make distinctions between less accurate and more accurate representations is the road to disaster.

Disaster can also result if we neglect the moral consequences of the extraordinary yet potentially dangerous inventions that result from our drive to learn. Reflecting on the giddy pace with which we seem to be embracing new technologies, Bill Joy writes: "Perhaps it is always hard to see the bigger impact while you are in the vortex of a change. Failing to understand the consequences of our inventions while we are in the rapture of discovery and innovation seems to be a common fault of scientists and technologists; we have long been driven by the overarching desire to know that is the nature of science's quest, not stopping to notice that the progress to newer and more powerful technologies can take on a life of its own."[28] We experienced the dangers of this unquestioned drive to learn with the Manhattan project and nuclear technology. We created a force that could wipe out humanity. As we embrace genetic cloning, nanotechnology, and other new technologies we might unwittingly find ourselves in similarly dangerous territory. The dark side of the drive to learn is that we can learn to destroy humanity itself.

Our attraction to novelty must always be disciplined by the practical question "so what?" and the moral question "will humanity be better off?" It is essential to check the wonderful human creative capacity, the species' ability to imagine almost anything, against the empirical world of reality. Fortunately the drive to learn pushes each individual to make this reality check all the time: not only to imagine a vast number of possibilities (V) but also to select the representation that best fits sensory observations of the external world (S) before storing the selected representation in memory (R). This is why we can feel somewhat optimistic about this hazard. If as a society we push our drive to learn through the complete learning cycle, and reinforce it in our educational system, we will be true to our human nature and avoid this hazard. In doing so we would simply be building on the great asset our genetic heritage has given us. After all, human genes did not survive by creating brains with a bias toward selecting untested and inaccurate mental representations of the world. And the discoveries still to be made by scientific curiosity can know no bounds.

~

The study of learning by a variety of disciplines has recently converged on the information-gap explanation of the activation of the learning drive, insatiable curiosity. This theory and the empirical findings that support it portray the learning drive as a potent and independent force behind humans' accumulation of information and knowledge of all kinds. It leads people into specialization and the mastery of crafts and all other bodies of knowledge. It accounts for the intrinsic attraction of work and for the drive behind creative, innovative achievements. It explains how humans build ideologies, broad explanations of their lives and their environment. It links the human mind not only to the development of science but also to religion and to the humanities. It provides one of the sturdy pillars in our developing account of the basis of human behavior. We hope this view of learning will have displaced any conventional wisdom in your mind about the newborn's brain as an empty sponge for cultural knowledge and motivated only by the D1 drive.

The drive to learn also throws fresh light on the puzzle we posed in Chapter Two: How can we account for the burst of social and technical achievement in the Upper Paleolithic period? Now we can hypothesize that this technical flowering was associated not only with the gradual strengthening of the learning drive but, in particular, with the emergence of the reasoning skill of abstract symbolization. The building of knowledge spurted ahead. Humans could even learn to symbolize the abstract concept of "the people," the tribe, and by this symbolization make it a concrete entity.

# THE DRIVE TO DEFEND (D4)

*We shall defend our island, whatever the cost may be, we shall fight on the beaches, we shall fight on the landing grounds, we shall fight in the fields and in the streets, we shall fight in the hills; we shall never surrender.*

—WINSTON CHURCHILL

Here's a mental experiment. Given a set of cards that have letters on one side and numbers on the other, the idea is to test whether the following statement is true: "If a card has a D on one side, it has a 3 on the other." Which of these cards would you need to turn over?

D F 3 7

Most people choose either the D card or the D card and the 3 card. The correct answer is D and 7. The 3 card is irrelevant; the rule said that D's have 3's, not that 3's have D's. The 7 card is crucial; if it has a D on the other side, the rule would be dead.

It turns out that only about 5 percent to 10 percent of people who try this test select the right cards. Even people who have taken logic courses get it wrong. This test was developed by psychologist Peter Wason, and it threw some serious doubt on human reasoning capacity. However, Leda Cosmides, now a leader in the growing subdiscipline of evolutionary psychology, found it hard to believe that humans had not evolved an innate skill set to help them with logical problem solving. She developed a test for the same problem-solving skills in a different context.[1]

Cosmides discovered that people get the answer right when the rule is a social contract that specifies an exchange of benefits. In those circumstances, showing that the rule is false is equivalent to finding cheaters who are breaking the social contract. In her experiment Cosmides told people, "You are a bouncer in a bar, and are enforcing the rule 'If a person is drinking beer, he must be eighteen or older.' You may check what people are drinking or how old they are. Which do you have to check: a beer drinker, a Coke drinker, a twenty-five-year-old, or a sixteen-year-old?" Most people correctly select the beer drinker and the sixteen-year-old. This question is logically identical to the one involving abstract symbols on cards. Cosmides discovered that humans have skill sets that come readily into play for defending themselves against cheaters but not such good skills for solving similar forms of abstract logical problems. Identifying cheaters was an important skill to early humans, helping them defend their valuables of all kinds.

## OVERVIEW OF THE DRIVE TO DEFEND

We hypothesize that humans have an innate drive to defend themselves and their valued accomplishments whenever they perceive them to be endangered. The fundamental emotion manifested by this subconscious drive is alarm, which in turn triggers fear or anger. The drive to defend has been selected for in the course of evolution as essential for survival of the genes.

This drive may well have been the very first to evolve—preceding even the drive to acquire. Probably the first function of the primitive central nervous system in multicellular creatures was to mobilize a systemic reaction to signals of external threats of harm.

These alarm signals were fed to the central nervous system through nerves from primitive sense organs. This simple defense system would have mobilized some limited reflexive defensive routines— to hide or to fight back—that were activated by chemical signals as well as electronic ones. As animals acquired the mental drive to acquire, the drive to defend evolved to protect valued acquisitions of all varieties, such as food sources. That is, the drive to defend began to evolve secondary emotions and skill sets focused around the defense of acquisitions. As the hominid line began to evolve independent drives to bond and learn, once again the drive to defend, we hypothesize, would have evolved secondary emotions and skill sets to protect accomplishments in each of these domains.

The drive to defend manifests itself in modern life in many ways. Indeed, much of human activity is generated by this drive. It is activated by perceived threats to not only one's own body and physical and experiential possessions (D1) but also by threats to one's bonded relationships (D2), and by threats to one's own cognitive representations of one's environment and of one's self (D3). The emotions aroused are experienced as fear escalating to terror, anger escalating to rage, loss escalating to despair, anxiety escalating to panic, loneliness escalating to depression. The human mind is probably preconditioned to enact a variety of defensive responses to threats, skill sets that develop further with acquired cultural knowledge and individual history. The kind of defensive routines enacted can be expected to vary depending on the severity of the perceived threat.

In response to mild threats humans can be expected to enact the kinds of defenses that are studied by psychologists and psychopathologists. These include such mechanisms as resistance to change, caution, and anxiety. As threats strengthen, humans may engage in denial, rationalization, and withdrawal, as well as in counterattack. As a result of long periods of high threat and stress, individuals can slip into a chronic defensive condition expressed by passivity and helplessness, with adverse health and performance consequences.

Similar defensive responses can be identified as operating at the collective or organizational level.[2] Defenses against mild threats can be expressed as intergroup rivalry, with verbal sparring and trickery; defenses against stronger threats can escalate into all-out conflict. At even higher levels, organizations and nation states can escalate matters to full-scale, all-out warfare.

At times the drive to defend clearly has the positive effect of conserving useful and constructive achievements associated with the other three drives. It serves to guard against hasty, ill-considered changes. If, after defensive delays, the threats turn out to have the potential for generating gains in D1, D2, and D3 terms, resistance can be expected to disappear.

With this overview of the drive to defend in mind, we can turn to the remarkable recent findings about the neural network and the brain centers that support this drive.

## Neuroscience and the Drive to Defend

More is undoubtedly known about the neural mechanisms of the human defense system than about any of the other three drives. A number of modern research techniques have been brought to bear on this mental apparatus and the findings are coming in with a rush. Some of this is turning up in the popular press.[3]

The newer findings about mental defense mechanisms grew out of animal studies. One of the pioneers of this work, Joseph LeDoux, a neuroscientist at New York University, started by conditioning rats to anticipate a mild electrical shock that would routinely be administered following the sound of a tone. Then he would sound the tone and trace the neural circuit by which the rat's brain would convert the sound into an alarm response. After years of patient work, his laboratory has been able to trace the tone message to a module in the limbic area of the brain known as the sensory thalamus, which seems to be an essential switching station for all incoming information about the world. The message is then sent immediately on to the amygdala, a small module also located in the limbic area of the brains of both rats and humans. In rats, the tone message arrives at the amygdala in twelve milliseconds. Cells in this part of the rat brain's emotional center can memorize signals such as the tone with great rapidity and tenacity.[4]

Another researcher, Bruce Kapp of the University of Vermont, started tracking the circuitry of alarm at the other end, and with rabbits instead of rats. He knew that one of the bodily responses to alarm was an acceleration of the heartbeat. By following the nerves that control the heart rate back from the brain stem, he found they led right to the amygdala. This indicates that, in both rats and rabbits, the alarm message flows from the sense organs to the amygdala and directly on to the organs that serve to alert the system to danger, all very quickly and without reference to the cortex or what might be called the conscious part of the brain.

The alarm connection noted in rats and rabbits also seems to be true in humans. Work on these circuits in humans is going forward in several laboratories with the use of MIR and PET equipment. Furthermore, it has been demonstrated that alarm-inducing messages can be fed into human sense organs in ways that are picked up and remembered by the human amygdala without being registered by human consciousness. In other words, people can have a bodily experience of panic—complete with the racing heart and the sweaty palms and the rest of the complex—without conscious awareness of the trigger. This clue to the workings of the human unconscious will be revisited in the next chapter.

Meanwhile, the laboratory of Michael Davis at Emory University has mapped out a different route that alarm signals can follow in humans. He has tracked alarm messages that flow from human sense organs directly to the cognitive centers of the cortex and only then move on to the amygdala. Davis's group thinks this may be the more routine processing route for fear-inspiring information in humans.

There are many more questions to be answered by this kind of research. Why do some alarm messages move in humans down one pathway to the cortex, while others move directly to the amygdala? What different consequences can be traced to the use of one route or another? At what point are alarm messages split into the signals humans consciously experience as the feeling of fear as against the feeling of anger? The answers to these questions are very relevant to the estimated twenty-three million Americans who suffer from some form of anxiety illness such as post-traumatic stress disorder or social phobia. Clues coming from these studies are already beginning to be used in clinical practice. For example, it seems to be helpful to patients suffering from panic disorder to combine drug therapies that weaken the amygdala's action with cognitive therapy that gradually accustoms the patient to the panic stimuli so as to form the habit of using the cortex pathway.

Regardless of the answers to these questions, it seems to be true that whenever humans experience extreme threats to their valued achievements, a pain avoidance reflex is activated by the amygdala, and humans experience intense fear or anger that is characterized by flight or fight, in a state of at least temporary irrationality. This is a fundamental, inborn reflex mechanism that seems to temporarily shut down the ability of the cortex to operate rationally in pursuit of the other three drives. It can be thought of as the coping mechanism of last resort. It seems to operate almost in a binary manner—on or off.[5]

The pain-avoidance mechanism accounts for the evidence that some human behavior seems to be irrational, in the sense of being self-defeating in terms of achieving goals set by the drives to acquire, bond, and learn. In the early stages of human development this reflex must have aided survival in a crisis by chemically activating and energizing the body's physical defense mechanisms. In the modern context it almost always causes harm. Goleman has assembled the extensive research record on the phenomenon.[6] He refers to the process as *emotional hijacking* or *flooding* and describes the educational process that can help people channel this emotional energy into the constructive pursuit of the other basic drives and away from the pain-avoidance reflex.

At the individual level the reflex can at times manifest itself in violence that has been labeled the *amok syndrome* or, more recently, the *postal syndrome.* It can also be a collective phenomenon. Both political and corporate history record all too many "reigns of terror."

This pioneering work on the detailed functioning of the mind in processing alarm stimuli provides leads to ways research can pursue an understanding of the mind's functioning in relation to the other drives to acquire, bond, and learn. Recall that Damasio hypothesized, as discussed in Chapter Three, that the drive modules of the limbic system code every incoming message from the sense organs with a marker that it carries on to the cognitive centers. The work on alarm signals suggests that the sensory thalamus is the first destination in the limbic area that switches signals to other modules of the limbic system, of which the amygdala is only one. We hypothesize that similar modules will be found in the limbic area that are the physical seat of the other three drives. Clearly more needs to be learned about the specific locus and function of such limbic modules.

## The Drive to Defend in Relation to the Other Drives

One feature of the drive to defend that clearly distinguishes it from the other three drives is that it is always reactive. The other drives, in contrast, are always proactive in the sense that they activate searching behavior, the seeking of some desired object, experience, or condition. Drive 4 keeps people alert to threats but obviously does not seek them—it provides an instinctive urge to avoid them. If signals from Drive 4 enter the consciousness the response is termed *reactive;* if it does not enter consciousness it is termed *reflexive.* Because it is a reactive/reflexive drive, it can best be described in more detail by considering how it works in relation to each of the other drives. It turns out that a significant number of individual behaviors and institutional responses derive from the single drive to defend, in interaction with the other three major drives.

### The Drive to Defend in Interaction with the Drive to Acquire

*Individual Level.* At the individual and interpersonal level the drive to defend is triggered and activated by any perceived threats of bodily harm, and also of damage or theft of valued possessions. These are the basic threats to D1 accomplishments. The feelings that such threats generate are not only the basic ones of fear or anger but the more particular derived one of anxiety that can escalate to paranoia. When triggered by a specific threat the response is glandular and muscular as well as mental. Heartbeat increases, adrenal and other glands become active, muscles tense, sense organs go on full alert, and so on.

The preferred response to such threats is usually to flee, to retreat, to seek shelter, and generally avoid the threat. The secondary response is to fight back, to attack and overcome the threat. Humans probably have some innate skill sets to pursue either of these strategies. They know how to run and hide. They know something about how to use fists, feet, teeth, and hand weapons in a fight. And human cultures have, of course, built up a vast array of methods and artifacts to build on and reinforce any innate skills. People have acquired elaborate security systems, with personal weapons, locks, alarms, and safes being only the most obvious ones. Legal systems also protect persons and possessions with associated punishments in terms of prisons and fines, and police forces and courts help cope with threats.

**Collective/Organizational Level.** At this level the drive to defend in regard to D1 gains is triggered in individuals when they perceive a threat to the resources of any group with which they are closely identified. Such threats can take the form of natural disasters such as earthquakes, hurricanes, and the like. Threats from other humans can appear as aggressive gangs or mobs or as hostile organizations or even subgroups of large organizations. They also appear in the form of hostile nation states oriented toward the plundering of D1 resources. Think of Iraq's attack on Kuwait. Intergroup conflict over resources is endemic in human life. The skill sets that humans seem to have evolved to deal with these threats are collective forms of the fight-or-flight skills seen at the individual level. They involve the process of closing ranks either to retreat to, or fight from, some kind of defensive position. Retreating and fighting can, of course, take many forms. Verbal battles rage in private and in public, in legislative halls and in courts. Within corporations the marketing people are often battling for their budget with production and engineering groups. Corporations also accumulate reserve funds, war chests to deal with hostile competitors. At the level of the nation state, these defenses take the form of military organizations that assemble a vast array of weapons ranging from simple firearms to nuclear warheads. Conflicts at the collective level can clearly escalate to the level of war—a complex issue that we will reserve for discussion later.

## The Drive to Defend in
## Interaction with the Drive to Bond

**Individual Level.** The drive to defend can be triggered in individuals by threats to any of their important bonded relationships. These threats can be to the life or well-being—or the possessions or beliefs or reputation—of a loved one, a family member, close friend, or business partner. This could be from natural causes such as ill health or from unnatural causes such as assault. They can be threats to the relationship itself, triggered by infidelity in a marriage or by disloyal behavior or threats of such by a friend or professional colleague.

The human response to threats to bonded relationships is more apt to be anger and fight rather than flight. Violence has often been a socially condoned response to marital infidelity. Disloyalty in a friend can trigger an angry and vengeful reaction, often leading to termination of the relationship. Even an accidental snub or slight will often lead to hurt feelings requiring remedial effort to restore the relationship. Think of the quantities of flowers and lunches that are bought to help restore damaged relationships.

Chapter Five described how the termination of an important relationship by death or other permanent cause can generate pain with deep sorrow, lasting grief, and sometimes depression. Humans go to great length to avoid or at least delay such experiences. As was true with the defense of acquisitions, the defense of relationships has led to aspects of the legal system such as marriage and divorce law, with its associated judicial institutions.

Some leading psychotherapists have talked recently about a pathology among younger patients that they label "fear of commitment." One of the more obvious ways this fear manifests itself is in the delayed marriages of couples with a long history of living together. Therapists often say that the lives of such couples would move forward in a positive way if only they could bring themselves to make the public commitment of marriage. And yet the couples continue to hesitate. Why do they avoid making that most important bond in life, a lasting bond with a mate? The innate drive to bond means that they must feel an urge to make the commitment. Yet the drive to defend can lead them to anticipate the severe distress they might experience in the future if this bond were severed either by divorce or death. Perhaps an in-depth understanding of their own drives to both bond and to defend against the risk of loss might help such people embrace life with all its hazards and make the commitment to go forward.

***Collective/Organizational Level.*** Threats to bonded relationships at the collective level take the form of threats to groups with which individuals are closely identified. Humans tend to be especially sensitive to threats, even slights, to their bonded groups, and often react defensively. As pointed out in Chapter Five, the drive to bond predisposes humans to be joiners. And once someone becomes identified with a group, so that it becomes "my" group, they tend to be quick to take offense at behaviors that they perceive to be hostile toward that group.

Again, as at the individual level, when people perceive their bonded groups as threatened, the favored response is to be angry, to close ranks and counterattack in some form. Retreating is a comparatively rare event. In fact, groups seem more willing than individuals to counterattack, even in the face of unfavorable odds. People are notoriously braver in groups than alone—sometimes to the point of foolhardiness.

Group conflict that is tied to the defense of relationships is what lies behind feuds between families that sometimes go on for generations. It energizes the tribal and ethnic conflict that has been the cause of so much human suffering. On the positive side, competition between hostile groups can inspire extraordinary acts of creativity and of sacrifice for fellow group members. And then there are the benign forms of intergroup conflict, such as the mock battles of athletic events to defend the honor of a school or city.

## The Drive to Defend in
## Interaction with the Drive to Learn

**Individual Level.** As noted in Chapter Six, the drive to learn leads people to build up their own complex view of the world around them, alongside their beliefs about themselves. The drive to defend is activated to protect these worldviews and self-images whenever they are threatened. The threats can come in several ways. The focus may be on the self and come in the form of personal insults or slander. It may come as an attack on a closely held belief system such as a religious faith. Or it can come in much more trivial ways, as when a single observation about the world that one happens to believe is shown not to be true. These examples make it clear that the response to be expected from such threats can vary from a mild passing argument to a major persistent conflict that could turn violent. After all, belief systems are the hard-won result of an entire life's experiences and are deeply prized and defended possessions.

It's common to think of threats to one's beliefs as arriving as direct verbal arguments but, of course, in today's world they are more apt to arrive in books or the mass media. In the face of such threats to personal beliefs, humans are more apt to use the defense mechanism of denial rather than the flight or fight prevalent in the responses to D1 and D2 threats.

Denial is a well-known psychological defense, one of the many identified by Freud. It is a kind of trick that the brain is capable of playing, pretending the threat did not really happen. It can then be forgotten, at least consciously. It is probably easier to use denial if the message arrives via mass media than if it arrives in a face-to-face conversation. Of course, another response is to change beliefs to conform with those being promoted as superior, or to hold onto prior beliefs but make some adjustments to bring them more in line with the alternative being proposed. Or one can launch a counterattack by strongly defending the current set of beliefs by some form of rational argument. Finally, it is possible to feel so deeply threatened by the external attack on a set of beliefs that the response is to lash out in rage.

A less well-recognized modern manifestation of the interplay between D4 and D3 is the fear of believing. The drive to learn and make sense of the world pushes everyone toward choosing a belief system that helps answer the more fundamental questions about the meaning of human existence and their own personal place in the universe. Everyone shares a drive to have such a belief system, and many conduct a lifelong search for an ever more adequate system. This is what is generally called the spiritual life. But the history of ideas in the last 150 years has in many ways been a story of debunking one belief system after another. While Darwin offered a belief system that many have found meaningful, for many others it only seemed to undermine traditional religions. Freud tried to offer a belief system that could lead people to mental health, but for many it undercut their belief in the possibility of true love in primary family relationships and made them doubt any nobility in their fundamental motives. Einstein offered people fresh insights into the wonders of the universe—but in the popular version it came out as "everything is relative" and weakened their belief in any eternal laws of the universe. Finally, many people in this century were caught up in the positive promises of sharing and brotherly love offered by communism, only to see it grossly corrupted by the Leninist and Stalinist police state. Such shattering of belief systems is a painful process. The current disillusionment of the people of Russia is one important example. All these events have led people to a cynical and severely skeptical view of the world and even to a loss of faith in the possibility of further human development and progress. This has led them to a refusal to believe and to a fear of any general explanation of human existence or positive vision of the future.

On a more positive note, the dynamic interplay of the drive to defend in combination with the drive to learn can help explain why humans have been so adaptable and flexible in surviving success-fully in a wide range of environmental niches throughout the world. It is these two basic mental drives, along with the cognitive centers, that have made the mind into such a highly adaptive learn-ing machine employing the Darwinian algorithm. D3 supplies the courageous, exploratory urges at the same time that D4 pushes for a cautious approach. Thus the brain can initiate multiple mental experiments, select the most promising ones for actual trial, per-ceive which trial works relatively well, and remember and defend what works. This process encapsulates major parts of the philoso-phy of pragmatism developed by William James and John Dewey.[7]

**Collective/Organizational Level.** Belief systems, while they lodge in individual heads, are very much a group phenomenon. The vast majority of the ideas people carry in their brains have been con-veyed to them by their cultures through their various group memberships, their bonded relationships. So while threats to self-concept are truly an attack on uniquely personal beliefs, most of the hostile belief systems that people experience as threats to their own beliefs are, more accurately, threats to the beliefs of the groups with which they are identified. Just a preliminary list of such groups clarifies the source and extensiveness of these belief systems. Think of your extended family, your church, your nation, your ethnic or racial group, your gender group, your political party, your work organization, your favorite school or university, your favorite sports team, and so on and on. The belief systems of such groups are the ones people have internalized and share with other group members in a mutually reinforcing way. So when the beliefs they share with these groups are attacked, they not only tend to take it personally, they also have a ready-made group of allies to help defend these beliefs. This often leads humans, as in the case of attacks on bonded relationships, to respond to attacks on collective beliefs with anger and counterattacks. They know they will not be fighting alone. Be thankful that almost all these attacks and counterattacks are verbal! Of course, the world has, unfortunately, seen a fair number of wars that were heavily ideological. This brings us to comment on the negative side of the drive to defend, namely war.

## THE DARK SIDE OF THE DRIVE TO DEFEND

The dark side of the drive to defend is war. Since the development of the nuclear bomb, war risks human extinction. In modern times wars are fought between nation states or between some part of a nation that fights a civil war to become an independent state. Modern nations have been able to secure a monopoly on the use of physical force to maintain order and resolve conflicts within their boundaries. The world, as yet, in spite of many efforts, has not been able to establish a world government strong enough to establish and sustain a monopoly on the use of physical force. Until this happens it is always entirely possible, even likely, for wars to break out. Does the four-drive theory of human nature generate any reason to hope this could change in the future? We see two reasons for hope.

First, the drive we have identified as one of the most basic elements of human nature is the drive to *defend*, not to *aggress*. This is not to deny at all that nations have a record of starting wars of aggression. But such wars are, we would argue, a secondary means to fulfill the underlying drive to acquire, a drive that can be met in various ways. It follows that war will not happen if the costs are high and other, less risky ways of fulfilling D1 are available. In this lies one hope for avoiding war. We must caution, however, that it is fairly easy for the leaders of nations to convince themselves that an aggressive act on their part is really a defensive one. It is easy to change the name of the "War Department" to the "Defense Department," but just switching symbols goes only so far. We must constantly guard against unleashing violence in the name of defense when the real drive is to acquire.

A second basis for hope that four-drive theory holds out is based on the human drive to bond not only with individuals but also with collectives. So far in human history nation states are the largest collectives to which humans have strong emotional commitments of allegiance. Even these bonds of allegiance to nations are a relatively recent development. Before, the largest bonded collective was the tribe, and before that the kinship group and the primary family. The point is that the size of collectives to which humans bond directly has been increasing, albeit very gradually.

No contemporary nation, with the possible exception of Costa Rica, has been willing to disarm unilaterally and trust in regional alliances and the U.N. to defend it from aggression. However, the drive to bond with collectives—and the historical record of the enlargement of that circle of trust—both provide some hope that humanity can move once more to the final step of world government. This possibility brings to mind the choice that Robert E. Lee had to make when Abraham Lincoln asked him to take command of the federal troops after Fort Sumter. At the very same time Lee was also considering a request from Jefferson Davis to take command of the Confederate forces. Lee made his choice to serve the Confederacy based on his deep feeling that his primary bond of loyalty was to his native state of Virginia, even though he was a West Point graduate with an outstanding war record as a general in the U.S. Army. The record suggests his choice was made in spite of his views on slavery, not because of them. Today Americans take it for granted that their broadest strong emotional commitment is to the entire United States. This emotional shift has been made and it could happen again, given enough time. Nothing about the human drive to bond would preclude it—to the contrary. Perhaps this generation's great great-grandchildren will take a pledge of allegiance to the United Nations of the World with the same emotional fervor Americans now feel toward that pledge to the United States.

## FOUR DRIVES

The four-drive theory that we are proposing makes four critical assertions. First, the four drives are innate and universal, found in some physical form in the brains of all human beings. Second, the four drives are independent, in the sense that the goals they seek are not interchangeable, even though they are highly interactive with each other. Third, in the current configuration of the human brain, the drives are not derived from one another or from a single underlying mental drive. This is proposed even though D1 and D4 almost certainly predated D2 and D3. And finally, the four drives are a complete set; they are not missing any other important universal and independent human drives.

The assertion that these drives are innate and universal is a strong one, especially when we learn from biology that, except for identical twins, every human is truly unique. Perhaps there are some exceptions to the universality of the drives. A person without any D1 might well be labeled a saint; in fact, it is the goal of some Eastern religions to help people reach this elusive condition. A human without any D2 would be a true sociopath (or psychopath), a menace to others. Very few people, if any, truly deserve the label of sociopath. The fact that so very few individuals are saints or sociopaths demonstrates that the drives to acquire and to bond are at least nearly universal. As far as we know, no label exists for an individual with zero drive to learn (D3) or to defend (D4), except possibly automaton and wimp. The strongest evidence of the universality of the four drives comes from their prominence in the lists compiled by Murdock and Brown of the traits found by anthropologists to be present in all the cultures they have studied, evidence we will further consider in the next chapter.

We would argue further that the genetically determined independence of the four drives has, paradoxically, actually served to somewhat loosen the control of genes over human behavior and to increase the importance and influence of cultural and individual development. The independence of the drives puts the major burden on the individual and on social institutions to carry on the further development of the species. This is true first of all because significant genetic change has, biologists maintain, virtually stopped for humans. The species now shares such a large gene pool with no totally isolated pockets that any new genetic mutations have little chance to take hold in the population as a whole.

But even more important, the independence of the drives often forces them into conflict. When there is no conflict between or among the drives in regard to a given situation, the mind is capable of signaling the action to be taken to the motor centers with minimal, if any, conscious awareness. This process saves decision time and frees the conscious mind to consider more important things. For example, you can carry on most necessary, uncontested bodily functions without awareness. You are only aware of your heartbeat when it speeds up and you need to be alert to what is causing this.

On the other hand, when the inevitable conflict between mental drives occurs, the opposing signals are forced into awareness where they are subject to conscious consideration and resolution. Such conflicts can be troubling and painful. For example, think of the feelings one has when a loved one develops a strong religious belief that conflicts with one's own. To be clear, these conflicts are entirely internal, between two parts of one mind. These conflicts pose choices that are impossible to avoid without resorting to the abnormal psychological mechanisms such as repression. So our genes, by establishing the independence of the four drives, have guaranteed that humans have to make decisions that involve difficult trade-offs, difficult moral choices that other animals do not face. Since these are conscious choices (what is often called *free will*), and since our large memory and information processing capacity forces us to review the past and anticipate the future consequences of our choices, we cannot avoid seeing ourselves as causal agents. Our minds are designed to force us to feel responsible for all the consequences flowing from our decisions. This is what is called the human conscience. This is the highest level of consciousness that Damasio describes in his recent comprehensive book of the biological basis of humans' multiple levels of consciousness.[8]

~

Another fresh perspective is opened up by the four-drive theory on the amazing adaptability of the human species. How has our species been able, in so relatively short a time, not only to survive but to thrive in all parts of the earth, on and under the seas, in the sky, and now even in space? One way of addressing this question is not only by exploring the relevant scientific literature but also by conducting a thought experiment. We suggest that you use your imagination to search for any other combination of drives that would be superior in achieving flexibility of response to all varieties of environments. We have so far never found any superior combination. The adaptive power of the four drives comes from their interplay in framing the ultimate goals of human behavior (the what) even as innate skill sets give humans a head start on the how of behavior. The drives tend to create some balance between order and change, between exploration and prudence, as each individual makes the required choices in the never-ending search for ways to fulfill, not just one or two, but all of the four independent drives.

Human genes do not determine behavior; far from it. On the contrary, they actually require the exercise of free will, albeit as constrained by environmental conditions. They require us to make choices, over and over, in an essentially unpredictable and nondeterministic manner, choices of what to do in our search for a better life.

# PART THREE

## THE DRIVES IN ACTION

How Human Nature Works in Context

# CULTURE, SKILLS, EMOTIONS
## OTHER PIECES OF THE PUZZLE

*Any merely superficial ordering of life that leaves its deepest
needs unsatisfied is as ineffectual as if no attempt at order had
ever been made.*

—I CHING

The four independent drives and related skill sets were critical to human evolution. Once these drives and skills were
firmly and innately implanted in the brain, the stage was
set for the takeoff in human cultural development. With their drive
to learn and related skill sets such as language and abstract reasoning, humans could invent and design all varieties of new artifacts.[1]
They could reach out to explore the entire globe. They could eventually domesticate a variety of plants and animals, greatly increasing
their available resources. With their drive to bond and related skill
sets such as morals, they could create the stable large-scale social
institutions necessary for the big construction and irrigation proj-
ects of ancient civilizations. With their drive to acquire and related
skill sets such as the sense of ownership and property rights, they
could create and accumulate large stores of items of value. With the
drive to defend in place they could create weapons and other defensive artifacts. These four drives, which together made up what was
universal in human nature, provided the foundation for the rapid
development of all varieties of human cultures.

Probably the single strongest evidence of the role played by these universal drives in cultural development is the amazing similarity among the earliest human civilizations. The civilizations that arose totally independently in the Old World and the New World shared remarkably common elements. In 1940 the American archaeologist Alfred V. Kidder summarized what had been learned about these independent cultural developments and pointed out the features they shared.[2]

He noted that in both hemispheres, civilizations developed from the same cultural base of Stone Age, hunter-gatherer tribes. In both places, groups brought wild plants under cultivation, and this agricultural technology allowed their populations to increase in settled villages and, later, cities. People in both the Old and New Worlds invented pottery and wove plant fibers and wool into cloth. They both domesticated local wild animals for food and transport. They both worked metal into tools and ornaments—first gold and copper, then bronze. They both invented writing and used it to record their myths, wars, and noble lineages. They both invented musical instruments. They both created stratified societies with hereditary classes for nobles, priests, warriors, craftsmen, and peasants. They both reared huge temples adorned with painting and sculpture. They both constructed elaborate tombs for their priests and chiefs. They both created hierarchical organizations to the scale of empires.

Differences in cultural forms were also readily apparent. For instance, their art and architecture were different; the plants and animals they domesticated were much more numerous in the Old World. The New World civilization did not develop the use of iron, nor did people make much use of the wheel. But in the end, this historical record constitutes a powerful argument for the existence of an innate nature that is shared among all humans. This human nature does not deterministically dictate the form of cultural development but does channel it down some broad avenues with ample room for variation.

Asserting that our genetic heritage of drives and skill sets provides a base for the development of human culture does not say much about how these elements of nature and nurture combine and work together on an everyday basis. This issue has been addressed by scholars working in both the biological sciences (studying genetic nature) and the social sciences (studying cultural heritage). This issue involves both the mutual interaction of innate nature and culture in shaping human behavior at a point in time, and how they both coevolve and change over time.

## THE ROLE OF EMOTIONS

Emotions are an important link between human nature and culture. The analysis of the place of emotions in human behavior has an extensive history. It starts appropriately with Darwin and his 1872 book *Emotions in Man and Animals*.[3] Darwin believed that many, though not all, emotional expressions in humans are innate. In making his case, Darwin drew on four kinds of evidence. He pointed out that some emotional expressions appear in similar form in many nonhuman animals. Some emotions also appear in very young children before much opportunity for cultural learning has occurred. Moreover, some are expressed in identical ways by humans born blind and thus unable to mimic the appearance of a gesture or expression. Finally, many emotional expressions appear in similar form across all human groups. Smiling is an example of an emotion that offers all four of these kinds of evidence.

Freud went further than Darwin by specifying and classifying the very limited number of drives he believed were expressed as emotions. For him, the two basic drives were the ego drive and the sex drive. For Freud, the ego drive was the source for several secondary drives, including hunger, thirst, and aggression, as well as the impulse to control others, to wield power, to attack, and to flee from danger. Most psychoanalytic treatment following Freud has focused on negative emotions such as fear and anxiety, and has tended to ignore the positive ones. This has obscured the fact that Freud saw emotions as essential for survival, performing the function of arousing, sustaining, and directing human action.

The point that emotions are essential for survival is important, because it contradicts the conventional wisdom that emotions lead to impulsive and irrational behavior that usually gets humans into trouble. Emotions, according to the latter view, are carryovers from early evolutionary history and, although they may have aided survival in the primitive world of the hunter-gatherer, are largely dysfunctional in modern civilized life. We strongly disagree. This is not to deny that there are occasions when the fear reflex leads to some conspicuously irrational behavior such as a fear of flying. But we see these situations as the exception. Emotions are usually an accurate guide on the path to fulfilling ultimate drives. Wise people have learned to sense and apply their emotional responses as well as their rational analysis when they face important choices.

Robert Plutchik, in *Emotion: A Psychoevolutionary Synthesis,*[4] has developed a more general theory of the role of emotions in human behavior. He agrees with Darwin on the evolutionary source of many emotions, and with Freud in there being a small number of primary subconscious drives that are expressed in consciousness as emotions. He argues that all emotions are derived from primary drives and conceptualizes emotions as a bridge between the primary drives and cognition. Cognition, he believes, evolved to predict the future and thereby to serve in the fulfillment of both the emotions and the underlying biological drives from which they are derived. We agree with this formulation of the connection between drives, emotions, and cognition.

The best way to explicate Plutchik's categories of emotions is to array a sample of them on a grid formed by the four drives and the spaces around and between them. This we have done in Figure 8.1.

It should be apparent from this array that the placement of derived emotions is rather crude and to some extent arbitrary. This is probably inevitable—words are somewhat clumsy symbols for the underlying emotions. But the point should be clear that emotions do come in different intensities and different mixes (think of the analogy to the combinations of the three primary colors), and they do convey some of the emotional variations possible around the four drives.

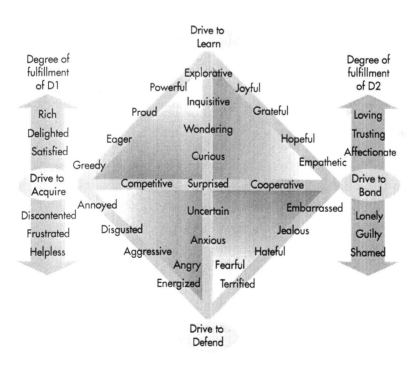

**Figure 8.1. Derived Emotions Arrayed on a Four-Drive Grid.**

## Cognition and Self-Determination

Edward Deci, in *The Psychology of Self-Determination*,[5] pushes Plutchik's treatment of the role of emotion in human behavior a significant step further by bringing up the age-old question of free will—from a psychologist's rather than a philosopher's perspective. He credits William James with being the first psychologist to treat the subject in some detail. For James, *will* was the desire for an outcome that the individual thought was attainable, in other words, a state of mind that preceded voluntary behavior.

Deci credits the well-known social psychologist Kurt Lewin with further clarifying these points. For Lewin, "there are three phases to an intentional action: a struggle between motives, a decision or intention that ends the struggle, and the . . . action itself."[6] The strength of the resulting action does not depend on the intensity of the *intention* but rather on the intensity of the *drives* upon which the intention rests. Lewin then stated that "an intention that is not based on a natural need (such as a drive) will surely fail." These observations are central to our argument as to how the four drives are combined with the conscious decision-making process in humans. In our terms, the independence of the four drives—that is, their non-interchangeable nature—necessitates an internal mental struggle among them that forces itself into consciousness for resolution. The struggle is resolved by the intentional act of will that leads to an action that is, in turn, energized by the relevant drives.

Deci describes this internal struggle in some detail, pointing out that people are frequently aware of more than one motive at a time:

> While it may be possible to select a goal that will satisfy all of these motives simultaneously, typically that will not be the case. People must therefore decide which one or ones to attempt to satisfy at that time; the others must be held

in abeyance. When there is only one motive, there is less need to recognize people's capacity for willing. However, with several motives, one must sift among the motives and select the one or ones that will be operative, and hold in abeyance the motives that were not chosen for satisfaction. It is particularly the function of holding motives in abeyance that necessitates the concept of will.[7]

Deci also strengthens our perspective by criticizing the rational choice theory favored by economists, or as psychologists say, the "cognitive theories of choice." Such theories, he argues, largely ignore the role of emotions in the choice process. On the contrary, Deci maintains, "emotions play a vital role in the motivation of behavior."[8]

Deci moves on to offer his own definition of will and self-determination that fits precisely with our thinking. "Will is the capacity of the human organism to choose how to satisfy its needs. . . . Self-determination is the process of utilizing one's will. . . . Willing is a necessary aspect of healthy human functioning." Thus, self-determination is a direct product of independent, non-interchangeable drives such as the four we hypothesize. This emphasizes the point of our theory that people desire to fulfill all four of their innate drives—people always look for smart ways to have it all. In some situations, of course, they cannot have it all and are forced to choose the fulfillment of one drive over another, perhaps choosing to alternate drive fulfillment to cope with this situation.

## SKILL SETS

In Chapter Three we drew heavily on the work of Pinker and other evolutionary psychologists in presenting the nature of innate skills and the role they play in mental activity. In discussing the four drives in Chapters Four through Seven, we also hypothesized about the skill sets that are closely identified with each of the drives. We took special note of the moral skills associated with the drive to bond and the abstract reasoning skills associated with the drive to learn. We now want to emphasize the special role skill sets play in bridging between the four drives and from the four drives to human cultural development. In essence these innate skill sets, as Pinker points out, give humans a wonderful head start in learning the multiple skills that cultures carry and pass on from one generation to the next throughout human history.

Another scholar of this subject is Howard Gardner. His work, *Frames of Mind: The Theory of Multiple Intelligences,*[9] highlights the way different intelligences, or what we call skill sets, interact with culture. Gardner summarizes his theory as follows: "In its strong form, multiple intelligence theory posits a small set of human intellectual potentials, of which all individuals are capable by virtue of their membership in the human species. Owing to heredity, early training, or, in all probability, a constant interaction between these factors, some individuals will develop certain intelligences far more than others; but every normal individual should develop each intelligence to some extent, given but a modest opportunity to do so." The six intelligences (skill sets) he discusses at length are linguistic, musical, logical-mathematical, spatial, bodily-kinesthetic, and personal or social. Around each of these skills he has assembled supporting evidence from various sources. The evidence is impressive but, as Gardner would be the first to say, his theory needs further testing.

Among the issues to be tested is the completeness of his list. There is some, but not total, overlap between Gardner's list of intelligences and Pinker's list of skill sets. This suggests that further research will discover additional skill sets. This field of research is just barely opening up.

To demonstrate the kind of analysis and evidence that Gardner assembled, we will use as an example some of the observations he cites in his treatment of musical intelligence. He reports that composers are particularly articulate about the origin of their skills.

Aaron Copeland indicates that composing is as natural as eating or sleeping: "It is something that the composer happens to have been born to do; and because of that it loses the character of a special virtue in the composer's eyes." Wagner said he composed like a cow producing milk, whereas Saint-Sans likened the process to an apple tree producing apples. The sole element of mystery, in Copeland's view, is the source of an initial musical idea: as he sees it, themes initially come to the composer as a gift from heaven, much like automatic writing. And that is the reason many composers keep a notebook around. Once the idea has come, the process of development and elaboration follows with surprising naturalness, eventually with inevitability, thanks in part to the many techniques available as well as to the accessibility of structural forms or "schemes" that have evolved over the years.[10]

A reading of Gardner's book will convince most people that the inherited skill sets he examines provide an impressive start for continued learning through cultural resources. They provide strong evidence that skill sets, in general, provide a sturdy bridge between basic drives and cultural inheritance.

We would caution, however, against any tendency to explain each and every human skill as an innate skill set. As an example of this hazard we are reminded of a comment about himself that John D. Rockefeller made, as cited in *Titan*.[11] Rockefeller noted the evidence that people often had special gifts, perhaps for music, or poetry writing, or similar skills. He felt strongly that it would be wrong for such people not to cultivate and develop these natural gifts. To do otherwise would be wasteful, even sinful in his strict Baptist terms. Rockefeller then explained that he had a gift for making money that would be sinful to waste. Probably those who were unfortunate enough to be his competitors in the oil business would grant that he had the gift—but still wished he would stop tilting the playing field.

## Skill Sets as Aids to Resolving Tensions Between the Four Drives

The work of Pinker and Gardner on innate skill sets has been built upon more recently by two other psychologists, Jordan Peterson and Alan Fiske, in a very original and useful fashion. Their work is of special interest in that it adds to our understanding of how skill sets can help people resolve conflicts between pairs of drives. Peterson's work shows how a particular skill set helps humans fulfill the drives to learn and to defend simultaneously, while Fiske's work shows how a group of four particular skill sets are of help to humans in fulfilling the drives to acquire and to bond simultaneously.

*Reconciling D3 and D4.* Peterson focuses his attention on how the mind is built to detect novelty or surprises in the environment.[12] He sees evidence that humans have a skill that helps them respond to novelty with a mixture of emotions—anxiety and curiosity. He believes this novelty detector skill serves to alert the entire body to attend or concentrate on the unknown event and explore it, but with caution—in four-drive terms, to approach and learn (D3) about the novel situation, but also with readiness to quickly go on the defensive and retreat or attack (D4). In this process the brain tries out different ways to form mental representations of the unknown object, searching for any preexisting representation that approximates the unknown and noting possible matches and mismatches.

As Peterson expresses it, "Human beings are prepared, biologically, to respond to anomalous information—to novelty. This instinctive response includes redirection of attention, generation of emotion (fear first, generally speaking, then curiosity), and behavioral compulsion (cessation of ongoing activity first, generally speaking, then, active approach and exploration)."[13] Later, "The simplest cognitive/exploratory maneuver that renders an unpredictable occurrence conditionally predictable or familiar is likely to be adopted. . . . If a solution 'works' it is 'right'." This fits in with Edelman's description of how neural sets employ the V/S/R process to develop more accurate representations, and with Loewenstein's discussion of how curiosity works (described in Chapter Six). Such a novelty detection and testing mechanism would certainly qualify as an important skill set that must make an important contribution to survival. It offers a clear understanding of how people combine and balance the drives of learning and of defending, of approaching and of avoiding, in action in the face of uncertainty.

**Reconciling D1 and D2.** Fiske's work has focused on developing an overview of the skill sets that humans use to relate to one another, which he calls the basic, universal forms of sociality.[14] He finds that all varieties of human relationships can be grouped into just four basic types, four skill sets.

Fiske made his initial observations on the four forms of sociality while doing extensive fieldwork among the Moose people of Burkina Faso in West Africa, among the poorest people on earth. He has subsequently tested his findings not only in other African tribes but also in several advanced industrial countries.

The four forms Fiske identifies are communal sharing (CS), authority ranking (AR), equality matching (EM), and market pricing (MP). Communal sharing (CS) is found universally in the primary family group. In this setting, people largely follow the exchange rule, "From each according to their ability and to each according to their need." This form is employed beyond the family only in an uneven way, sometimes to extended family and less frequently beyond it. Communism was an ill-fated experiment in trying to turn CS into an all-purpose ideology that extended this form of sociality far beyond the primary family group.

Authority ranking (AR), by contrast, is a relationship of inequality. In this form humans negotiate, over time, a rank ordering among themselves as to who has more social importance, status, or dominance over others. This is the pecking order that is so clearly evident in many animal species. Rank can be established in many ways—age, intelligence, brute strength, wealth, social skills, and various combinations of these attributes. Ranking relationships do involve a form of exchange between the parties, even though it is unequal. The dominance of one party provides entitlement to resource advantages, but also carries with it an obligation of some amount of support for the lesser party. Well-established hierarchies of this type have mixed costs and benefits for the participants. One benefit is a relatively stable place for everyone, and everyone—except for those at the very bottom—can dominate someone else. This basic form of human relations is, however, subject to destabilizing turmoil whenever any parties struggle to improve their ranking since anyone's gain is another person's loss. This mode is obviously conspicuous in formal hierarchical organizations, as well as in heavily class- or status-stratified societies such as medieval feudalism or the Indian caste system. Fiske argues again that this mode of sociality is universal to humans and presumably innate in its basic form.

Equality matching (EM), better known as long-term reciprocity, provides the ground rules that govern most peer relationships. This mode calls for an equality of exchange over an extended time period. You scratch my back, and then I have an obligation, sooner or later, to scratch yours. These are the ground rules for establishing lasting friendships. There is very strong evidence that all humans, in all cultures, use this form of sociality on a regular basis.

Finally, market pricing (MP) is exchange by bartering—or by a ratio to some medium of exchange. This can be the price negotiation that occurs in a standard, one-time commercial transaction that is done, for example, with a used car salesman, a Middle Eastern rug merchant or an African street vendor. This kind of bargaining involves bidding and counterbidding, often with bluffing and calling bluffs, while keeping one's rock-bottom or *reservation* price a secret. It lends itself to exchanges between strangers who do not expect to trade repeatedly, and Fiske asserts that all humans seem to have a basic understanding of how to play this game.

Fiske presents evidence to support his hypothesis that these four modes are universal and innate among all humans. In addition, he presents limited anecdotal evidence that these four modes are manifested in maturing children, in the order they have been presented, in a spontaneous, uncoached manner starting roughly with three-year-olds for CS and proceeding to eight-year-olds for MP.

He develops the idea that each of these modes carries its own set of ground rules or moral codes that people expect to be observed or sanctions will follow. For example, fairness and equality of exchange over time are the key rules for the EM mode, while "buyer beware" during the negotiations but abide by the resulting agreement or contract are the key rules for MP. CS invokes the rule of sharing generously with the others that are most closely bonded of one's kind, and placing the needs of this group on a par with personal needs. The morality of AR consists of an attitude of respect, deference, loyalty, and compliance by subordinates, complemented by the responsibility of the authority figure to provide protection for subordinates, a share of the resources available, and wise directive guidance.

In our terms, these four forms of social relations represent four skill sets or methods that people have innately available to them to develop and maintain bonded ties (D2) and simultaneously to exercise their drive to acquire (D1). The rules that are the essence of each of the four modes define them as a particular kind of social contract. When people are acting in MP or AR mode, it is experienced as primarily a competitive relationship, oriented mostly to fulfilling D1. When people are acting in EM or CS mode it is experienced primarily as a cooperative relationship, oriented mostly to fulfilling D2. Any given relationship between two people will always have some competitive elements and some cooperative elements. The weighting between the two aspects will depend on the history of the relationship and the immediate context of the current action.

Fiske ends his book by supporting our hypothesized drive to bond as follows: "This relational-models theory construes human beings as inherently sociable. People seek to relate to others in each of the four basic modes. . . . People understand their social life in terms of these four models, and they attempt to impose these relational structures on their social world. People want others to conform to the models. Consequently, conceptions of social relations, moral judgments, norms and relational motives often coincide. We are social by nature and by culture."[15]

We will return to these four forms of sociality in Chapter Ten, discussing the diversity of cultures, and in Chapter Eleven with regard to organizational life. For now, we will summarize our discussion by arraying a sample of possible skill sets we have discussed (some more speculative than others) on another grid of the four drives, shown in Figure 8.2.

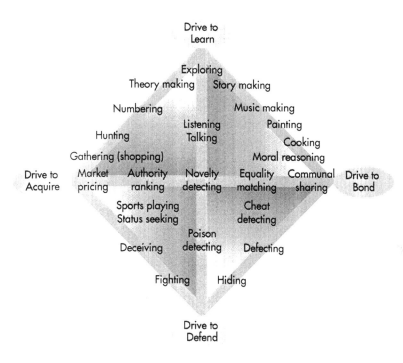

**Figure 8.2. Skill Sets Arrayed on a Four-Drive Grid.**

## Universal Cultural Traits

The final building block we need to put in place to understand coevolution has been provided by anthropologists. In particular, we will draw on the work of George Murdock and Donald Brown.[16] These anthropologists have given exceptional attention to seeking out the cultural universals that are present in every human culture that has been subject to careful study. It may seem surprising that so few anthropologists have carefully pursued the question of cultural universals, but the truth is that the discipline, very early in its history, became focused on the differences among cultures. This focus was consistent with the general doctrine of the social sciences that human behavior is completely malleable to environmental influences. Murdock and Brown each set out to correct this bias.

In 1945 Murdock produced a systematic list of the cultural traits that were practiced in every single one of the several hundred human societies that were documented in the Human Relations Area Files at Yale University. Table 8.1 presents his whole list, along with our assessment of the approximate connection of each item with one or more of the four drives. In so doing, we are not suggesting a strong causal relationship between these traits and the drives—only a potential or partial connection that should be studied further. They represent for us the items of culture that are candidates for having a genetic component along with specific content that is carried from generation to generation by acquired learning.

Precision of coding is not the point here. What we find especially interesting is that we had little trouble finding some connection between every one of Murdock's universal cultural traits and one or two drives. In addition, we find it somewhat surprising that more of Murdock's universal traits seem to be associated with the drive to bond than with the drive to defend. Perhaps Murdock, or the original anthropologists who did the underlying research, might not have noticed defensive behavior. Brown's work on this same subject is at a somewhat higher level of abstraction and is therefore difficult to compare with Murdock's, but in general, it agrees with his list. Our point in enumerating and encoding Murdock's list is to show that it is feasible to associate a list of universal cultural traits with the four drives that we propose are innate and universal among humans.

One of the founders of anthropology, Bronislaw Malinowski, in his classic study of the Trobriand Islanders, describes in detail the kula exchange process between the natives of different islands.[17] This is a gift-giving process that is carried out during periodic visits

**Table 8.1. Murdock's List of Universal Cultural Traits, Coded for Linkage to the Four Drives.**

| Cultural Trait | 1 | 2 | 3 | 4 |
|---|---|---|---|---|
| Age grading | D1 | | | |
| Athletic sports | D1 | D2 | | |
| Bodily adornment | D1 | | | |
| Calendar | | | D3 | |
| Cleanliness training | | | | D4 |
| Community organization | | D2 | | |
| Cooking | D1 | | | |
| Cooperative labor | D1 | D2 | | |
| Cosmology | | | D3 | |
| Courtship | | D2 | | |
| Dancing | | D2 | | |
| Decorative arts | | | D3 | |
| Divination | | | D3 | |
| Division of labor | D1 | D2 | | |
| Dream interpretation | | | D3 | |
| Education | | | D3 | |
| Eschatology | | | D3 | |
| Ethics | | D2 | | |
| Ethnobotany | D1 | | | |
| Etiquette | | D2 | | |
| Faith healing | D1 | | D3 | |
| Family feasting | | D2 | | |
| Fire making | D1 | | | |
| Folklore | | | D3 | |
| Food taboos | D1 | | | D4 |
| Funeral rites | | D2 | | |
| Games | | D2 | | |
| Gestures | | D2 | | |
| Gift-giving | | D2 | | |
| Government | | D2 | | |
| Greetings | | D2 | | |

| Cultural Trait | 1 | 2 | 3 | 4 |
|---|---|---|---|---|
| Hair styles | | D2 | | |
| Hospitality | | D2 | | |
| Housing | | | | D4 |
| Hygiene | | | | D4 |
| Incest taboos | | D2 | | |
| Inheritance rules | D1 | | | |
| Joking | | D2 | | |
| Kin-groups | | D2 | | |
| Kinship nomenclature | | | D3 | |
| Language | | D2 | D3 | |
| Law | | D2 | | D4 |
| Luck superstitions | | | D3 | |
| Magic | | | D3 | |
| Marriage | | D2 | | |
| Mealtimes | D1 | | | |
| Medicine | | | D3 | D4 |
| Obstetrics | | | D3 | D4 |
| Penal sanctions | | | | D4 |
| Personal propitiation of supernatural beings | | | D3 | D4 |
| Puberty customs | | D2 | | |
| Religious ritual | | | D3 | |
| Residence rules | D1 | | | |
| Sexual restrictions | D1 | D2 | | |
| Soul concepts | | | D3 | |
| Status differentiation | D1 | D2 | | |
| Surgery | D1 | | | D4 |
| Tool making | D1 | | | |
| Trade | D1 | D2 | | |
| Visiting | | D2 | | |
| Weather control | | | D3 | |
| Weaving | D1 | | | |

made between natives of adjacent islands. All of the islands together are positioned in the form of a ring. Ceremonial shell necklaces are passed in clock-wise direction around the ring, and shell bracelets are passed in the opposite, counter-clockwise, direction. The leaders of each island present these gifts to their counterparts, following the rules of equality matching (EM). Malinowski interprets these exchanges as a very important way of reinforcing a relationship of peaceable respect among the island groups, in our terms, a bonded relationship. As these exchanges take place around the complete ring of related islands, the entire regional community is formed and stabilized. After gifts are exchanged at the start of each visit, the visitors and the locals engage in bargaining for the exchange of useful commodities following the rules of market pricing (MP). Gift-giving is one of the universal features of all cultures—as is trade. The special role of the leaders of each island in this process demonstrates that the Trobriand Islanders were also employing the rules of authority ranking (AR). Finally these symbolic exchanges and the material exchanges that follow clearly represent culturally defined ways to fulfill the underlying drives, first to bond and then to acquire.

∼

We are now ready to summarize how the various aspects of our brain serve to bridge between biological drives and culture. These interactions are best understood by examining the diagram in Figure 8.3.

The diagram can be read as follows:

Information passes to the brain through the sense organs. This information may be in the form of cultural cues (such as the raised eyebrow of an elder), observations of well-known things (such as a coveted sports car), or observations about a new situation (such as

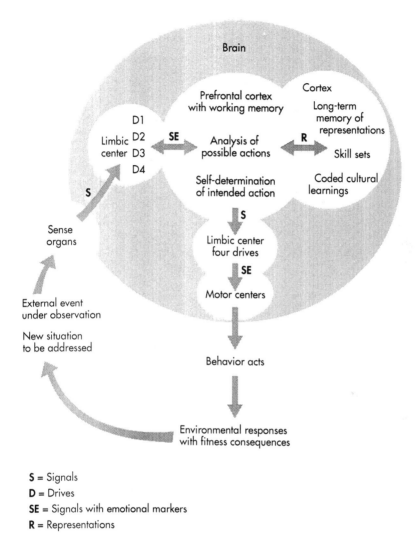

Figure 8.3. Schematic of How the Mind Works.

the cultural practices of an unfamiliar human group). Though our examples will deal with visual information processed through the eyes, the model would equally apply to information processed through the nose, the skin, and so on.

The signals the brain receives from the sense organs are processed through the limbic system, where the four drives reside. Here these signals are loaded with emotional markers depending on which of the four drives they trigger. Of course any signal may be loaded with more than one emotion, as when the drive to acquire the coveted sports car competes with the bonded obligation to save money and be safe for one's family.

The emotionally loaded signals are next processed in the prefrontal cortex, the home of working memory and cognitive capacities that help individuals choose courses of action that would satisfy the drives. This process is mediated by relevant inputs from long-term memory, the home of representations of skill-sets and cultural learnings.

Once a tentative action (for example, to postpone buying the sports car) is chosen through the exercise of human will, this signal feeds back through the limbic center to pick up the emotional energy provided by the drives. These energized signals are then relayed to motor centers that control the muscles and other bodily parts. These actions are what we recognize as human behavior (such as walking away from the showroom in which the tempting car is being displayed).

These behaviors in turn generate environmental responses with survival consequences (such as a spouse's loving appreciation)—a new situation with which the individual must now deal. All this can happen very quickly, and such cycles are repeated over and over in our everyday lives.

# 9

## ORIGINS OF THE
## SOCIAL CONTRACT

*It is not the strongest of the species that survive, nor the most intelligent. It is the one most adaptable to change.*

—CHARLES DARWIN

Most—though not all—of the pieces are on the table now. A pattern of why and how humans act as they do is beginning to emerge. In this chapter, we need to put a few last pieces in place, step back, and see if the pattern is complete and if the mystery is, at least tentatively, solved. What was the mechanism that turned humans into social beings that universally forge social contracts to order their relationships?

### HOW THE DRIVES EVOLVED

In Chapter Four, we discussed the issue of how the independent drive to bond could have evolved in the Upper Paleolithic period in a way that was consistent with modern biological theory of the evolutionary process. We did not attend to the other three drives because their evolutionary mechanisms seemed more obvious. But we should not take for granted how any of the four drives evolved, since we have argued that these four drives, in their current configuration, are the most critical and most recently evolved features of the modern human mind. This now needs to be addressed, in terms not only of specific scientific evidence but also as a story that rings true to modern minds. The story, for now, will have to be somewhat speculative, with many of the empirical facts lost in time until and unless the analysis of the human genome can identify and date the critical changes. The story is, therefore, vulnerable to being attacked as a Kipling-style "just so story," as Stephen Jay Gould might say.[1] But if the minds of our ancestors of seventy-five thousand years ago were genetically modern, as most biologists agree, then our contemporary minds can provide a useful test of the story—does the story have face validity?

Ian Tattersall, an eminent British archeologist, provides some interesting support for this kind of test. In *Becoming Human,* he reviews the most recent archeological evidence in searching for an answer to the mystery of the Great Leap. He concludes that it will never be possible to find a firm answer in the fossil record. He is optimistic, however, that with the newer tools of neuroscience and evolutionary psychology, an answer may well be found right behind your nose, in the analysis of the contemporary human mind.[2]

Recent findings of evolutionary biologists provide four additional clues. The first supports the hypothesis that at some time in the development of the hominid line, the selection process started to favor genes that delayed maturation, especially of the brain. This is evidenced by the fact that the skulls of human infants at birth are more pliable than those of chimpanzees. Thus the brains of humans can continue to grow in size after birth, in contrast to those of other primates, and as a result their mature brains can be much larger than the size of the female birth canal would otherwise permit. However, the fragility of the brain case of human infants and other aspects of delayed maturation means that they require a much longer period of intense nurturing by adults. It also means, not so incidentally, that humans will look younger—that is, more like baby apes—throughout life. This whole process is called the *neotony effect*. Finally, it means that mothers of human infants—unlike chimp mothers who do essentially all the nurturing of their young—need significant help from other adults if they are to be successful in raising their infants to adulthood. And fathers, the suppliers of half of each infant's genes, are the logical candidates to be recruited for this job.

The second clue that biologists have found is that there always seems to be more variability in those body parts that are most critical to the adaptability of the entire organism. For example, the Grants found in their detailed study of the finches of the Galapagos Islands that the birds' beaks varied more in size and shape than any other anatomical feature that they regularly measured. And there is no question, since Darwin's original discoveries, that beaks are the key to the adaptability of finches to their various niches in the Galapagos. This greater variability means that beaks can genetically adapt more quickly to environmental change than other features of finches. Similar results have been found in other species as different as insects and fish. And since the brains of humans are unquestionably the critical feature of their adaptability, they can be expected to exhibit more variability and be subject to faster adaptation than other human features.

The third clue found by biologists is that genes can guide not only the physical form of organisms but also behavior traits. The pioneer of this line of research is Seymour Benzer.[3] He and his students at the California Institute of Technology have demonstrated that certain genes specify behavioral drives in fruit flies. For example, they discovered flies carrying mutant genes that drove them to avoid light, unlike the regular flies that move toward light. When cross-bred, these mutant flies passed on their light-avoidance drive to their children and grandchildren. There is good reason to think that some of the genes of humans specify behavioral drives—consistent with four-drive theory.

The final and most important clue from modern biology is that, in many species, mate selection has been found to be a very powerful engine of genetic change, in some cases more powerful than natural selection. Darwin called it "sex selection," but we believe our label is more descriptive of what he proposed was an essential mechanism in the evolutionary process. In Darwin's theory of evolution, three hurdles must be cleared for genes to be passed from one generation of mammals to the next. First, each individual organism must survive all environmental hazards and reach reproductive age. Second, for their genes to persist, each individual must also find a consenting mate with whom to consummate the reproductive act. This is the mate selection step. And finally, their offspring must receive the nurturing essential for surviving to adulthood. Only by clearing all three hurdles will the genes of any given individual organism survive beyond its lifetime. In humans, success with both the second and third hurdles is largely determined by the mate selection choice.

The particular circumstances of archaic *Homo sapiens* in the Upper Paleolithic period would, most likely, have greatly enhanced the power of mate selection compared to natural selection. Those smart hominids would have mastered most of the hazards of natural selection caused by predators, food and water shortages, and the like, leaving the hurdle of mate selection determinative.

All these clues speak to the critical power of mate selection in the evolution of the human mind in the Upper Paleolithic period. The issue is clear. Hominids could not have known exactly how babies were made, but their genes had, obviously, provided them with an urge to experience the pleasures of sex. They must have been observant enough to have figured out that sexual intercourse had a causal relationship to pregnancy. And since human infants were maturing more slowly, the females figured out that it was not to their advantage to mate with the first male who expressed an interest in them but to be selective. Why? They had figured out that when babies arrived that it was very much in their interest to get some help. They could see that they would have to experience several months of pregnancy, and then two to four years of breast-feeding the baby, and even more years of protecting, feeding, and training the child. This would require considerable time and attention and it would be difficult and at times impossible for the mother to provide it all. They could also see that their mates could stick with them and help in this process, or could wander off in search of other females. Female hominids realized that they had the power to choose which male they would mate with. And it dawned on them that this was no minor power, given the obvious strong urges of males to find some willing mate. Their minds were perfectly competent to realize, most likely with help from their mothers, that they were the gatekeepers to what males badly wanted. They could be choosy simply because men were not as choosy. Men had little at risk by engaging in the pleasures of sex compared to women. Evolutionary biologists term this *investment theory;* they conclude that the greater investment of women in the mating process placed most of the control of mate selection in their hands.

Given their power of mate selection, what kind of a mate would it be in the best interest of the women of the Upper Paleolithic to select? What would define a good hominid husband? Their choice would make the crucial determination of which male genes would make it into the next generation. We submit that the answer is rather obvious. They would select the kind of mate that, in actual fact, research tells us that women all over the world still prefer today. First, they would select a male with wealth and status or, at least, a likely bread-winner with ambition; a person with a drive to acquire. But that is not all. Second, they would also select a male who had fallen in love with them. A person who, beyond all rational considerations, simply felt driven to bond with them in a long-term—in fact, lifelong—commitment. A person who could say with conviction, total sincerity, that he wanted to live together with his mate in sickness or in health, for richer or poorer, for better or worse until death did them part. They wanted a mate who had found the "sincerity" solution to the problem of making credible commitments that Frank discussed (see Chapter Four). They wanted not only a good hunter but one who would actually bring the bacon *home;* a person with a drive to bond. Third, they would be looking for someone who was not only smart but who seemed reliable, committed to using his brain to figure things out on a consistent basis; a person with a drive to learn. Fourth and finally, these females would be looking for someone who was healthy and strong and prepared to protect them from all hazards; a person with a drive to defend. These four features together would make a really good husband and mate. Furthermore women were getting very clever at separating the cheaters and the pretenders from the truly sincere young suitors. Now the point is clear that the female power of mate selection must have had a tremendous influence on what hominid genes survived into the next generation and all four of the drives would, in all likelihood, have been favored, as they are still favored by contemporary women around the world.

Darwin was always very interested in the practitioners of animal and plant selective breeding. From observing these professionals going about their trade, he realized he was watching the evolutionary process being guided by a purposive mind. And the results were dramatic. By selective breeding, plants and animals could be guided to develop desired characteristics in a relatively limited number of generations. Dogs could be selected for breeding so that their line developed special innate skills such as hunting for birds rather than boar. The same was true of plants.

One person, Luther Burbank, became world famous for his skill at selective plant breeding. His key method was to spend most of every day roaming his extensive gardens in the Sonoma Valley looking for plant specimens that happened, by chance, to display some trait he thought would be of value. Once he spotted it, he crossbred this particular specimen to develop a new line that could over time predictably produce the traits he desired.

The females of the advanced hominid line had the mental capacity to act as selective breeders. They acted like Luther Burbank, looking over the whole field for the males who displayed the innate traits they wanted in a mate. They were practicing eugenics at least a hundred thousand years before the term was invented. This was an awesome power and, in a small intermarrying group, within only a thousand generations (twenty thousand years) this power could convert smart hominids into human beings. Any manifestation of genes that called for a strong independent bonding drive or an independent learning drive that these choosy females could spot would inevitably wind up in their offspring.

The offspring would not only tend to carry forward the kind of drives their mothers wanted, but these drives would be powerful. Humans are distinctive not only for their acquisitive, bonding, learning, and defending traits, but also for how powerful their drives are. Humans are doers, not coasters. By contrast, chimps are inclined to relax for hours in a quiet spot whenever they are not picking up the next meal or chasing a mate. They simply do not display the drive that humans universally do. The females of the hominid line were not looking for lazy, dumb, fickle, or cowardly males. They wanted mates that were motivated by all four drives.

This point about all four drives is not a minor one. Think how a female hominid would judge a male who only displayed one of the drives, even strongly. A male with only a strong drive to acquire, for example, might accumulate wealth, but if he was not loving, caring, and trustworthy, what could the female count on? And if a male displayed only a drive to bond, that would be a plus until the female realized that she was likely to starve with a romantic dreamer. If a male had only a drive to learn, it would result in great thoughts but no action. And finally, if the male had only a drive to defend, one would be married to a great fighter who had nothing he would want to defend but his own body. And he could turn into a mate-abuser. The point is clear, a male with a great deal of just one drive would be a big loser in comparison to one with all four.

Meanwhile, males had some say in the mate selection process, albeit a weaker one. Evolutionary biologists have argued that male mate selection, guided by the gene survival process, has biased selection toward female beauty—roughly meaning young and healthy, that is, able to bear more children. This selection bias toward youth also favored genes that delayed maturation, since any delay of the maturation process produced younger looks—as well as, not so incidentally, bigger brains.

As suggested earlier, the strongest evidence that the mate selection process had a major effect on developing distinctly human traits, the four independent drives, comes from the study of what traits men and especially women currently seek in their mates. David Buss of the University of Texas has studied this question in great detail. He set the stage for his detailed findings on mate selection as follows, "A woman who preferred to mate with a reliable man who was willing to commit to her presumably would have had children who survived, and thrived, and multiplied. Over thousands of generations, a preference for men who showed signs of being willing and able to commit evolved in women."[4] Buss hypothesized that this skill set would be present in all contemporary women.

Buss decided to test this hypothesis directly by asking American women to rank the qualities they most preferred in a mate. Buss summarized the findings of his research and those of other similar studies as follows: Women seek out mates with resources but they "may be less influenced by money per se than by qualities that lead to resources, such as ambition, intelligence, and somewhat older age. Women scrutinize these personal qualities carefully because they reveal a man's potential."[5] We code this cluster of features as strongly favoring D1 and D3. Buss continues, "Potential, however, is not enough. Because many men with a rich resource potential are themselves highly discriminating and are at times content with casual sex, women are faced with the problem of commitment. Seeking love is one solution to the commitment problem. Acts of love signal that a man has in fact committed to a particular woman."[6] "Direct studies of preferences in a mate confirm the centrality of love."[7] We code these findings as strongly favoring D2. Finally, Buss reports that women select for men who are strong and healthy. We code this for D4.

Thinking that American women might have different preferences from those of other humans, Buss asked his questions of thirty-seven different samples from thirty-three countries and found essentially the same results. Buss concluded that the consistency of these patterns from multiple cultures must mean that these selection criteria were an innate skill set of ancient origin. However, he seemed to have largely missed the point that this mate selection process, when carried on for multiple generations, would have had a decisive role in the spread of the genetic traits that women were seeking, the four independent drives. This mate selection pressure would have created a self-reinforcing cycle, an autocatalytic process that is the most powerful change mechanism in organic life.

Buss found that the men in his studies, in terms of their long-term mating choices, preferred beauty and youth (D1), love and faithfulness (D2), and intelligence (D3). However, he found that men, unlike women, also showed evidence of employing at times what he termed a "short-term" mating strategy—with sheer sexual accessibility being the criterion of choice. This short-term strategy could better be termed the "ancient" strategy since it mirrors that of male chimpanzees.

Studies of the sexual behavior of chimpanzees have made it very clear that their sexual behavior is radically different from that of humans. Long-term bonding between sexual partners has, to the best of our knowledge, never been observed among chimpanzees nor among pigmy chimpanzees, the bonobos. To the contrary, both genders in both species are promiscuous. Careful observers of the behavior of chimpanzees in the wild and in captivity cannot determine the paternity of newborns except by laborious DNA testing—and there is no reason to believe the mothers can either. In sharp contrast, among humans, mate bonding—in other words, monogamy—is the norm. Marriage is observed as a long-term commitment in all cultures. Polygamy is rare in hunter-gatherer bands and has only been widely practiced among the elite in highly stratified agricultural systems. While marital infidelity is practiced to some degree in all recorded cultures, it is seen as deviant behavior to be engaged in surreptitiously. Sexual infidelity, while it certainly does happen, is a somewhat dangerous game in all cultures. Men who have been cuckolded become violent with some frequency. Women, if they learn that their husbands are unfaithful, may well end the marriage. Biologists have, unfortunately, tended to underplay these remarkable differences between the genetically based sexual behavior of humans and chimpanzees.

Many biologists who have studied chimpanzees have also noted that they are perfectly capable of deceiving, cheating, and double-crossing each other. In reporting these behaviors, they sometimes observe that in this regard chimps are not much different from humans. This largely misses the point that, yes, humans do cheat and deceive, but they do it much less frequently than adult chimpanzees do. Biologists also report that chimp mothers take loving care of their babies, and that chimpanzee males occasionally collaborate with each other in hunting and pursuing females. But they miss the point that not only human mothers but also human fathers regularly devote loving care to their children, while no chimpanzee father has been so observed. And also, human males do a great deal more cooperating with other humans of both sexes than male chimpanzees do.

The question of the role of innate gender differences and family structure has been carefully studied by the biologist Sarah Hrdy and is reported in *The Woman That Never Evolved,* and, much more recently, in *Mother Nature: A History of Mothers, Infants, and Natural Selection.*[8] She draws on recent studies of a large variety of primates and other mammals in the wild. Hrdy observes that the difference in size between males and females is closely correlated with family structure, with greater relative size in males associated with polygamy, and greater equality of size with monogamy. The basis for this causal association is fairly obvious. When males are larger than females, sexual practices will evolve toward polygamy, since the largest males will be able to drive smaller males away and then dominate a harem of smaller females. Such males will pass on genes for size and thereby reinforce polygamy, *as long as their offspring can survive to reproductive age without the help of paternal care.* Sexual practices, however, evolve toward monogamy when conditions favor the survival of the genes, not of the larger males, *but of those males who offer paternal care.* This will tend to happen with humans given the long-term dependence of human infants on intensive care. Both forms of family structure can be found in different mammalian species. Our most closely related primates by DNA analysis are chimpanzees, and male chimps are 25 percent larger than females. Among humans, the size differential is estimated to be between 5 percent and 12 percent. This clearly indicates, according to Hrdy, that humans are well along on the road to monogamy—but not all the way there.

The latest studies of ancient human family structure report that monogamous pair-bonding and nuclear families were dominant throughout human history in hunter-gatherer societies.[9] Among contemporary hunter-gatherer people, Australian aborigines, the Trobriand Islanders, pygmies, Kalahari bushmen, and Amazonian Indian tribes all organize themselves into nuclear families.[10]

The most straightforward explanation of the trend toward monogamy is that smart female hominids went to work on chimp-like hominid males and—step by step, mate-selection by mate-selection—shaped them up into loving husbands and fathers with true family values. In genetic terms, accomplishing this would not have been all that difficult; infant chimps, male as well as female, demonstrate a very strong drive to bond with their primary caregivers. Their very lives depend upon establishing such bonds. And these infant drives to bond have nothing to do with the sex drive. To humanize hominids the only change that would be required would be genetic coding for the persistence of this characteristic into adulthood among males. By this process the innate foundation of the nuclear family would be established, locked in by *both* the sex drive stemming from D1 and now also by the independent bonding drive (D2).

We would also argue that, as the drive to bond with mates strengthened toward monogamy, it further generalized as a drive to bond with other humans as commitments to friends and work associates as well as loyalties to the extended family. In Chapter Five, in discussing the origin of the independent drive to bond, we cited the recent work of biologists that demonstrates how this general drive could have arisen through natural selection. But their argument was based on the assumption that genes favoring the bonding drive would have become established in a significant population of some intermarrying group of hominids. From that point onward it could have been extended to the wider population by the improved survival rate of the entire original group and by genetic mixing between groups. Now we can add the all-important argument that the original small population of humans carrying the bonding drive could have been established by the mate selection process. Once so established in a small group, it could then be extended to other groups by the multilevel selection process described by Sober and Wilson.[11]

This hypothesis of the power of female mate selection in the evolution of the four drives has not as yet been demonstrated by direct proof. It is, however, the strongest explanation available for the creation of the first of three mechanisms that triggered the evolutionary advance called the Great Leap. The sequence of self-reinforcing causation that is behind the bonding and learning drives is diagrammed in Figure 9.1. The figure illustrates our conclusion that at this stage of evolution, hominids—through the mate-selection process—were using their brains to select the brains of the next generation.

For billions of years evolution was a blind, mindless, trial-and-error process. Now, in the last few steps toward evolving humans, it was being guided by a purposive mind. Hominids were, in effect, pulling themselves up by their bootstraps. And females, the so-called weaker sex, were in charge of the design team. Their mate choices, in time, led males themselves to include faithfulness and intelligence in their mate-selection criteria. This, we hypothesize, is a major piece of the solution to the mystery of the Great Leap. And as human males, the authors are exceedingly grateful women did it, and fervently hope that they will retain their grip on mate selection and their wise selection criteria. We much prefer being human, rather than very smart, totally opportunistic apes. The genetically based drive of humans to develop trustful bonds with others

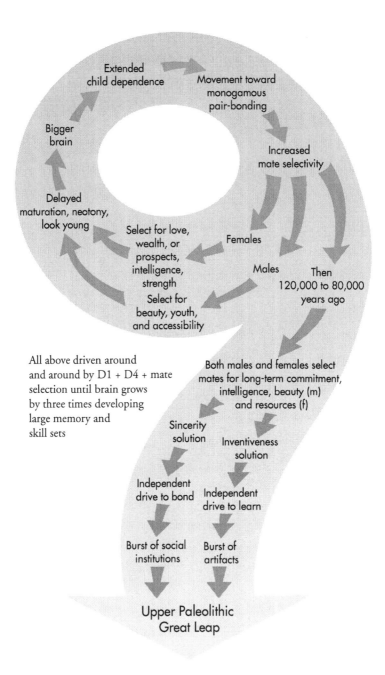

**Figure 9.1. Hypothesis of Evolution of Independent Drives to Bond and to Learn.**

relieves us all of a considerable burden of anxiety. And the drive of humans to actually use their gray matter to learn provides us all with the pleasures and power of comprehending so much of the universe around us and of ourselves.

As a final argument on the role of female mate selection in the evolution of the four drives, we turn once more to Darwin. On a careful rereading of Darwin, we discovered to our surprise, that he had in fact briefly discussed the power of women's choice of mate in human evolution.

Darwin's thinking on the subject was somewhat confused by his sharing the assumption of his culture that the choice of a mate was dominated by males and that women were of lesser intelligence. But some observations on the mate selection process from his voluntary amateur anthropological friends from around the globe gave him the necessary clues that women played a larger role in mate selection than his cultural beliefs recognized:

> With respect to the other form of sexual selection . . ., namely, when the females are the selectors, and accept only those males which excite or charm them most, we have reason to believe that it formerly acted on our progenitors. . . . But this form of selection may have occasionally acted during later times; for in utterly barbarous tribes the women have more power in choosing, rejecting, and tempting their lovers, or of afterwards changing their husbands, than might have been expected. As this is a point of some importance, I will give in detail such evidence as I have been able to collect.[12]

Some of his examples are quite humorous from our current perspective. "With the Kalmucks there is a regular race between the bride and bridegroom, the former having a fair start; and Clarke was assured that no instance occurs of a girl being caught, unless she has a partiality to the pursuer." Among the wild tribes of the Malay Archipelago there is also a racing match; and it appears from M. Burin's account, as Sir J. Lubbock remarks, that "the race is not to the swift, nor the battle to the strong, but to the young man who has the good fortune to please his intended bride." A similar custom, with the same result, prevails with the Koraks of northeastern Asia. Another example:

> Turning to Africa: the Kafirs buy their wives, and girls are severely beaten by their fathers if they will not accept a chosen husband; but it is manifest from many facts given by the Rev. Mr. Shooter, that they have considerable power of choice. Thus very ugly, though rich men, have been known to fail in getting wives. The girls, before consenting to be betrothed, compel the men to show themselves off first in front and then behind, and "exhibit their paces." They have been known to propose to a man, and they not rarely run away with a favored lover.

Darwin concludes, "We thus see that with savages the women are not in quite so abject a state in relation to marriage as has often been supposed. They can tempt the men whom they prefer, and can sometimes reject those whom they dislike, either before or after marriage."[13]

Finally, and most important, Darwin reveals that he could have explained the mystery of the Great Leap Forward even though he had no knowledge of its existence. He understood that female mate selection might have been critical to the rapid evolutionary changes that produced the modern human mind. He also understood that evolution at the human level could well have stopped being a blind, mindless process and that it could have been guided by a purposive mind, primarily a female mind. And he got all of this in one sentence. Darwin writes, "Preference on the part of the women steadily acting in any one direction, would ultimately affect the character of the tribe; for the women would generally choose not merely the handsomest men, according to their standard of taste, but those who were at the same time best able to defend and support them."[14]

These insights of Darwin's are truly amazing when one realizes that he made them without the benefit of knowing many things that are clear today. He worked without any knowledge about how genes work. He had practically no archeological information about hominid fossils, very limited and often erroneous ideas about the behavior of primates in the wild, no anthropological information except from his amateur recruits, and no knowledge of the inner workings of the brain. In spite of all of these limitations, he got so much right that we are only now developing more complete maps of the virgin terrain that he first pioneered and surveyed. He spent his entire life puzzling through the mysteries he had observed as a young man voyaging on the *Beagle.* His brain must have carried a powerful loading on the drive to learn.

There is a second penultimate piece of the puzzle to put in place. Even while the gradual buildup of the genetic drives to bond and to learn was proceeding, there was also a gradual buildup of the language and symbolization skills of these advanced hominids, building on their drive to learn. Deacon, to whom we referred in Chapter Two, argues that the growth of the brain, especially the prefrontal cortex, coevolved with the increasing capacity of hominids to use symbols. He concludes, "Human beings approach the world of sensory stimuli and motor demands differently from other species, particularly with respect to higher-order learning processes."[15] By using symbols, humans became able to condense representations and to construct abstract models of external events.

This was a new way to learn—one that went well beyond conditioned learning and first-level symbolization. Deacon captures what we call the drive to learn very clearly: "We find pleasure in manipulating the world so that it fits into a symbolic Procrustean bed, and when it does fit and seems to obey symbolic rules, we find the result comforting, even beautiful."[16] This is the skill set of multilevel abstract reasoning at work pushed on by the subconscious drive to learn.

We argue that it was the buildup of these mental capacities for abstract thinking that made it possible for the first time for humans to symbolize, literally to name, their tribe as a concrete collective entity. This was a conceptual leap to a higher level of abstraction than was possible for any hominid up to this point. Once accomplished it must have been quickly reinforced with physical symbols and rituals. These two innate developments—extended bonding and collective symbolization—when simultaneously in place, must have suddenly sparked the first bonding of individuals directly to the newly symbolized tribe. This was the first formation of the social contract at the societal level.

## THE ULTIMATE SOLUTION

This was the third and final step to the solution of the Great Leap puzzle, the bonding of the individual directly to the newly conceptualized collective, the tribe, in the form of an implicit social contract. It was initially an emotional step of mutual commitment to caring and support. It was secondarily reinforced with a more cognitive understanding of the rules of the relationship, the rights and responsibilities of each party to the other. The symbolization of the contract gradually took the many forms used today: creeds, pledges, constitutions, flags, songs, sculptures, paintings, group rituals. It was the beginning of the passion we call tribalism and patriotism.

The social contract would have been established and reinforced with relevant innate skills. This event signaled a critical social invention, the first large human institution with bonded membership.

Humans tend to take the existence of a world full of institutions and organizations for granted, as if the species had always had them. Not true. They had to be invented. This, we propose, was the last step in the human evolutionary breakthrough that made the Great Leap possible. We propose that this was the event that actually produced modern humans. Organizations at all levels from work organizations through social, religious, and recreational organizations to tribes and nation states were impossible without the buildup of the extended bonding drive. Organizations literally were inconceivable until the learning drive pushed symbolization skills to the necessary level of abstraction. Both developments had to be in place for humans to develop the innate capacity to order relationships by social contracts. We believe humans have, in fact, evolved a skill for creating the rules and norms that are the substance of the social contract. The four forms of sociality described by Fiske are, we argue, four modes of the general social contract of human interaction.

Once humans were able to symbolize and bond with collective entities, much else followed quickly. Our ancestors then were able to develop complex systems of social norms and moral codes that could be steadily reinforced by relatively low-cost rewards and sanctions. They could create myths of the creation of the tribe and rites of initiation into membership. Religions arose to provide answers to the ultimate questions. Artistic symbolization of the collective flowered, and, not least, the groupwide collaborative efforts that followed were able to generate and then rapidly disseminate technical advances. Cultural development for the first time took over the lead role in coevolution. Civilization was launched. The uniquely human form of culture that can conceptualize information into concrete entities and create complex social structures emerged at last.

If, as proposed by archeologists, all this happened in a small intermarrying group (estimated to have held as few as four to ten thousand people), then this original group with modern human minds would have probably shared a common language, a common religion, and common tribal symbolism.[17] All members could have been at least superficially acquainted with all other members. Members of this group would have been tightly bonded to each other. They would have started sharing a common tradition of art, music, dance, cuisine, and every other aspect of social life. Domestic violence would almost certainly have existed, but probably not many other forms of violence. Life among early humans has been described as brutish and short, but we believe that for this primordial group it was closer to peaceful and prosperous, with no other species providing much of a threat. But these were the humans who, because of the independence of the four drives, were forced to make real choices. Not the easy choices of chimpanzees between bananas or mangos for lunch but the difficult moral choices of whether to be loyal to friends or pull off an important acquisition at their expense. These were the choices that involve the knowledge of good and evil discussed in Genesis, the choices that people meditate about, perhaps to secure guidance from their deepest feelings, from their subconscious drives.

The unified original tribe in its "Garden of Eden" could not, however, have lasted long. The Great Leap would have triggered a population increase and thus an inevitable pressure to move out to fulfill the drive to acquire and the drive to learn, which would have pushed early humans to find out what was across the mountain and the sea. The great exodus to all parts of the earth would have started—with geographical separation, in turn, generating the gradual differentiation of languages, religions, and all the other cultural and even physical features that characterize the modern population.

~

At the beginning of Chapter Two we quoted Aristotle's seven-word definition of humans. Now we can more fully appreciate the depth of his insight. He said, "Humans are social animals endowed with reason." All multicelled animals, including humans, are distinct from plants in having a nervous system that is the seat of the drives to acquire and to defend. Aristotle is saying that, in addition, humans are distinguished by being basically social—in our terms, having a drive to bond. Finally he adds that humans are "endowed with reason," that is, they have the capacity for abstract symbolization that differentiated our drive to learn from that of other species. Elsewhere Aristotle characterized humans as political beings, beings, in our terms, capable of creating and abiding by social contracts.

Our intellectual journey has come full circle. We have defined a unified human race, operating everywhere from four basic drives. Why then is there so much difference from one person and one culture to another?

# 10

## WHY SO MUCH DIVERSITY?

*If we cannot end now our differences, at least we can help make the world safe for diversity.*

—JOHN F. KENNEDY

If we are right that all humans share a common set of innate drives and related skill sets that help explain much of their behavior in our modern world, how can there be so much diversity? It turns out that environmental contingencies can account for most of the great variety that is readily observable among human cultures, organizations, and individuals. We will start with Jared Diamond, a physiologist at the UCLA Medical School, who has done a remarkable job of pulling together all the evidence of the major influence of biogeographical differences on the form and pace of cultural development around the world.

Diamond tells a marvelous story of a conversation he had with a close friend, a native of New Guinea where Diamond did research for several years. New Guineans valued and enjoyed all the equipment and gadgets arriving from the rest of the world—the watches, jeans, cola drinks, cameras, radios, and the like—referring to these imports as "cargo." Diamond's friend asked a simple but provocative question: "How come you guys got all the cargo?" Diamond has spent a great deal of time pondering this question.[1]

His answer is both clear and persuasive. He found that differences in the rates at which civilizations evolved were, to a great extent, caused by regional differences in biogeographic conditions. These biogeographic differences were the contingencies that explained the variability in civilizations that arose as people learned to adapt to very different environments. Why did some regions produce civilizations with lots of cargo, and others did not? It was not that some places had a few geniuses, and others did not. It was not the result of average differences among whole peoples in inventiveness; there is no evidence for such differences. It was not the result of biological differences. The most recent findings about the complete human genome estimate that 99.9 percent of the genes of all humans are the same. It was simply that some parts of the world offered humans significantly different biogeographic conditions—more or less resources to work with, if you will.

## Biogeographic Resources and Coevolution

Diamond starts his analysis by summarizing the obvious large differences in technical and social development that existed between Eurasia and the rest of the world at the time of Columbus. Most Eurasians used iron tools, had writing, advanced agriculture, and multiple domesticated animals. They were organized in large centralized states and employed oceangoing ships, muskets, and cannons. Meanwhile, the people of the Americas lacked iron tools, and had less developed agriculture and more limited means of writing. Australians were still in the Stone Age without agriculture. He writes:

> Nineteenth-century Europeans had a simple, racist answer
> to such questions. They concluded that they acquired their

cultural head start through being inherently more intelligent, and that they therefore had a manifest destiny to conquer, displace, or kill "inferior" peoples. The trouble with this answer is that it is not just loathsome and arrogant, but also wrong. It's obvious that people differ enormously in the knowledge they acquire, depending on their circumstances as they grow up. But no convincing evidence of genetic differences in mental ability among peoples has been found, despite much effort. Because of this legacy of racist explanations, the whole subject of the human differences in level of civilization still reeks of racism. Yet there are obvious reasons why the subject begs to be properly explained. Those technological differences led to great tragedies in the past five hundred years, and their legacies of colonialism and conquest still powerfully shape our world today. Until we can come up with a convincing alternative explanation, the suspicion that racist genetic theories might be true will linger.[2]

Diamond argues that technological levels differ because of the way the continents differed in the resources on which civilization depends—especially in the wild animal and plant species that proved useful for domestication. Continents also differed in the ease with which domesticated species could spread from one area to another. Wherever it was practiced, agriculture vastly increased the carrying capacity of the land in terms of human population, releasing many individuals from food production to specialize in other skills. At the same time, domestic animals provided richer food, a steadier supply of clothing materials, and power to transport people and goods and to pull plows.

But domestic animals differ from place to place—most mammalian species cannot be domesticated no matter how hard anyone

tries, and at the time the possibility was discovered, the luck of
the draw placed a significant fraction of the surviving opportunities
on the Eurasian land mass. Diamond writes, none of these animals
were available for domestication outside Eurasia. "By around 4000
B.C. west Eurasia already had its 'Big Five' domestic livestock that
continue to dominate today: sheep, goats, pigs, cows, and horses
. . . . These animals provided food, power, and clothing, while the
horse was also of incalculable military value. (It was the tank, the
truck, and the jeep of warfare until the nineteenth century)."[3] The
llamas and guanacos of South America can be used as beasts of
burden but not ridden, and no one has succeeded in getting
kangaroos to do anything useful besides breed in captivity.

Plants pose similar problems. Self-pollinators like wheat are
easier to domesticate than cross-pollinators like rye, and were
brought under cultivation far earlier. Australia has very few wild
plants suitable for domestication. Although the Americas are rich
in native species that are now important to worldwide agriculture,
the chief crop—corn—posed considerable difficulties. Diamond
explores these problems at length, concluding, "Characteristics of
the New World's staple food crop made its potential value much
harder to discern in the wild plant, harder to develop by domestication, and harder to extract even after domestication. Much of the
lag between New World and Old World civilization may have been
due to those peculiarities of one plant."[4]

Finally Diamond points out the major effect that landforms
have had on the spread of domesticated plants and animals. Being
adapted to specific climates, plants and animals transfer fairly readily in the same latitude, where seasonal conditions are apt to be
similar. At any rate, east-west moves are far easier than north-south
moves, as conditions change far more rapidly from one zone to
another in the latter direction. Eurasia lies largely on an east-west
axis, while the Americas run north-south. Thus it was much harder

for people in the Americas to take advantage of discoveries and developments made elsewhere in the hemisphere.

And it's not just plants and animals that travel more easily between east and west—people do too, and so do their diseases. The more elaborate agriculture of Eurasia encouraged the growth of the human population to unprecedented density. As Diamond observes, "Dense populations also promoted the evolution of infectious diseases, to which exposed populations then evolved some resistance but other populations didn't. All these factors determined who colonized and conquered whom. Europeans' conquest of America and Australia was due not to their better genes but to their worse germs (especially smallpox), more advanced technology (including weapons and ships), information storage through writing, and political organization—all stemming ultimately from continental differences in geography."[5]

Diamond does not claim that biogeography is the only contingency that caused the world's current cultural diversity. The distribution of mineral resources and chance historical events also help account for the timing of the transition from hunter-gatherer to agricultural-pastoral life. Diamond has, however, made a very convincing argument for the way that the biogeographic contingency has had a significant impact on the timing of the shift and the consequent rate at which civilizations have developed around the world. He has given his New Guinea friend's question about cargo a valid and important answer—an answer to a question that has plagued humans for a very long time.

## Physical Isolation and Coevolution

Closely related to the contingency of biogeography is that of physical isolation. The idea behind this contingency is very simple. Once the core group of modern *Homo sapiens* began the great exodus from Africa, the migration process spread these early humans across the globe, isolating them from each other. The most dramatic example involved the humans who, between forty thousand and fifty thousand years ago, crossed some sixty miles of water from Southeast Asia to the then connected continent of Australia/New Guinea. These people were without contact with other humans until the arrival of the European explorers in the eighteenth century. The second most notable case of isolation was that of the American Indians who came across the land bridge at the Bering Straits at least twelve thousand years ago, and thereafter became cut off from the rest of humanity until the fifteenth century. The story has been repeated more recently with the South Sea Islanders (who probably came originally from Taiwan), and, by and large, by the peoples of sub-Saharan Africa. The simple fact of this environmental isolation was the contingency that is the best available explanation of the variability of human external appearance. It was accomplished primarily through the process of human mate selection.

Among the current scholars of human behavior from an evolutionary perspective, the one who has focused the most on the process of mate selection is Matt Ridley.[6] Ridley assembles the evidence from many sources that one of the chief criteria that human males universally use in selecting a mate is beauty.

A few aspects of what human males define as beauty seem quite universal. For instance, all males seem to prefer females with waists smaller than their hips and chests. The Darwinian process would have selected for the preference for this form of beauty since such women would, on average, bear more children. Presumably for the same reason, men seem to universally equate beauty with signs of youthfulness.

However, many aspects of human ideas about beauty are variable. People in different parts of the world do not agree on the most

beautiful skin color, the prettiest type and color of hair, the loveli-
est configuration of facial features, or many other variables. It is
easy to note that, at the individual level, people of both sexes often
prefer those who look a good deal like the members of their immediate family. This, in itself, does not do much to advance the search
for the answer to the original question of why the appearance of
people varies across the earth. After all, a man may seek a mate who
looks like his mother, but how did his mother get the features that
make her different in appearance from mothers living in other parts
of the world in the first place?

Very recently a study of this issue seems to provide a definitive
answer to this ancient question. Two scientists of the California
Academy of Sciences, Nina Jablonski and George Chaplin, published their findings in the July 2000 issue of the *Journal of Human
Evolution.*[7] They employed very modern methodologies to test an
old theory that had fallen into disrepute, namely, that skin color
varies with climate. Recent biological studies have demonstrated
that to remain healthy human skin must absorb enough ultraviolet
light to generate adequate amounts of folate (folic acid) and vitamin D-3—but not too much. Folate is needed for the proper
development of the nervous system in fetuses and for sperm production in adult males. Vitamin D-3 helps develop strong bones
and an alert immune system. However, too much UV risks triggering skin cancer and even the destruction of the needed
biochemicals. As has long been known, skin color is created by the
amount of melanin in the skin—the more the darker. Melanin, it
not so surprisingly turns out, moderates the rate at which skin
absorbs UV rays. Now add the latest methodology, the tracking of
UV levels around the globe by NASA satellites. When this information was compared to the record of local skin color recorded by
anthropologists over the years, the puzzle disappears. Jablonski and
Chaplin found a strong correlation between local skin color and the

amount of UV light that hits the earth in various locations. Thus the most conspicuous difference between the races, skin color, has a straightforward explanation based on geography and the Darwinian natural selection process.

There are, however, differences in the external features of people of different races other than skin color. What explains features such as differences in texture and color of hair, facial features, and so on? The general explanation most widely accepted today is that such variations in human external appearance are basically random fluctuations. But how can this be? The hair type and nose shape of every new baby is not determined like a random lottery. It is obvious that the genes of the two parents prescribe such features. Over many generations, however, such external features are largely ruled by the same kind of random process that governs cultural fashions. Think of trends in clothing, as an example. The first few moves in clothing fashions are probably determined randomly when some few conspicuous people happen to make similar selections. But once this happens, a small trend can be set up that gradually creates a fad and then a pervasive fashion—which persists until it is displaced by another fashion.

In the world of biologists a favorite example of this process at work among animals is the preference of peahens for peacocks that have large, brilliantly colored tail feathers. No one can say how this well-established genetic preference was started, but, once it was, it has continued to create larger, brighter tail feathers in each successive generation of males. It is at the point now that this feature of peacocks has practically disabled them from flying. This preference of females could in time wipe out the species in the wild. Humans can be grateful their process of mate selection has not taken such a turn. In the case of peacocks, a single feature, apparently insignificant from a natural selection standpoint but conspicuous from a mate selection standpoint, emerged as a mate selection preference that became genetically established over a long sequence of generations. A similar process may have occurred in human populations.

This process could not have happened if humans had not moved to isolated parts of the globe and stayed separated for long periods of time. It seems that in this way human variability of nonessential external features has come about. The old adage that beauty is in the eye of the beholder is true for such features, as well as the adage that beauty is only skin deep. Thus we can thank the contingency of human isolation for the variability in humans of superficial external appearances. The effect of this contingency, in addition to the effect of the biogeographic contingency, should put questions about racial differences to rest. They are really of no significance.

## STAGES OF TECHNOLOGY AND COEVOLUTION

In Diamond's account, the biogeographic resources of regions had a major influence on the timing of the shift in human societies from hunter-gatherer technology to the technology of agriculture and herding. This shift, in turn, led to population increases and to the development of all the artifacts of civilization that enabled these agricultural societies to overrun and displace the hunter-gatherer societies. This displacement has proceeded on every continent; even in Africa, where the agriculturally sophisticated Bantu people overran the original hunter-gatherer bushmen in most parts of central and southern Africa. This technological shift not only changed the artifacts of the time but also generated a major shift in the way people were organized to perform the work at the heart of their cultures, their core way of making a living.

Of course, the shift to agricultural technology was not the last of these major shifts of core technology. In many places, the dominant technology has evolved from agriculture to workshop crafts and trading to the industrial age (with its factories and pow-ered machinery), and now to the computerized information age. In each instance, the shift from one dominant technology to another was driven by a combination of built-in technical requisites and the logic of sequential inventions. We argue that the dominant tech-nology is an important contingency that impacts coevolution, the interplay of a persistent genetic base with a changing culture that produces much of the great range of human variability.

Anthropology has given us our clearest understanding of how humans who employ a hunter-gatherer technology go about organ-izing themselves in their everyday life. While exceptions exist, there is a central tendency. The four universal social skill sets that Fiske identified (described in Chapter Eight) are of great help in general-izing about this pattern. The typical hunter-gatherer band is made up of 100 to 150 people of varied ages. The men usually hunt wild animals and the women gather wild plants. Both tasks involve a sig-nificant amount of uncertainty. The wild animals and plants are usually scarce and often scattered over a considerable area. It takes a significant amount of skill and knowledge to perform each task successfully. Strength, physical agility, and perseverance are neces-sary, but knowledge is probably needed most. Some aspects of each job can not be specified in advance by a formula, since each situa-tion has unique aspects. All healthy members of the band are expected to contribute in whatever way they can to the search for food. These task characteristics and the relatively small size of the total group indicate that, while all four forms of sociality will be used, community sharing (CS)—as expected in the extended family—will dominate. A secondary use of equality matching (EM) has been found in the reciprocity within the smaller hunting and gathering parties. Some element of authority ranking (AR), based primarily on expertise and age, has been found in the deliberative decisions of the entire band. Often the leadership of the group passes from individual to individual depending primarily on specialized expertise concerning the issue at hand. Some market pricing (MP) occurs in the bartering between bands.

Anthropologists have found this pattern in most of the relatively few hunter-gatherer bands that have survived and have been subject to careful study. Christopher Boehm, an eminent anthropologist, reviewed the ethnographic literature on small-scale societies and concluded, "The data do leave us with some ambiguities, but I believe that as of 40,000 years ago, with the advent of anatomically modern humans who continued to live in small groups and had not yet domesticated plants and animals, it is very likely that all human societies practiced egalitarian behavior and that most of the time they did so very successfully."[8] We do not want to idealize this way of life, but it was clearly more egalitarian, less sexist, and more communitarian than the societies that followed. This was not because of any special nobility on the part of the hunter-gatherers, but because that life pattern best met all four basic drives under conditions of hunter-gatherer technology. This kind of life pattern probably persisted as it moved gradually into small-scale farming and herding, but, as larger-scale agriculture took hold, all that changed.

The domestication of plants and animals enabled people to produce more food on a given amount of land. It also enabled them to store food in large quantities for the first time in the form of grain and live animals. A person could become specialized in producing a particular type of food and sell or trade most of it. The tasks involved in this form of food production were less risky than hunting and gathering. A person who had gained possession of a sizable piece of arable land by any means, including the use of force, could pressure the landless into doing the necessary heavy physical labor for a fraction of the food produced. After all, almost anyone could pick up the limited skill involved in doing the routine work involved in this type of large-scale food production. The surplus of food produced enabled more people to undertake other roles such as soldiering or ruling. In general, authority ranking (AR) became the dominant mode of sociality, with market pricing (MP) a secondary mode. The use of communal sharing (CS) retreated to the primary family, and the use of equality matching (EM) to relations among personal friends. Class stratification and the rise of elites became common. States and empires formed, along with large cities. Inequality between the sexes grew. This new pattern developed in the ancient, classical civilizations and persisted in medieval times in the form of feudalism. All in all, these complex changes constituted a massive shift in the life of the average person. Even though the shift offered a more predictable and stable life, for many it surely must not have felt like progress. But it happened because of a slow momentum of its own with each step toward the new lifestyle promising more certain fulfillment of the four drives.

The next big step in this sequence of broad technologies came with the expansion of crafts and trading that reached its apex in the Renaissance. The roots of this technology started much earlier with the growth of arts and crafts in the Middle East and in the imperial cities of Classical times. But crafts and trading did not become the dominant technology until it took off in northern Italy and spread throughout Europe and North Africa, gradually rolling back the institutions of feudalism. This shift in technical dominance brought an upsurge in skill requirements and a burst of inventiveness. The small artisan workshop, with its master craftsman, journeymen, and apprentices, became the modal organization. The craft guilds became strong. The merchants who conducted the trading became wealthy and socially dominant. The traditional hierarchies of authority gradually weakened.

Lacy and Danziger, in their fascinating look at the year 1000, provide a vivid description of life in a craft and trading society. In the English town of Winchester, they write, the town records "show a hosier, a shoemaker, and a soapmaker in position to sell their wares to the visitors, along with two meeting halls where the prosperous citizens gathered to feast and drink." They add, "Trade was the life of the town, and by the year 1000 England's merchants had been trading for some time in goods that came from exotic and faraway places." Goods came in largely from Pavia, in what is now Italy, the major commercial center for trade between northwestern Europe and the East. "Prominent among the merchants [of Pavia] were the gens Anglicorum et Saxorum, who haggled over silks, spices, ivory, goldwork and precious stones with merchants from Venice."[9]

This account clearly illustrates the forms of sociality that accompanied the shift to a craft and trading technology. In the towns of turn-of-the-millennium Europe, equality matching (EM)—reciprocity among skilled peers—was becoming the dominant form, along with market pricing (MP)—the haggling carried on with the "merchants of Venice." As a result authority ranking (AR) lost its clear dominance. We argue that the craft and trading technology served the four drives better than its antecedent by increasing the fulfillment of the drive to learn.

In Western Europe, craft and trading technology was superseded by the emergence of industrialism with its widespread use of powered machinery. The positive and negative effects of industrialization are well known. It brought an increase in the size of the basic production unit, the factory. Jobs were typically deskilled, even as productivity shot up. The simpler jobs could be efficiently controlled by a hierarchy with rules and regulations. Authority ranking (AR) returned to the forefront, backed up this time by market pricing (MP). Stratification increased along with gender inequality. For the average person industrialism provided a more predictable way to fulfill at least minimally the drive to acquire but fewer ways to meet the drives to learn and bond. These issues have, of course, created an enormous literature.

Today the Western countries, joined by many in Asia, are moving through another shift, with information technology rapidly becoming dominant. It already seems clear that the sociality of equality matching (EM) is becoming dominant, with the other three modes playing backup roles. This shift will again change many aspects of everyday life for people. Culture will take on a different character, as hierarchies shrink and more of life's important relationships become long-term, reciprocal networks among peers. The spirit of entrepreneurship will grow as people invent and produce more information-loaded services that are of value to others, and perhaps fewer hard-goods. We will explore this transition further in Chapter Eleven.

This rapid tour through ten thousand years of human history has risked error and oversimplification to establish the general idea that much of the variability in human cultures is caused by the powerful contingency of step-by-step shifts in core technology. The world is, of course, still occupied by societies that even now are adapted primarily to one or the other of these five basic technologies. There are hunter-gatherer societies, albeit few; there are agriculturally dominated societies; those that feature crafts; and, of course, industrial as well as the emerging informational societies. Under the conditions of these dominant technologies, different forms of culture have emerged that emphasize different forms of sociality. It should also be emphasized that in every one of these five technologies all four of the sociality forms are active; they vary only in weight.

We briefly discussed one classic example of this cultural variability in Chapter Five when we wrote of Robert Putnam's study of the often-noted sharp cultural contrast between southern and northern Italy.[10] The south has a reputation for poverty, violence, rigid hierarchy, and even Mafia-ridden commerce and politics. Meanwhile, the north is well known for its civility, entrepreneurship, art, fine craftsmanship, architecture, and music. Putnam found that these differences have persisted for around a thousand years. The north seems dominated by the reciprocity of the craft era, while the south seems dominated by some of the worst (AR) features of the hierarchical agricultural era. He presents evidence that it all started with a sequence of historical events that occurred almost by chance. Once established, these cultures have had a sobering persistence. Putnam reports that the contemporary reform effort in the south has met with only limited success. Meanwhile, the north seems to be skipping most of the industrial phase and moving rather painlessly from the culture of the craft age directly into the culture of the emerging information age, with its similar emphasis on long-term reciprocal (EM) relationships.

In presenting the story of technology as a powerful contingency we have shifted from the natural environment, the biogeographic factor, to the human-made resource of technology. The core technologies have become a major contingency to which people are adapting their cultures. Each new discovery, each important new invention lays the essential groundwork for the next discovery. The drive to learn as well as to acquire keeps pushing individuals and societies on to that next step. The culture part of coevolution is changing at what seems to be an accelerating pace, even as our innate human nature—the basic drives embedded in the limbic system of every human brain (as discussed in Chapter Three)—provides the same steady, constant base through it all.

We also shift in our analysis back and forth from the societal level of analysis to the nation state level, and at times to the organization level (note the reference to workshops and factories). We believe that the four-drive framework and its associated skill sets will prove helpful in explaining phenomena at all these levels.

## Ideology and Coevolution

The contingency of ideology is certainly less tangible than that of either biogeography or technology, but nevertheless we believe it has a significant, and probably comparable, impact in contemporary times. For example, we believe ideological factors can largely explain why a rather outmoded cultural system has persisted in southern Italy over these many years. We think it can also help explain the persistence of prescientific beliefs such as creationism, as well as some of the variability in political systems. And not to let scientists be an exception, we will also discuss the role ideology might play in the persistence of some scientific theories.

In our discussion of the drive to learn and make sense of the world in Chapter Six, we argued that the human mind seems to have a strong distaste for inconsistencies or lack of congruence. People seek an explanation for events consistent with the observations of their sense organs and with their prior knowledge. Whenever an explanation seems sensible, people lock onto it and store it in long-term memory. From then on, whenever something similar comes along, they note it as the same and the original explanation is reinforced.

This usually works just fine. But sometimes a person encounters an idea, perhaps on a random basis, that strikes them as new—an original explanation of some important matter that makes sense. Unfortunately, it might well make sense for reasons other than its accuracy or its completeness. Perhaps its logic is aesthetically pleasing in its elegance and purity. And this simple idea might appeal to others who learn of it for the same reason. But what if it is not a reasonably accurate representation of the real world? Therein lies a significant hazard. Often in human history, incorrect or misleading ideas have taken hold and gained favor. As people find an idea appealing and keep talking about it positively, it becomes further locked in the collective memory with many favorable associations. What if it is truly difficult to check out this particular idea with empirical data? Let's say that confirming or disconfirming facts are difficult to come by and somewhat ambiguous. Now let us call this idea an ideology. It may have appeared originally by chance, but the way it is propagated and persists is not by chance. It is based on how the human mind is designed to work.

Such ideas can be passed on by the usual kinds of cultural transmission. People come to believe they are true. They, of course, then act on them as if they *are* true. They must do this because these ideas provide the only guide to action for the domain in which they apply. People have no other choice but to act on what they believe to be true. People for countless years believed that the earth was flat. It was the way it appeared, and that is what other people told them when asked. They had no practical way to check this belief for accuracy. In any event, when they acted on this belief it did them no harm. They were not trying to navigate across the ocean. Flatness was lodged as a fact in their heads. Once so firmly lodged, it was hard to remove. Being told in a classroom that the world was round did not always change matters. It was more effective to take people to the coast and show them how an approaching boat shows its sails before its hull. Taking them up in a space ship would have undoubtedly been even better. But best of all would have been to explain that the earth was round the very first time the question came up. Then the idea could be implanted without the need to displace a prior idea.

Human brains seem to be built in a way that makes it difficult to displace prior ideas. When others try, it triggers the drive to defend current beliefs more often than the drive to learn new ones. As a conservative assumption, this makes good sense. Why abandon an old idea that has stood the test of time unless you are very sure the new idea is more accurate or useful? Humans have to struggle to keep an "open mind." And, as we said earlier, an ideology that is hard to test is the most persistent of all. Such ideologies, once they get rolling, can build up a lot of momentum and become, in themselves, a major contingency that can shape the development of whole cultures.

Once this process has been described, it is not difficult to think of examples. But great care must be taken about the process of calling any particular belief system an ideology. We caution that doing so is certain to be taken as a serious insult by any true believer. However, in spite of this hazard, people do need to help one another as best they can to avoid false ideologies, at least ones that can cause harm.

We picked as our first example the idea that the world is flat because we knew that all our readers have always known that the earth is round. So we can be sure no one is insulted yet.

Now let us try one that will probably upset some readers, but probably not too many at this stage of world history. Take the idea of communism. It clearly can be classified as an ideology. Why has it been appealing to so many people? Perhaps because it has a simple, elegant logic: "From each according to their ability, to each according to their need." This statement probably resonates at some deep level with our need to bond with others. It certainly mirrors the form of sociality that Fiske calls communal sharing and identifies as one of the four universal forms of sociality that we believe are innate skill sets. It appeals to a mind looking for simple explanations to lock onto as an anchor in a sea of confusion.

Beyond the appeal of their simple logic, such ideas also set a trap for the mind because they have some element of truth in them. In the context of the primary family, the rule about communal sharing works fine. Who would argue with the idea that within the immediate family whoever can put food on the table should do so, and whoever is hungry should eat it? But, as we can clearly see in the case of communism, if such ideas are taken as the total truth, the one right way to run all aspects of life, they can be deadly. At the time of the Russian Revolution in 1917, most Russians were no more than two or three generations removed from the small village *mir,* with its traditions of communal living in the isolation of the northern forest. The ideology of communal sharing had some resonance in their minds, and the Bolsheviks traded on it. Many minds became hooked on the ideal state of communism. The Red/White civil war was fought on the energy of that ideology. The idea boiled down to the proposal that a few laws that transferred all possessions except personal effects to the state would lead to the perfect ideal of communal sharing throughout the land. But when the fanatically committed Lenin, and later Stalin, tried to implement the ideology, they ran into stiff opposition from people unwilling to forgo their inherent drive to acquire and possess something—at least their own home and a bit of land. Eventually, Stalin employed the draconian measures of the police state to get people to give up their private property and completely embrace communal sharing. The rest is well known: the genocide of the kulaks, the purges, the gulags, the pogroms, and finally the collapse of the whole system. We know now, of course, that using communal sharing as the only rule for running a society is a road to disaster. Such mistakes can be extremely costly in terms of human suffering.

The Irish Potato Famine of the mid-1840s provides another example of the possible negative effects of the human tendency to lock onto incomplete ideologies. It is estimated that a million people died of starvation and related diseases, while another million were forced to emigrate to avoid a similar fate. The underlying cause of this tragedy was the outbreak of a blight that destroyed the potato crops. But there was also another intervening variable, a more proximate cause that was ideological in nature. Ireland at the time was producing a bounty of other food stocks—mostly wheat, meat, and dairy products that large landowners customarily harvested and shipped to England. At the highest level of the British government a decision was made not to divert these food stocks to relieve the mass starvation. To do so would have violated the dominant ideology of the times, the dogmatic belief in laissez-faire capitalism as the best and only method for running an economy. This belief was so strongly held that British policymakers of the time seriously argued that to do other than let the free market run its course would be immoral, against God's will. The scars from this sad episode are still felt in Ireland.

Are there any such massive hazards, such mind traps, comparable ideologies, still floating around at the start of the twenty-first century? We do not know, but we have to wonder. Every major religion has an extremist wing, alive and well. Are those groups such hazards? Certainly each has its corps of fanatical believers. There are also extreme libertarians who to some extent mirror the opposite of the beliefs of the committed communists of the past, arguing that market pricing is an ideal pattern to be applied in all social relations. And we still have outbreaks of pure fanatical cultism, epitomized by the Jonestown, Heaven's Gate, and Rwanda cults.

To move to a mild case of mental lock-in, think of the division of labor among the various social sciences. It is not much of an exaggeration, we believe, to say that each of the social sciences currently expects the normal practitioner to stick fairly closely to the central paradigm of that discipline. For economics, the principal paradigm is that the unfettered, laissez-faire market will work out all transactions between people in everyone's best interest. This sounds like market pricing (MP) is the single means with the drive to acquire as the single motive. The dominant paradigm for anthropologists is that humans are programmed entirely by their culture; this would suggest that all cultures are equally valid and valuable and should be left intact. The political scientists of the seventeenth century, known as philosophers, had a paradigm focused entirely on authority ranking that asserted the divine right of kings. Today's orthodox political scientists seem to focus on interest group politics using market pricing models. Sociologists tend to expect their professional colleagues to subscribe to one or both of two paradigms: either human behavior can be explained by the network of bonded social commitments that humans make to each other, or human life is made up of the perceptions we borrow from one another, the "social constructions" we create and exchange with each other. In sociological terms, these two paradigms are known respectively as network theory and institutional theory.

The theories of each of these social sciences contain a strong element of truth. All have a simple and elegant logic. They are all plausible. They all have attracted some very fine scholars who wish to push these theories' logic to the limit as part of the scientific process. All these people mean well and want to make a contribution to the store of human knowledge. But all of these theories suffer from being incomplete. The hazard is that some of their practitioners do not recognize this.

To grasp the full hazard of incompleteness, think for a bit about Karl Marx—probably the most maligned social scientist of the last two hundred years. Marx was a very sensitive, well-meaning and smart German essentially living in exile in England. He wrote extensively about the nature of society. He was greatly distressed by the suffering caused among working people by the early forms of industrial capitalism. He hit on a simple but profound idea. Wouldn't the world be better if everyone could live by the simple rule of communal sharing? Like any good scientist, he felt a drive to test his idea to discover its limits. The elegance of the idea excited his friends and companions and they pushed Marx to try to put it to the test. Marx would certainly have been totally appalled with the test of his ideas that was eventually carried out (long after he died) in the Soviet Union, with all its accompanying terror and suffering. He would have wanted anything but a police state and genocide.

This morality story should give anyone who attempts to generate all-encompassing ideas serious pause. We see this example of the fate of the idea of communism as a powerful argument for the search for consilience among all the scientific disciplines. We believe it also demonstrates how ideology—based on the human mind's tendency to grasp and lock onto elegant, logical, and partially true ideas—is another major contingency that helps account for the full diversity of human cultures. Just look around the contemporary world and ask how many societies are significantly influenced by the logic of an essentially untested and seriously incomplete ideology that may well have been launched utterly by chance. In the modern world, where culture and technology increasingly buffer people from the raw impact of nature and natural selection, everyone can expect to be exposed again and again to the hazards created by the mind's attraction to ideologies.

## INDIVIDUAL DIFFERENCES AND COEVOLUTION

Now it is time to move on to the last level of analysis, the examination of any contingency that, in spite of our shared human nature, creates variability in human behavior at the level of the individual. We have only one in mind, an obvious one that might be overlooked for that very reason.

We are referring to the two-sex reproduction system that humans share with almost all animals. Biology has established that, when the female DNA joins with the male DNA at conception, there is a random sorting out of the genes that will determine the heritage of the new individual, with 50 percent of the genes selected from each parent. This device of nature ensures that there is a tremendous mixing of genes as each generation succeeds the last. Thus the two-sex system of reproduction is a contingency that automatically creates diversity among individual human beings. The unique mix of genes each person carries, as well as each person's unique life history, generates individual differences.

Twins (and the still rarer larger multiple births) are the only exception to the natural diversity-generating engine built into the human two-sex reproduction system. Studying twins has thus long been viewed as one way to determine the relative influence of genes versus the environment in shaping individual differences.[11] Twins can be identical (genetic duplicates) or fraternal (share 50 percent of their genes). By comparing identical and fraternal twins with each other and with other sibling pairs, it is possible to estimate how genes and environment interact to influence such things as intelligence, personality, character, and even values. Studies of twins rely on the following contrasts: same genes, same environment (identical twins living in the same family) versus different genes, same environment (fraternal twins living in the same environment) or same genes, different environment (identical twins that have been reared in different households). Despite the seeming simplicity of their design, studies of twins suffer from a large number of methodological problems. Yet the preponderance of evidence gathered to date suggests that both genes and environment have their influence. On some dimensions, as with a person's choice of desired mate, the genetic influence is negligible. On other dimensions, such as intelligence, personality, interests, and attitudes, the genetic influence is substantial. However, even on dimensions where genetic nature appears to have a substantial influence, there is clear evidence that the environment matters as well. In sum, the research on twins suggests that there is no simple answer to the nature versus nurture question. Both matter.

Because most people have different genes and different life experiences, it is hardly surprising that there is so much diversity among human beings. Everyone's genes certainly shape the trajectories their lives take—but they don't do so deterministically. Their material and cultural environment have a powerful influence as well. Human behavior is thus a product of the coevolution of genes and the physical and social environment.

The genetic differences mean that the brain of each individual has a somewhat different weighting or strength among the basic drives, and a somewhat different mix and weighting of skill sets. For example, to state this point in purely speculative terms, if the drive to acquire module in humans averaged 25 percent of the total number of neurons committed to drives, you might find that there was a plus-or-minus variation of 5 percent around the mean. This has to be one source of the variability observed in human behavior, in spite of the fact that we all share the same drives from the same human gene pool.

The variety created by each individual's life history is also clear. Think of the impact that different early life experiences can have, whether diseases, trauma such as abuse or malnutrition, or, at the other end of the spectrum, intensive educational experiences or gifted mentors.

A second feature of two-sex biology also creates variability in behavior. Some of the genes supplied to humans from their parents are coded for sex. This means that these genes will, at some developmental stage of life, generate differences in the bodies of males and females, including their minds. Not a great deal is known about the specifics of these mental differences between the sexes. It might turn out, for example, that males are apt to have more skills for mechanics, and females are apt to have more social skills. It would be surprising if some such differences in these head-start-for-learning skills did not exist, given the millions of years that women have specialized in gathering, as well as in carrying and nurturing children, and that men have specialized in hunting and other more mechanical duties. These differences have nothing to do with mental capacity or brainpower, only for the weight given to different modules of the mind. It might also be found, for instance, that the average woman has a somewhat heavier weighting on D2 than the average man, and the opposite might be true for D1. This would tend to reinforce the stereotype of gender roles. But the opposite might also be found, if the stereotype is wrong or only based on culture. In any event, the variance within the population of women and within the population of men will in all probability minimize the importance of any difference in the averages.

If the four-drive theory is, in due course, verified, it will probably be possible to invent ways to roughly measure the strength of the four drives and associated skill sets on an individual basis. Those who specialize in studying personality differences could explore how well the more broadly accepted typologies of personality, such as the Meyer-Briggs personality typology that builds on Jung's theories, map onto the four drives. Such measures might help people plan their education and careers by building on their special gifts.

In our view, five contingencies—biogeography, physical isolation, stages of technology, ideology, and individual genetic differences—explain much of the great variability in human behavior that occurs in spite of our shared genetic heritage as a species. These contingencies significantly impact the diverse ways our common innate drives are manifested in everyday behavior. We do not pretend to have identified all of the major influences of this kind. Further inquiry will, we would hope, discover others.

# Part Four

## HUMAN NATURE AND SOCIETY

# 11

# HUMAN NATURE IN ORGANIZATIONAL LIFE

*The return from your work must be the satisfaction which that work brings you and the world's need of that work. With it, life is heaven, or as near heaven as you can get. Without this— with work which you despise, which bores you, and which the world does not need—this life is hell.*

—W.E.B. DU BOIS

In the organizational context, the four-drive theory implies that every person, from the CEO to the most junior employee, will bring a predictable set of mental equipment to work each and every day. This mental apparatus will be engaged in every item of behavior that takes place at work. Likewise, all the other people engaged with the focal organization—its customers, its shareholders and creditors, its suppliers, it neighbors and its regulators—will have this same mental equipment.

What would an organization look like that was explicitly designed to effectively engage the drives, the skills, the smarts, and the emotions of such people in a collaborative effort to design, produce, and sell products and services of value to the wider world? After we have deduced what such an organization would be like, we will compare it to a well-known and admired model of industrial organization—General Motors. We will also compare the theoretical model to a much-admired high-technology firm—Hewlett-Packard. Finally we will propose a research project that would test the four-drive theory's relevance to organizations by predicting outcomes instead of explaining events with hindsight.

## An Organization Designed for Four-Drive People

What is the most basic thing employees of all levels must come to terms with at work? The nature of their individual jobs. How would individual jobs be designed to best engage the four-drive person? Once this question is asked it is quite amazingly simple to answer. Clearly, every job must provide an opportunity to fulfill, to some reasonable degree, all four drives. In other words, *every* job needs to provide an opportunity for the incumbent to acquire, to learn, to bond, and to defend. A job that fulfills only one or two drives, no matter how lavishly, would not be a substitute for a job that provides a balanced opportunity to fulfill all four drives. This simple design rule is the fundamental and primary one that should guide the work of the organizational leader throughout the design process.

This design rule is easy to state, but it is difficult to follow for two basic reasons. First, some core production technologies are less amenable to applying the rule than others. Second, organizations have a tendency to veer to an extreme emphasis on the achievement of some one drive to the neglect of the others. When this happens, even the emphasized drive will in time become frustrated. To maintain a reasonable balance among the drives requires hands-on steering by the leadership of the organization. Like riding a unicycle, it takes constant adjustment to move forward without falling right, left, front, or back.

Let us now assume that the organization leader has done the design work and that the organizational roles have been planned so that every job has four-drive potential. Further we will assume that the interconnections between roles are also planned so as to achieve the overall objectives of the firm in relation to customers, investors, and regulators. Now people are chosen to step into these roles and the organization is set in motion. What will happen in real time?

Once on the job, the bonding drive will lead every person to search for others with whom they can evolve mutual caring commitments. These others will, in all likelihood, be in their immediate work area. When these one-to-one bonded relationships form a cluster, the participants will begin to see themselves as a group, *their* bonded group that is distinct from other groups. If the individuals in this primary group have interlocking tasks, their bonds of trust will facilitate their joint task performance and they can be officially recognized as a work group or team. The more extended bonding drive of employees will also predispose them to bond with organizational groupings beyond their immediate work team. They will bond, if such opportunities have been wisely provided by the leaders, with their department, their plant, their division, and even with the entire firm. Other things being equal, these multiple bonds will lead the people involved into friendly support of one another. However, without other counterbalancing drives at work, this would in time lead to a tension-free, collusive set of relationships with everyone attending to everyone else's comfort instead of attending to their acquiring drive by focusing on job performance. One problematic form this excessive bonding can take is the "group think" process described by Irving Janis.[1] But, of course, the bonding drive is not alone in the human psyche; the drive to acquire will especially unsettle any such cozy equilibrium.

The acquiring drive will lead to ongoing competition as everyone in the organization seeks to boost their relative share of the scarce resources. This competitive drive to excel others is the greatest source of the restless energy that people bring to the workplace. If this were the only drive in play, it would lead inevitably to an all-out struggle of each against all. Everyone would act as a free agent in a winner-take-all contest. Opportunism and selfish political behavior would be rampant. A great deal of frantic effort would be expended—but little of it would be the kind of coordinated effort that would result in completed tasks for the overall firm. In other words, all this energy probably would not be harnessed efficiently to the goals of the larger enterprise.

It is clearly in the interest of the organizational leader to align the competitive energies of individuals with the integrated goals of the organization. To do this the leader would need, on an ongoing basis, to moderate the competitive energies of D1 with the mutual caring generated by D2. This need for balancing the acquisitive and bonding drives sets up the second guiding principle for the leader: such a balance needs to be struck in every key relationship in the firm—within each primary work group, between all primary groups that are interdependent, between any larger groups such as departments and divisions, and directly in the social contract between all employees and the overall firm. Think of it as seeking the tension of *respectful competition* in all relationships.

Keeping all these relationships in balance is much easier to say than to do. Relationships can all too readily slide into cutthroat competition or totally collusive bonding. Either extreme will harm the firm's performance. These swings can occur because each of the four drives was created by evolution to improve the odds of gene survival. When any one drive gains dominance for whatever reason in a given social setting, it soon becomes self-reinforcing. A spiraling arms race can be created with everyone seeking more and more of a good thing. There seems to never be enough of the good thing—until a crisis breaks up the cycle. Individuals can be expected to try to maintain a balance among their drives in their own personal lives, but they often need the help of well-managed social institutions to succeed.

Leaders have several structural devices they can use to promote this balance. For example, they can balance financial and symbolic rewards for both individual achievement and teamwork. They can arrange the physical layout to place interdependent groups in adjacent space to encourage trustful bonding. Individuals can be assigned the full-time job of maintaining balanced relationships within and between groups. Of course, these same structural devices can be misused and thereby contribute to the extremes. For example, offering large financial incentives to the winners of intergroup contests would predictably pull these relationships into cutthroat competition.

In addition, in an effort to keep the competition from becoming cutthroat or the bonding from becoming collusive, the designer can foster the identification of every employee with the firm as a whole and its overall goals. Remember that four-drive theory argues that the innate pressure to fulfill all four drives together has served to evolve a social contracting skill as a means to this end. People are predisposed to bond with their firm both in a mutual caring way and also to help their firm to excel. The designer can encourage this by fostering firmwide symbols, rituals, and norms. However, any such social contract must be a mutual commitment to be effective. The leadership group must make their own strong and visible commitment to the welfare of the overall firm and to its members if less powerful participants are to follow.

So far we have focused on the implications of the drives to bond and to acquire and the interplay between them. The drives to learn and to defend must receive equivalent consideration. For individual jobs to offer opportunities for learning they would have to entail enough variety of content to generate novel or problematic situations that trigger the itch of curiosity. It is this itch in the incumbent's mind that activates the drive to resolve the gap between the known and the new perception. Of course, the variety can be too great and the gaps so large that confusion results. But if the variety is in a zone of moderate stimulation, creative new solutions to problems will be fostered that can be gratifying to the individual as well as useful for the organization. Learning of this same kind also moves along well in a group or intergroup context when the participants are diverse enough to trigger the curiosity itch, but not so different as to be threatening. What constitutes "too much" diversity is moderated by the quality of the social skills participants are able to exercise toward keeping the learning dialogue open and flowing.

In relation to the drive to defend, work groups must be provided with the means to fend off external attacks. They must be able to press their legitimate claims for resources and support from the overall firm. They must be able to defend their identity and reputation from unjust attacks. And the firm as a whole needs a similar defensive capacity for its dealings with hostile competitive firms, community groups, or governmental agencies.

The defending and learning drives can also veer to dysfunctional extremes. Individuals can become defensive to the point of paranoia, and so can organizations—building fortresses so strong they have trouble learning about and relating to customers and investors. Likewise, individuals can become so obsessed with learning that they forget to eat or sleep or take vacations—and this can happen to whole organizations. The organizational leader needs to balance D3 and D4. The goal is to encourage prudent risk taking, not reckless exploration, and to encourage boundaries between groups that are permeable rather than impregnable. Certainly work shared between individuals or between groups can best be conducted without a heavily defensive mood inhibiting the desirable spirit of mutual learning and inquiry between the parties. One of the critical roles of a leader of any given group is to facilitate open-minded relations with other parts of the organization while defending the group from outside challenges as needed. Part of the challenge of organization design is to lay out the architecture of the organization so that barriers between groups—physical distance, organizational lines, and skill differences—do not pile up at any single interface to handicap the needed relationship.

Beyond the question of drives, *every* job in our theoretical four-drive organization would offer an opportunity for the incumbent to employ some personal skills, skills for which they not only have an innate head start but also a personal history of further developing and refining. Since individuals will differ in regard to the skill sets they have developed, this step will necessitate a one-to-one matching of skills and job requirements. As people with the needed skills and interests are selected for employment and as they further evolve their skills on the job, differences in this regard will appear between people and groups that complicate the process of sustaining healthy working relationships.

Any organization has design issues posed by the innate nature of its employees and also by the same innate nature of its customers, suppliers, investors, and regulators. Much the same issues arise here as with employees. For example, most firms depend on the continuing high regard of their customers. Repeat sales are essential. To achieve this the product or service needs to engage customers in terms of all four drives. Hence firms need to cultivate identifying brands for their products that represent a kind of social contract, a promise of a certain mix of quality (D1), service (D2), novelty (D3), and reliability (D4) that adds up to a value that justifies the price.

Of course, shareholders have always been seen as caring only about the acquiring opportunities provided by share ownership. But this ignores their defending drive to avoid significant losses of their capital, and often their satisfaction from simply being associated with a distinguished and interesting firm.

The relation between firms and their suppliers, to be sound over the long haul, needs to allow both buyers and sellers a chance to fulfill all four drives. Addressing their acquiring drives is necessary but not sufficient to create an ongoing healthy relationship. The variety of issues and problems generated by the interaction of the parties can stimulate the joint problem solving of both to their mutual benefit. They can come to the defense of one another by providing help in times of crisis. They can take significant satisfaction in developing bonds of partnership and friendship and feel free of concerns about being double-crossed. Relations of this rich four-drive type can be planned for and evolved between firms in the supply chain to their mutual advantage.

Finally, while it might be more difficult to achieve, a very similar relationship can evolve between direct competitors and between firms and their government regulators. It may come as a surprise to some business leaders, but regulators can actually help competing firms avoid the perils of cutthroat competition on one hand and price-fixing collusion on the other. The government can thus help them achieve the balance of healthy competition that is vital to sustained prosperity.

Consider the commercial fishing industry. All fishermen can be expected to try to fill up their own vessels with fish on each voyage—to do less would not be in their competitive interest. Yet if every fisherman acts this way, all will lose out as the overall stock becomes depleted. Economists call this dynamic dilemma the "Tragedy of the Commons." Nothing short of the government with its power of regulating an industry for the common good can stop such an outbreak of cutthroat competition. The government can take the lead in negotiating a sensible social contract, binding on all participants in the industry, that sets helpful constraints on competition. This type of problem arises again and again in economic activity. Think of the problem of pollution control, of lumbering, of soil conservation—the list goes on and on.

To the extent that a living organization managed to follow this blueprint, we predict that it would achieve long-term success in terms of all the major outcomes by which organizations are judged. Since all four human drives are being fulfilled by this design one might think that it would not be all that difficult to achieve. Certainly once such a blueprint is understood as a desirable target, it should be easier to achieve. However, it turns out to be a difficult target to hit. Organizations as well as individuals easily drift into an overemphasis on one drive. This leads in time to the frustration of all drives. In addition, some core technologies make it very awkward to follow this blueprint.

## GENERAL MOTORS AND THE FOUR-DRIVE BLUEPRINT

The auto industry was at the center of America's industrial experience throughout the twentieth century and was at the peak of its influence at mid-century. Its leading firm at the time, General Motors, was the world's largest industrial employer. General Motors has epitomized the social institutions of the industrial age. The industrial wave of development with its mass production and mass distribution was still growing at mid-century. Few realized it was nearing its peak and was about to give way to the information age. Well hidden from sight, seeds were beginning to sprout that would transform organizational life in the next fifty years. At Bell Labs, the transistor was under development. At IBM, punch-card calculators were just beginning to be challenged by computers. In Japan, the postwar auto industry was being born afresh.

American auto industry virtually started with the start of the twentieth century. In 1900, a total of 4,192 cars rolled out of plants consisting of a few dozen self-taught mechanics operating out of a large garage, each car essentially handmade. By 1910, about 250 firms produced a total of some 180,000 cars. The story of the decade was innovation, experimentation, start-up and failure, trial and error. Not much is known of the daily details of what went on inside those small start-up auto firms, but it cannot have been much different from the familiar start-ups of today's software and Internet firms. The early automakers would have been exciting places to work, with close, friendly relations developing as people shared their creative ideas and tested them to see which ones worked. By the decade's end a great mix of auto choices had been generated for Americans, including an Averageman's Car, an Everybody's, an Electrobat, a Harvard, and two different Yales, all with different styles, sizes, features, power plants, and prices.[2] Many of the features of the modern automobile were already in place, albeit in a primitive form.

If the first decade of autos was one of learning innovation, the second was one of acquisitions as the tests of market share and profitability thinned the ranks. The firms that could achieve economies of scale came to the front. Ford led the way with new manufacturing systems that followed Fredrick Taylor's rules for making the core technology of *mass production* a reality. The most notable innovation was the moving assembly line Ford introduced in 1913. In 1912 Ford produced 78,611 cars. When the assembly line was fully operative in 1914, it produced 260,720 Model T's. Costs and prices plummeted. The Model T sold for $850 when introduced in 1908. By 1916, when Ford built more than half a million significantly improved cars, the price had fallen to $360.

The moving assembly line did a great deal more than cut costs. It made a fundamental change in the nature of the job and the relationship of the autoworker to management and the entire organization. Where innovative ideas had been shared and help exchanged between boss and worker, now a strict authority-ranking system took over. The organization of work was determined exclusively by the boss. Once the wage bargain (market pricing) had been struck, workers were expected to act as mindless robots doing simple, repetitive jobs to keep the line moving. Whatever innovations had been coming from the bottom of the organization were quickly shut down. Instead the mechanically paced work made it virtually unnecessary for managers and workers to talk to each other. The assembly line fostered obedience but certainly no bonding between management and workers. Loyalty became virtually unknown in either direction, down or up. One worker told Edmund Wilson in the thirties: "Ye get the wages, but ye sell your soul at Ford's—ye're worked like a slave all day, and when ye get out ye're too tired to do anything. . . . A man checks his brains and his freedom at the door when he goes to work at Ford's."[3] Most workers deeply resented these jobs and turned their resentment toward management. Their underutilized thinking capacity often went into finding ways to ease the pressure of the moving line by cutting corners, often at the expense of quality.[4] The price to be paid for these production methods came much later. During the glory years, Ford was king, with its market share soaring to a peak in 1921 of 56 percent. Ford's methods were undoubtedly the best way known at the time to deliver on the promise of mass production to fulfill the acquiring drives of the company owner—and also of his customers and even his workers. But these auto jobs clearly did not help employees fulfill any other drives. No one had figured out a way to design mass production jobs so as to address human drives to bond or learn or defend. Even though the successful (though bitter and at times violent) unionization drives of the late thirties helped address the security needs of the workforce, they did not bring any change in the social contract that was built into the assembly line process itself. That process continued to generate hostility in worker-management relations.

Meanwhile, the emphasis on acquiring was also dominant at General Motors, but in a very different form. GM was buying up other firms as they were squeezed out of business by Ford. Whipped into action by the driving ambition of its chief executive, William Durant, GM went through two periods of feverish combination. The first wave captured Buick and Olds; the second, Cadillac, Oakland (now Pontiac), and Chevrolet. Among the firms GM acquired was Hyatt Roller Bearing—and with it, Alfred Sloan, the company's guiding force for the next twenty-five years. The brief recession of 1920 forced Durant out of GM. Pierre DuPont, representing the DuPont stock holdings, took over the leadership. DuPont quickly recognized Sloan's managerial talent and gave him operational control of the firm. It was Sloan's policies that turned the odd conglomeration of GM's acquisitions into a unified firm that fairly rapidly overtook Ford's commanding lead.

The General Motors that Sloan stitched together followed Ford's example in its production methods, including the moving assembly line. GM made the same implicit social contract with its workers as Ford did—to help fulfill their D1 drive but not the other drives. However, in terms of customer relations and management relations, Sloan was a true innovator.

Sloan's marketing was highly successful. Ford had essentially offered his car to the public on a take-it-or-leave-it basis. His social contract with the public was very clear: "Ford offers a standard, one-type-fits-all car at a fixed price—no discussion needed." Sloan worked to achieve a much more reciprocal relationship with GM customers; first learning about them and then providing the cars that different clusters of customers really wanted. Over time, these policies developed a bond between the firm and its customers; they developed strong brand loyalty. GM customers came to believe they not only got a good car for their money (D1) but also a trusted friend (D2) who offered a reliable vehicle (D4) tailored to their desires (D3).

Sloan was also one of a very few industrial leaders who pioneered a major innovation, the multidivisional form of organization.[5] For a time this innovation paid off handsomely for GM, but the particular way the company implemented the structure proved, over time, to be very costly. GM divisions were provided with most of the resources they needed to operate as independent units that could be judged by their overall profitability. Each division was encouraged to develop its own car brands and to compete with the others for market share, and executives received annual bonuses keyed to divisional profits.

This management method did unleash a lot of energy, but—as four-drive theory predicts—the financial rewards induced fierce interdivisional competition. The exchange of innovative ideas between divisions ground to a halt. What division executive would think of passing on good ideas to a prime rival? Each division also came to see it as in its best interest to go for the large middle-class market. Product differences between divisions tended to shrink as all divisions converged on this one market and neglected both the high-price and low-price ends. By the fifties and sixties GM divisional executives were reenacting the Tragedy of the Commons in their relations to one another.

Sloan's GM also led the industry in the way it managed vital external relationships, such as those with suppliers. GM combined the use of wholly owned parts suppliers with the purchase of parts from independent suppliers. With the independents, GM offered the chance to bid on short-term contracts. The contracts usually went to the low bidder, following the classic market pricing (MP) system. This system tended to drive down costs (D1), but often at the expense of innovation and quality. The sheer volume of GM orders gave the firm tremendous power to drive down suppliers' prices and profits, even forcing some suppliers to adopt sweatshop conditions to survive. The classic example in Detroit is the infamous "Lopez Incident," where GM reputedly told all its suppliers that GM would be paying 15 percent less for parts—effective immediately. Suppliers, to defend against such high-pressure tactics, undoubtedly cut corners on quality, passed on extra charges by all means possible, and withheld valuable information. One auto-part supplier explained to us that he had candidly told a senior GM executive that GM would be the last to hear about any of the supplier's design improvements. The reason was simple: the GM purchasing officer would inevitably follow company policy and call other suppliers with the new idea and ask for lower bids. Supply relationships became a form of cold war similar to that conducted with the hourly workforce on the factory floor.

Throughout the century, the relationship of GM with federal and state governments has been both cooperative and adversarial. The firm has, of course, been enormously helped by the continuing commitment of public funds to constructing the road systems required for auto traffic. Gasoline taxes, although they somewhat dampened the growth of the industry, were much less in the United States than in other countries—far from covering the expense of roads. These decisions of public policymakers greatly helped the auto industry in general and GM in particular.

GM's relations with the government turned adversarial over auto safety, fuel efficiency, and emission control regulations. Like businesses in many other fields, GM resisted these governmental controls. This resistance came dramatically to public attention through the Nader episode. GM was greatly embarrassed by the revelation that it had hired a public relations firm that, in turn, tried to discredit Ralph Nader and his auto safety campaign by attempting to compromise him with a hired call girl. GM seems to have consistently rejected the option of cooperating with regulators in the drafting of sensible controls that could have served all the auto firms equally by establishing a level playing field for competition while still honoring legitimate public concerns.

GM's record in its relationships with its auto industry competitors also involved its relations with regulators. By the end of the twenties, GM, Ford, and Chrysler had established an oligopoly that proved to be remarkably enduring, together sharing approximately 90 percent of the U.S. market. In 1931 GM had 43 percent of the market, Ford 25 percent, and Chrysler 19 percent. These respective shares did not vary much over the next forty years. The pattern held largely because true competition between the major firms had essentially ended. GM was so dominant that they could unilaterally set the prices they would charge in each new model year. They could calculate their cost of production for each model and then deliberately add the profit margin that they thought fell just short of seeming excessive. They did this knowing full well that Ford and Chrysler would not rock the boat. The other automakers had no incentive to undercut GM's prices because, even though their own unit costs were higher, GM's prices were high enough to cover their own costs handily. For the twenty years between 1946 and 1967, GM had a widely envied average profit return on net worth of 20.7 percent. Meanwhile the average of all three firms for these years was 16.7 percent, in itself nearly twice the rate earned by all manufacturing corporations.

One of GM's CEOs during this time is reputed to have said that his biggest problem was keeping his subordinates from squeezing Ford and Chrysler out of business and thereby bringing the antitrust people down on his head. In fact, the government antitrust people are not known to have brought any action against GM throughout this period. It seems fair to say that during this period GM had, in four-drive terms, generated collusive D2 relations with its external competitors—but, as time would reveal, at the price of internal stagnation.

The prosperous stability of the postwar period masked vital weaknesses that left U.S. automakers vulnerable to the onslaught of imported cars, mostly Japanese, that came in the 1970s. As it turned out, the Japanese auto industry, as it rebuilt from the ground up after World War II, adopted very different ways to relate to its five key constituencies, to its frontline workforce, to its own managerial workforce, to its suppliers, to its customers, and to government regulators. In essence, while the American approach appealed almost exclusively to the acquiring drive of its constituent groups, the Japanese methods went far beyond by appealing to all four drives. How did this work?

## The Nature of the Japanese Challenge

As the seventies unfolded it finally became clear that the chronically hostile labor relations at GM were creating a major strategic problem for the company, a product quality problem. As the higher quality of the Japanese imports became apparent to the American public, loyalty to domestic products gradually waned. And the differential in quality can largely be explained by the differential in the quality of labor relations in the two systems. As is well known, Japanese managers were treating their workers very differently and getting big benefits, not only in product quality but also in innovative ideas.

The Japanese firms had worked out a way to segment their assembly lines, with each segment managed by a small team. Each team of workers was held responsible not only for the volume of output but also for its quality. Each team was given the power to stop the line if necessary to meet its responsibilities. Teams were also urged to come up with their own ideas for improving quality and efficiency. These practices gave Japanese workers not only a relatively well-paying job but also a job that contributed to their drive to learn and to bond.

The Japanese also found many ways to foster worker loyalty to the firm as a whole. The most obvious way was to enter into a commitment that was tantamount to lifetime employment. Beyond this strong commitment, Japanese customs, such as the group exercises and company songs that were perceived as odd by many Americans, provided an opportunity for workers to feel bonded to the entire organization. These expressions of loyalty of the firm to the worker were reciprocated by the loyalty of the worker to the company. They worked diligently, they innovated, and they did not go on strike.

It came naturally to Japanese workers to honor anyone in their group who passed on to management an idea that could cut costs or improve product quality. Any GM worker who proposed any such idea to management would have been ostracized as a sellout. The bitter hostility between management and labor became so ingrained and persistent at GM that observers judged it to be completely inevitable. Then the Japanese showed that there was a more effective way to manage the workforce. During the eighties and nineties GM and the other U.S. firms strove to emulate the Japanese model of workforce relations—with only mixed success. The biggest remaining roadblock is probably the U.S. firms' persistence in running their assembly lines the traditional way.

Another source of weakness in GM that showed up when contrasted to the Japanese approach was in the relations between divisional and functional managerial groups within the firm. The Japanese evolved an executive reward system and a decision-making system that promoted cooperation rather than competition between units. The Japanese tied their executive reward system almost exclusively to overall firm performance, rather than to the performance of any subunit. Beyond this their decision system, called *ronji,* involved developing a position paper on important company-wide topics, which was then circulated for consideration and comment down through the ranks and laterally across divisional lines. This system was somewhat time consuming, but this was more than offset by the consensus built, the quality of the plans evolved, and the cooperative manner in which the final decisions were implemented. Furthermore, the Japanese led the industry in the fine art of creating multifunctional design teams that improved the quality and the timeliness of new car designs.[6]

These two structural features, plus the team-based assembly line, helped Japanese organizations achieve the respectful competitive relationships called for by four-drive theory from top to bottom and from side to side. The structures fostered open communication channels as well as learning and innovation in all parts of the organization. For Japanese auto employees at all levels, the only intense competition was with other auto firms. The advantages of these internal practices became even greater as the pace of change picked up speed. During the late eighties and into the nineties U.S. auto firms have finally moved to adopt their own versions of the managerial relations practiced by the Japanese firms.

In regard to supplier relations, the Japanese auto industry adopted the practice of cultivating long-term relationships with independent auto parts firms. As it turned out, this type of social contract also provided the Japanese with a major advantage over the GM model. Japanese supply networks were based on bonded ties that followed the rule of long-term reciprocity in help and advice. The major Japanese auto firms did dominate these relationships, but they did not use their power to squeeze profits out of their suppliers. This system greatly aided the automakers in securing high-quality parts at reasonable cost—along with a continuous flow of ideas for product improvements.

Once the Japanese supply system network took hold, the disadvantages of the U.S. arrangements gradually became apparent. Led by Chrysler and Ford, the U.S. industry has responded by spinning off wholly owned suppliers and entering into long-term bonded relations with them and other external suppliers.

In regard to customer relations, the Japanese firms largely copied the practices that GM under Sloan's leadership pioneered in the twenties. As noted, GM at that time led the way in demonstrating how to build a solid, long-term relationship with customers in terms of brand loyalty. GM designed its car lines around customer segments, provided options that enabled customers to customize their cars, offered follow-up services and warranties—a complete four-drive relationship. However, during the long period of Big Three oligopoly, complacency set in. GM started taking its customers for granted and, with the divisions' product lines converging on look-alike cars, it lost track of changing tastes. When the foreign cars came on in strength with a fresh effort to address customer desires, GM was caught napping and the vaunted loyalty of its customers evaporated. Brands proved to represent a promise of caring attention and service that required constant renewal to be of real value.

Japanese auto firms are also well known for the cooperative relationship that has existed over the years in their dealings with government regulators. They not only complied with regulations on emissions, safety, and fuel conservation, they helped to write the rules. Beyond these important issues, it has been the policy of the postwar Japanese government to steer each industrial sector away from either too little or too much competition, away from either monopolistic or cutthroat competition. They understood that the great advantage of competitive markets, as economists have well established, is that they provide strong incentives for firms to strive to be effective and efficient, to avoid waste and to seek creative solutions to market opportunities. This advantage is lost if firms are allowed to move into a quasi-monopolistic position without real competitive pressures. At the other extreme, the Japanese government was steering firms away from cutthroat competition, from using power plays such as predatory spot pricing and product bundling to destroy the competition rather than simply outperforming them on a level playing field.

In the case of the U.S. auto industry, the federal government was lax in enforcing monopoly controls. For all practical purposes, GM had monopoly powers for about three decades. The government did not intervene and, as a consequence of the lack of competitive pressures, the industry did predictably slide into waste and stagnation. Meanwhile, although cutthroat competition has never been a major problem among the Big Three, it has cropped up in their relations with suppliers.

In the nineties, some serious limitations of the Japanese management methods emerged. In retrospect, it seems evident that carrying company-wide bonding to the point of offering lifetime employment went too far. This also seems to be true of their very closely bonded relations with long-time suppliers. When various technological and market changes resulted in a need for reassigning and in some cases reducing the number of employees and in a need for shifting among suppliers, Japanese firms were torn between these pressures to change and even downsize and their strong traditional commitments. With hindsight, it is clear that it would have been preferable to make long-term but not lifetime commitments to employees and suppliers that could have been fairly and humanely altered as requirements changed—without shattering the valuable bonds of mutual trust. This downturn in the affairs of the Japanese firms demonstrates that excessive stress on D2 and D4 can lead to trouble, just as much as excessive stress on D1.

A century of history in the auto industry has provided many opportunities to illustrate the usefulness of the four-drive theory as a means to understand and, as a consequence, better manage and lead organizational life. It took the massive competitive victory of the Japanese firms to expose the weaknesses in GM and the other U.S. auto firms in all of these relationships. The Big Three thrived for four decades with their cozy pricing formula only because, until the Japanese arrived on the scene, there were no competitors that were demonstrating better ways to make and sell cars. The Japanese firms were able to out-compete their American counterparts because they worked out a social contract with their workers that made it possible for them to fulfill, at least to some extent, all four drives on the job. They did the same for their suppliers, for their interdivisional relations, and in their relations with governmental bodies. The innovations and superior quality that flowed from these social contracts made for an enormous competitive difference. And with all of these factors in place, it is no surprise that the shareholders were very well served as well. Later, however, they encountered conditions where their emphasis on the bonding drive dangerously reduced their agility in the market. This review supports the argument of the four-drive theory that businesses succeed to the extent to which they find a way to offer opportunities to fulfill all four of the drives to all their various participants and partners. It also supports the argument that undue attention to any of the four drives can lead to trouble.

The auto industry example also illustrates how, in four-drive terms, organizations take on a life of their own beyond the life of their individual participants. Like systems at all other levels of life from the cell to the complex organism, organizations have a boundary that encloses differentiated parts that are joined by a set of integrating systems. The combination of the network of social bonds, shared property rights, and shared representations or culture within an organization acts as the connective tissue that gives the firm its systemic or quasi-organic properties.[7] To a limited extent it becomes reasonable to characterize entire organizations by their emphasis on and success at acquiring, at learning, at bonding, and at defending. Organizations as totalities can bond with other organizations as allies with mutual concerns. Organizations can learn in the sense of creating collective knowledge and know-how. They can internally develop a network of bonded relations that can be conceptualized as social capital, or in everyday language, as trust. Francis Fukuyama has made the strongest and broadest case for the importance of trust for economic success in *Trust: The Social Virtues and the Creation of Prosperity*.[8] This overall way of thinking, which deals with the four basic drives within a straightforward systems framework, holds out the hope of creating a more unified complete theory of the firm, of organizational life.

### The Challenge of Transformational Change

As of the turn of the twenty-first century, the U.S. auto firms have taken many of the steps needed to catch up with Japanese management practice. They still need further changes in assembly-line technology and in developing more environmentally friendly power systems. Beyond this, the newer electronic technologies and the Internet offer an opportunity for the U.S. firms to take the lead by developing stronger and more responsive bonds with their customers. These technologies offer new, low-cost ways to further customize cars to the preferences of customers and to personalize an ongoing service relationship with the customer.

The transformation of the U.S. auto firms over the last thirty years is but one example of a very similar process that has been quietly proceeding throughout the U.S. manufacturing sector during these same years. The changes have been uneven and are incomplete but there is a clear direction toward which all these changes are heading:

- Redesign the more routine jobs so that they contain some variety and some responsibility for problem solving so that all employees can to some extent be knowledge workers, using their brains to learn and to invent ways to enhance performance.
- Centralize decisions about objectives after wide discussion and delegate decisions about means to all parts of the organization.
- Flatten and downsize the managerial hierarchy and reduce the power and status gap from top to bottom so as to improve the flow of good ideas.
- Foster the development of bonded work teams that jointly tackle production problems or the challenges of new product development.
- Encourage lateral lines of collaborative communication between functional and divisional groups by drawing them into the decision process and by designing reward systems that moderate intergroup competition.
- Earn the bonded loyalty of every employee to the firm as a whole as well as to their immediate work group.
- Focus the firm on excellent performance of its core technology while outsourcing other tasks and processes to long-term, trusted suppliers.
- Build long-term customer relations around brands that stand for quality, value, and reliability.
- Work with regulatory bodies to develop sensible guidelines to ensure a level competitive playing field and the protection of legitimate public concerns.

These changes have begun to take hold across U.S. manufacturing. They have arrived under a number of reform banners—*total quality, team building, management by objectives, quality of work life, reengineering, job enrichment, gain-sharing, empowerment,* and a host of others. Today firms that are not moving down this reform road are simply no longer competitive. All these changes have a common theme: they are structures and processes designed to help all participants fulfill all four drives on the job. They make it possible to achieve simultaneous improvements in productivity, in work satisfaction, and in innovation. They also allow companies to work around the constraints that have historically gone with the core technology of mass production.

Although the example of Japanese success played a major role in changing the U.S. auto industry, the stimulus for change in other manufacturing sectors has come from many other sources. It has come from the research and teaching of professional business schools. It has come from the successful examples of early adopters in each of the manufacturing sectors. But perhaps the single strongest pressure for change has come from the new firms springing up in the high-technology sector.

## The High-Tech Sector and Four-Drive Theory

Our extended analysis of the auto industry has simplified our discussion of the high-tech sector in four-drive terms. We are referring here to the entire information age combination of computers, software, telecommunication, biotechnology, Internet, e-commerce, financial, legal, consulting, and other professional services, and health care. This is the combination that has exploded in growth in the last half decade. It is the mega-sector that has been the major force, much more than the Japanese model, pushing the restructuring of the industrial manufacturing sector along the lines outlined earlier. This is true because from the start the pace-setting firms of the information age have been built for information-intensive work, for the best deployment of knowledge workers. All nine of the design features listed in the preceding section are basic to effectiveness in high technology. The fact that these organizational practices are so well understood and applied in U.S. high technology is what has given U.S. firms a clear lead in this sector on a worldwide basis. They are now employed in the United States with a good deal more sophistication than elsewhere, well exceeding their use in Japan or Europe. These practices are, we believe, what is powering the "New Economy" with its record years of growth and gains in productivity and innovation. These firms have become the leaders in finding ways to help fulfill all four drives at all levels. Their chief deficiency may come from the fact that they are engaging so much of the attention and energy of their participants that they are unbalancing the tradeoff between work and family and community life.[9]

## HEWLETT-PACKARD AND THE FOUR-DRIVE BLUEPRINT

The one firm that many observers would credit with being the pioneer in creating the organizational methods that characterize high-tech firms is Hewlett-Packard. Although others have certainly contributed to the new way of doing business, HP seems to have been on this track first with the most inventive features.

In 1939, Bill Hewlett and Dave Packard set up shop in the one-car garage of Dave's rented house in Palo Alto. They had $538 in capital then; at the end of 2000 their firm had $48.8 billion in annual sales, $3.7 billion in profits, and eighty-nine thousand employees worldwide. The first product Hewlett-Packard chose to make was an electronic instrument, an audio oscillator used to test sound equipment. This choice of technology helped greatly in getting HP off to a strong start toward creating a firm consistent with the four-drive blueprint, assuring that HP would be a knowledge-based firm whose products tightly focused on measurement, computation, and communication—all aspects of information processing. Most tasks at HP required people to be skilled at information processing. HP needed the brains of its employees over and above their brawn or their manual dexterity. It became essential that people be on-the-job learners.

In addition, designing, producing, and selling electronic instruments required tight coordination, not just the one-step-to-the-next sequential process of the assembly line but reciprocal coordination, checking back and forth between tasks to achieve the right answer. This technology, therefore, required that individuals and groups bond to one another in trustful relations simply to get the job done.

As a result, most jobs at HP of necessity provided an opportunity to fulfill all four drives. Such jobs would be powerfully attractive to all people with the necessary starting qualifications. The founders of HP, however, had to build on these initial advantages—and Bill and Dave, as they were known at HP, turned out to be experts at gaining the most from these advantages. Many other high-tech managers at the time, trapped in the managerial habits of traditional industry, allowed similar advantages to slip away.

What follows will be a sampling of observations and quotations that illustrate how HP has run its organization. The sample should provide a feel for HP culture, "The HP Way," and other features of HP that can be tested for fit with the four-drive organizational blueprint.[10] Do the HP leaders seem to be striving to follow the two primary rules for four-drive organizational design? First, do they really design into every job a way to fulfill all four drives? Second, do they manage the ongoing relationships at all levels so as to balance the emphasis on all four drives? The source or topic is given at the beginning of each paragraph, with our commentary in brackets where needed.

## GUIDELINES FROM THE FOUNDERS

*Dave Packard [placing emphasis on D1 for everyone]:* Early in the history of the company, while thinking about how a company like this should be managed, I kept getting back to one concept: If we could simply get everybody to agree on what our objectives were and to understand what we were trying to do, then we could turn everybody loose, and they would move along in a common direction.[11]

*Dave Packard [placing emphasis on D2 for everyone]:* One of the things we have tried to achieve, and I think have achieved thus far, is this concept of teamwork. The only way this company is going to run successfully is if we can ensure that there is a maximum flow of information and cooperation between all the elements of it.[12]

*Bill Hewlett [insisting that all jobs have four-drive potential]:* At HP we believe that a manager, a supervisor, a foreman, given the proper support and guidance (that is, the objectives), is probably better able to make decisions about the problems he/she is directly concerned with than some executive way up the line, no matter how smart or able that executive may be. This system places great responsibility on the individuals concerned, but it also makes their work more interesting and challenging. It makes them feel that they are a part of the company and can have a direct effect on its performance.[13]

## CREATING FOUR-DRIVE JOBS FOR EVERYONE

*HP group VP:* You said you don't think making printed circuit boards is much different here from other places; I think probably it is. People making PC boards here don't punch time clocks and haven't for the many years I've been here. They do have flexible work hours. They got them as soon as I did. They've got considerable freedom of input about how they are doing their job. They make suggestions for changes. They have every bit as much access to HP's president as I do.[14]

*HP employee:* There's a conditioning period for people who have worked other places. Maybe it's the informality they see or the nondirectiveness of HP. Instead of your being told point by point what you're supposed to do, your boss is relying on you to able to use your head. I think maybe that's sort of frightening to some people.[15]

## ENCOURAGING BONDING (D2) AMONG ALL EMPLOYEES

*Physical plant:* HP used a variety of techniques to encourage an ongoing dialogue among all its employees. Almost all individual offices had no doors. Top executives had modest-sized offices within large administrative areas, divided only by freestanding, low partitions.[16]

*Management practice:* Managers at all levels were encouraged to spend part of each day wandering through the organization, even if only to see what was going on and to build new channels of communication with other employees. Management by wandering around [MBWA as it was called] . . . was spread through company publications, meetings, training sessions, and by the example of upper management.[17]

*Career movement [as a way to encourage bonding across groups]:* Employees referred to career paths at HP as "the career maze." This phrase acknowledged the normalcy of cross-functional and cross-divisional promotions and lateral moves, based on performance and potential, that often occurred over the course of a career. . . . Not only did HP believe this was the best use of people, but the constant fertilization across functions helped coordinate the design, manufacturing and distribution processes.[18]

## ENCOURAGING LEARNING (D3) AMONG ALL EMPLOYEES

*HP manager:* When I first came to HP, I started to wonder how I was going to get any work done with people going by my office and telephone conversations going on around me. But I got used to it. It's really about creating a learning organization. . . . Best practices are widely talked about and spread around the organization.[19]

## DEFENDING JOBS AND INCOME (D4)

*Financing:* It has been HP's policy to finance its growth entirely through the profits it generated by its regular operations and thereby undertake only a minimum of long-term debt. HP's self-financing policy was intended to support its human resource philosophy and policies, particularly employment security. Although employees could be fired for poor perform-ance, HP has never laid off anyone even when its profits suffered in an economic downturn.[20]

## BALANCING D1 WITH D2 AT THE TEAM LEVEL

*HP manager:* Working at HP is about feeling the responsi-bility to express your opinion. It is about contributing as an individual while at the same working in a team.

As result, there is an important value of trust and freedom at HP that employees need to work successfully as
an individual and a team member. This inherent feeling within HP makes it a very special place to work.

## BALANCING D1 WITH D2
## AT THE INTERGROUP LEVEL

*HP group manager:* We use a lot of task forces. It's an
important vehicle for getting things done. It's a way we
get along with a relatively small staff. We sometimes
call this real people involved in solving real problems.
First of all, it gets work done. As a matter of fact, it is
a very, very important part of the way we do business.
But it also gives a lot of visibility to people.[21]

## BALANCING D1 WITH D2
## AT THE INTERDIVISIONAL LEVEL

*HP Organization Manual:* The division [by a recent count
HP has fifty-eight divisions] . . . is an integrated, self-
sustaining organization with a great deal of independence. The aim is to create a working atmosphere that
encourages solving problems as close as possible to the
level where they occur. To that end, HP has striven to
keep divisions relatively small and well defined.[22]

*HP division manager:* The magic of HP is the critical
balance between being one company and being a
conglomerate. In many respects, it can't survive on
either end of the spectrum. It must accomplish the
tricky task of managing its opposites to create the
momentum that will take it into the next decade and
beyond.[23]

## BALANCING D1 WITH D2
## AT THE OVERALL FIRM LEVEL

*Pay policy:* HP managers invested considerable time and energy ensuring that an individual's pay level within their salary range reflected their performance when compared to others. Individuals whose performance was ranked in the top quartile, for example, were given larger and more frequent raises. . . . Those whose performances had declined were given small or no increases. Constant placement in the lowest quartile resulted in job counseling and quick improvement, repositioning, or involuntary termination.[24]

*Status:* The company went to great lengths to build an egalitarian atmosphere of rewards beyond salary. Executives didn't have the usual privileges of position like enclosed offices. . . . Nor did they have special executive incentive plans. All employees were on the same profit-sharing plan and all were eligible for stock options. There were no annual executive performance bonuses. . . . The share of profits was the same percentage of pay regardless of level, but no one contended that the stock options should be the same for everyone—that was a function of contribution.[25]

## BALANCING D1 WITH D4 DURING
## DOWNTURNS

*Sharing the trouble:* During the 1970 business downturn, when electronics companies across the United States were laying off employees, every HP employee took a 10 percent pay cut and worked nine out of ten days, taking every other Friday off. There were no layoffs.[26]

*Downsizing and redeployment:* During the mid-80s economic dip, downsizing was accomplished through
early retirement packages and voluntary severance
incentives. Employees with the least amount of senior-
ity were chosen for redeployment. They were given
three paid months to find another job within HP. If
they were unsuccessful at doing so, HP found one for
them anywhere in the company, if necessary at another
location and/or at lower pay. If the employees did not
accept the new job, then they would have to leave the
company with a severance package. While HP had still
been able to avoid outright layoffs, the CEO at the
time explained that HP could not guarantee never to
make layoffs. In the final analysis that depended on
individual and company performance. [HP was avoiding the excessive emphasis on D2 and D4 that contributed to the Japanese slump of the 90s.][27]

## ADJUSTING TO FOREIGN CULTURES

*Adaptability:* In the early 90s concerns by Samsung, its
joint venture partner in Korea, about HP's management practices in that country raised the question of
whether the HP Way would work in countries with
cultures and traditions very different from the U.S.
This was an important question as HP continued to
expand internationally. . . . Management in the U.S.
and Korea was persuaded that HP's core values and
objectives should and could remain in place in the
Korea subsidiary. It realized, however, that certain
management practices associated with the HP Way
would have to be compromised due to continual

rejection of them. Certain aspects of Korean business culture were accepted such as the tradition of addressing someone by their corporate title. Employee response was very positive.[28]

## EXPRESSING THE BOND HP PEOPLE FEEL WITH HP AS A WHOLE

*Corporate sales manager:* The HP Way is difficult to explain because it's woven into the fabric of our organization. It's really about the inherent feeling that you just have to do the right thing for the company, the people, and the customer. It can take the form of teamwork, respect, or even just a smile. This doesn't change at HP.[29]

*HP model maker:* I thought these people are putting me on. Why, there's not a shop in the world where someone isn't bad-mouthing the management. So it bothered me that no one was saying anything really bad about HP. I still can't say I really understand why it works, but it does. Peer pressure has something to do with it. New people with bad attitudes quickly learn that it is not acceptable to be that way at HP.[30]

*HP employee of the year:* We hear about the "HP Way" almost ad nauseam. It's sort of "truth, justice, and the HP Way." I went through a real struggle with the concept. Initially exposed to it, I thought: Boy, there's an awful lot that makes sense. But I guess I came to the point where I said this is overindoctrination. Some of it must be baloney. I've come not quite full circle but partway back to the realization that, gee, there is an awful lot that is distinctive and good in the "HP Way" that as an employee I feel grateful for.[31]

For the sixty-two years of its history HP has been required to adapt to many environmental changes. It has entered new fields such as minicomputers, desktop machines, and personal computers and peripherals. It has had to weather swings in the business cycle, the challenge of going global, enduring intensified competition, and the acceleration of product changes. The record shows that this organization has been amazingly capable of changing and adapting its business practices in response. But these necessary changes have not changed the core values that Bill and Dave laid down at the start that have become known as the HP Way. HP is an organization that fits the four-drive blueprint remarkably well—and the HP record of success provides empirical evidence of the value of the four-drive theory as a guide to organizational performance. The very recent setbacks at HP under new outside leadership make us wonder whether they are losing the HP Way. Additional rigorous research needs to be done on a larger sample of firms to adequately test this proposition.

## CORPORATE LEADERSHIP

In the last analysis the story behind the ups and downs of organizational life is one of leadership. Recent years have seen a flood of writing about leadership. This complex and often confusing literature can be clarified and simplified by seeing it all in four-drive terms. The existing literature has identified two key aspects of leadership, the instrumental and the social or charismatic. In four-drive terms, the instrumental aspect refers to acts of leadership that help others fulfill their acquiring drives (D1). The social aspect refers to acts of leadership that help others fulfill their bonding drives (D2). Four-drive theory suggests two more aspects to be added to leadership theory: acts of leadership that help others fulfill their learning drives (D3),[32] and acts that help people defend their accomplishments (D4). This last aspect of leadership needs additional comment.

Some leaders have relied heavily on the negative side of the drive to defend, using threats and inducing fear in an effort to motivate followers to obey directions. This does work, but at a price. In general it produces rote compliance—not the intelligent, eager response that can be secured from followers motivated by a combination of the other drives. On the positive side, leaders can, of course, greatly help their followers cope with outside threats. In organizations, this involves sticking up for one's subordinates, a basic part of leadership that can easily be forgotten in the contemporary business context. HP, for example, has gone to great lengths to help employees cope with economic uncertainties. It must also be recognized, however, that almost any act of leadership will inevitably involve changes that trigger some D4 defenses that will need to be addressed. Leaders would be wise, of course, to avoid ruthless acts that could trigger the extreme of the pain avoidance reflex in followers. One way of harnessing the potential energy of D4 is to rally the organization to fight the enemy outside. Leaders have employed this strategy with great success on occasion. But the energy unleashed this way is short-lived. Once the heat of the battle is over, leaders have to find a way of tapping into the three other drives to maintain a vibrant and adaptive organization.

The key lesson from GM is that when leaders cut off the opportunity of any of their firm's participants to fulfill any of the four drives, that firm is headed, in time, for trouble. More effective leadership is the kind that addresses to some degree the drive of humans to fulfill all four of the basic drives. The Japanese auto firms happened to be the first in that sector to address all four drives simultaneously, and their reward was competitive success. Belatedly, the U.S. firms are following their example. HP was the first in the emerging high-tech sector to take full advantage of that sector's special need for knowledge workers. To put it differently, if all humans are experiencing all four drives, all four will need to be addressed by leaders if they expect to have eager and responsive followers.

One way for leaders to address their followers' drive to bond needs special attention. It is by no means just the process of forming paired bonding relationships throughout the organization, although this is part of the story. The most powerful way leaders can induce bonding in others is by *their own* clear and unambiguous bonding directly to the institution itself. Do the leaders link their personal fate with that of the collective? Followers watch closely for evidence of leaders' sincerity in this regard before they make an organizational commitment themselves. When the leaders plan for the cash-out at the time of the IPO, they are clearly not providing an example of such a commitment. Such practices may well have contributed to the bursting of some of the dot-com bubbles.

A key insight growing out of the newer understanding of human nature is the role of leadership in negotiating and renegotiating the multiple social contracts the firm is a party to with its various constituencies. A recent book by Thomas Donaldson and Thomas Dunfee, *The Ties that Bind: A Social Contracts Approach to Business Ethics,*[33] provides a clear and practical guide for managers in this area. The book highlights the fact that the firm is inevitably embedded in a complex array of explicit and implicit social contracts that govern its relations with all related parties. These contracts express norms for appropriate, expected behavior between the parties. They contain promises of an ethical nature.

Donaldson and Dunfee make an important and useful distinction between two kinds of norms. On one hand, they identify the most general and universal human norms (called *hypernorms*) that are rooted in innate moral sense. These are the kind of universal morals discussed in Chapter Five and the kind that HP chose to maintain in its overseas operations. On the other hand, they identify the specific local norms that are created by all human communities. These local norms reflect local history and circumstances and hence vary greatly across institutions and cultures. These are the norms, for example, that specify where the line should be drawn between bribes, which are judged to be wrong by all cultures, and symbolic gifts of friendship. These are the types of norms that HP chose to comply with in its Korean operations. Firms that operate in multiple cultures around the globe are especially vulnerable to costly errors as they try to negotiate their way through these complex norms. But business managers are by no means powerless. They can take the initiative to open up these local social contracts and renegotiate their terms to enable the better fulfillment of the drives of all participants.

~

One additional observation about corporate leadership falls out of our four-drive analysis. Any firm that establishes social contracts that provide all participants with good opportunities to fulfill their drives will, in all likelihood, grow to dominate its industry. This could be accomplished while sticking faithfully to the rules of fair competition. But then comes the rub. Success will lead toward monopoly—which, in turn, will lead to complacency, stagnation, and, almost inevitably, some abuses of power. This is roughly what happened to GM. Think of the GM leader who felt it was necessary to convince his subordinates to stop trying to put Ford and Chrysler out of business. He apparently was so effective at this task that he created the complacency that made GM so vulnerable to Japanese competition. What choice does an effective leader have?

Our approach would suggest an organic solution: declare victory and voluntarily subdivide the firm into two or more independent firms. It could work like cell division, with management making sure that each new cell gets a full set of parts necessary for success. Who would not be a winner? The stockholders would probably benefit like those who hung onto the divided-up shares of Standard Oil and AT&T in the years immediately after their breakup. The customers would in all likelihood benefit. Employees and managers would have improved career opportunities. The government would be saved the hassle of forcing the breakup. Of course, the lawyers would lose and perhaps the incumbent CEO— but no one else. Would this not have been a wiser leadership step for GM to have taken after World War II than the course it followed, a course that has moved it from No. 1 to No. 69 in market capitalization among U.S. firms? Would it not currently be a better step for Microsoft?

# 12

# THE ROAD FORWARD

*Human nature will not change. In any future great national trial, compared with the men of this, we shall have as weak and as strong, as silly and as wise, as bad and as good.*

—ABRAHAM LINCOLN

A unified theory of human behavior must meet several demanding criteria. It must be valid across different cultural settings, simple and parsimonious, and empirically testable and falsifiable. It must work across levels of analysis from individual to societal, and it must be action-oriented (that is, *practical* in the sense of being both teachable and usable) and consilient with the findings of the various social and natural sciences, especially human biology.

To what extent does our four-drive theory meet these criteria? Have we come closer in our search for a better understanding of human nature? What are the opportunities and the obstacles that lie on the road ahead?

## IS THE THEORY UNIVERSAL?

Although human behavior is certainly greatly influenced by culture, our four drives are universal. Their roots lie in humanity's common evolutionary heritage. They are the essence of what makes people human, regardless of where they were born or the circumstances in which they grew up. The four basic drives, combined with numerous skill sets and the capacity to reason, unite all human beings—making each person in many ways the same, even as each one is in many ways different. In our reading of the anthropological literature, we could find no example of a society or culture where people did not display some measure of each of the four drives.

The tendency for people to seek status distinctions, which satisfies their drive to acquire (D1), is universal. As the sociologist Robert Michels discovered, even in the most egalitarian societies, some measure of distinction or status—the iron law of oligarchy—inevitably surfaces.[1]

As hard as it is to create a communal utopia in which everyone is equal, it is equally hard to create a true Hobbesian state in which everyone is at war with everyone else. Even in highly competitive arenas, people develop bonded relationships (D2) with some selected others and respect the mutual commitment implied by these relationships. Putnam's study of the perennial strife that has characterized the history of southern Italy shows that even in this landscape of vicious competition, there are bonds that unite people into tightly knit groups.[2]

Nor can any society stamp out the universal drive to learn (D3). Whether it was the Inquisition in the Middle Ages, the Cultural Revolution in China, or the Pol Pot regime in Cambodia, efforts to suppress the drive to learn inevitably end in failure. It is tempting to imagine that somewhere in the world there are remote societies, disconnected from modern civilization and frozen in time, where nothing has changed or been learned in centuries. However, whenever an apparently primitive society has been found, the anthropologist Claude Levi-Strauss has noted that the so-called savage mind is inevitably engaged in active bricolage—

forever seeking to learn and draw new patterns, much like our so-called civilized minds. The drive to learn is found in every society.[3]

So is the drive to defend (D4). When their property, loved ones, or beliefs are under attack, the members of even the most peaceful societies will defend themselves. This universal tendency to defend against aggression has been underscored by E. O. Wilson, who arrived at this conclusion after a comprehensive review of the available anthropological evidence.[4]

## Is the Theory Simple and Parsimonious?

Good theories must follow Occam's razor: use as few variables as you can; as many as you must. So why four drives? Why not three? Or seven? Or maybe just one? When discussing our theory with others this question invariably comes up.

Occam's rule of parsimony tempts us to reduce the number by treating one or two of the drives as derivative. The most obvious way would be to treat D2 and D3 as derivative of D1. But this would remove from our innate nature the very traits that we believe make people truly human, different from the other primates. The independence of these drives is what has created the capacity and need for conscious choice—producing the surge of adaptability that is the great competitive advantage humans have over other earthly creatures. But the term *competitive advantage* is itself now outmoded by four-drive theory. We could as accurately call it "cooperative advantage" or "learning advantage" or "defensive advantage." People need all four drives, all four directions on the human navigational compass. Let us simply call the four drives the human *adaptive advantage*.

When it comes to adding more drives, we respond that we would be glad to do so, if others can be proposed that are independent, cannot be derived from the basic four, and have a significant influence on human behavior. So far we have not thought of any drive or heard of any that meets this test. Therefore we believe the available evidence does not allow us to increase the number of drives.

We think a parsimonious set of drives is far better than a long list. We remember as a cautionary tale the drive theory that some psychologists introduced in the twenties. The original idea was to have a short list headed by such drives as hunger and sex. Then candidates for more drives came in from all directions. With no clear criteria for what constituted a drive and what constituted evidence of its existence, the list quickly expanded to a ridiculous length and the theory became useless.

## Is the Theory Testable and Falsifiable?

Defending neoclassical economics, Milton Friedman argued that it is not crucial to test the axiom that human beings are rational, self-interest-maximizing actors. What is far more important is to test the predictions that derive from this axiom. If human beings behave in ways that appear consistent with this assumption, Friedman contends, we should embrace neoclassical economics because of its brevity and predictive power.[5]

Setting aside the point that neoclassical economics has been seen to fail on tests of Friedman's assertions, we believe a valid theory should be testable both in terms of its axioms and in terms of its predictions. The axioms of our theory—that human behavior is motivated by four basic drives—can be tested because of their concrete biological basis. Human drives are rooted in the physical structure of human brains. We are not neuroscientists. But we think our argument can be verified or falsified by some imaginative experiments that employ electronic brain scanning methods to observe how the limbic center of the brain reacts to various stimuli.[6] We would expect that different parts of the brain's limbic center will record activity when the stimulus triggers the drive to acquire (perhaps with pictures of highly coveted acquisitions such as luxury cars, fine jewelry, or chocolate desserts), the drive to bond (with pictures of family and friends), the drive to learn (with abstract pattern recognition puzzles), or the drive to defend (with pictures of hazardous circumstances). That is, we would hypothesize that different modules within the limbic center of the brain will be responsible for activating and channeling the four drives we have discussed. If experiments along these lines show that the exact same area of the brain responds to all these stimuli, the independence of our four drives (or the idea that the limbic area of the brain comprises four specific drive modules) would be called into question. Moreover, if, taken together, these four types of stimuli activate only a small area of the limbic center, there would be a need to consider additional independent drives that we have not identified here. We suggest it might also be possible for evolutionary psychologists to contribute to this effort by conducting carefully designed experiments while observing the eye movements of human infants.

In addition to testing the biological micro-foundations of our four-drive theory, it is also possible to test our theory's macro-predictions. Our theory does not predict how an individual human will respond in a specific situation. In any given situation, human beings will behave in ways that attempt to reconcile the different and sometimes competing tugs of their four drives, but their final specific choice of resolution is not predictable. In some circumstances, an individual's choice may reflect only one of these drives, in others it may reflect some combination of all four drives acting in concert. Therefore, our theory allows one to talk only in terms of probabilities in regard to the prediction of the response of a specific person to a specific situation. What the theory does predict with assurance, however, is that, if observed over time, any normal individual will behave in ways that reflect all four drives.

The theory also predicts what makes individuals and social institutions more or less adaptive. In general, individuals and social institutions will enjoy an adaptive advantage to the extent that they are able to fulfill all four basic human drives. Individuals and institutions that focus on satisfying one drive to the exclusion of others will be less adaptive and fare less well than those that succeed in the pursuit of all four drives.

## DOES THE THEORY WORK ACROSS MULTIPLE LEVELS OF ANALYSIS?

In Chapter Eleven we discussed briefly how empirical studies can be devised at the organizational level of analysis to test the four-drive theory. Similar studies could also be conducted in relation to the family, the small group, the community, or the nation state. Researchers could also, for instance, look at the adaptive well-being of a panel of individuals over time. We might focus, for instance, on their mortality or their morbidity rates. In this regard four-drive theory would predict that individuals who found ways of fulfilling (at least in some reasonable measure) all four of their drives would do better than those that had managed to fulfill only one or two, even to abundance. Of course, for each level of analysis it would be necessary to select a different set of measures that captured the adaptive capacity of the chosen unit as well as the ability of the chosen unit to meet the four drives of its constituent members. In the Afterword, we go into more detail on how such studies could be designed at various levels of analysis.

In moving across levels of analysis we must be careful not to anthropomorphize social institutions. We must be wary of saying, for example, that organizations or nations have a drive to acquire or to bond. Only human beings have the four drives. Of course, to the extent they organize through social contracts into smaller or larger entities (like organizations or nation states) to pursue their drives, these larger entities will reflect these drives. Both firms and nations do make efforts to acquire desired resources. They also form bonds such as strategic alliances with other firms or nations, as the case might be. They engage in learning through investments in such areas as R&D and education. And they go to war against each other to defend themselves. It is tempting, therefore, to conclude that social institutions, at any level of analysis, have four drives analogous to the drives that people have as individuals. The difficulty with such analogies is that they require the equivalent of the human brain that is the source of the individual drives to exist at each level of analysis. Is it meaningful to talk of an organization's mind or a nation's mind? We don't think so.

Instead, we think it is more appropriate to think of institutions as being the product of social contracts among their individual members. These social contracts are ways in which human beings try to coordinate their actions with others to meet their four drives. Some social contracts work better than others do at satisfying these drives. Social contracts (and by implication social institutions) thrive to the extent that they provide their members opportunities to reasonably satisfy their four drives. They are eventually changed if they don't. Thus the viability of social contracts, at any level of analysis, can be assessed using four-drive theory even though organizations don't themselves experience human drives.

## Is the Theory Useful in Practice?

We will address this question by returning to the Russian reform example and comparing it to the reform experience in Ireland.

## The Russian Debacle

The continuing failure of Russia's reform efforts provided a strong motivation for writing this book. It gave us an urgent reason to search for a consilience among the human sciences to develop a more complete understanding of human nature. As discussed in Chapter One, the reform effort was influenced heavily by the logic of neoclassical economics. We will now consider in four-drive terms how the reform disaster unfolded, and what, if anything, could have been done differently in the light of four-drive theory.

In early 1991, the Russian people were in a state of almost total disillusionment with the overall belief system they had been taught over the preceding seventy years. They had been taught that communal sharing was the one and only true way to order social life. At the same time, they had observed the opposite extreme in practice: the exercise of totalitarian power by a police state, an extreme authority ranking system, and reliance on draconian sanctions to enforce Communist rules. The complete disconnect between ideology and practice had made Russians cynical about their government. In addition, their drive to acquire—to own even small amounts of personal property—had been systematically and utterly frustrated. They felt starved for some form of personal ownership, a modest home, a scrap of land. Their skills of dealing with one another in long-term reciprocal relations had atrophied (D2); almost all of their social relationships, other than those in their immediate families and friendship networks, were hierarchical. Furthermore, their drive to learn (D3), to engage in open discussions aimed at understanding the world around them had been systematically frustrated by severe government censorship. Russians' main preoccupation was keeping out of trouble (D4). A vast army of formal and informal enforcers—by some estimates, as much as 50 percent of the population—was engaged in monitoring and policing this extreme system. All of this had driven people into a state of continuous fear. Finally, all these distortions on the expression of their normal human drives led to the atrophy of their central skill of making reasoned choices about better ways of fulfilling all four drives in a balanced fashion.

At the institutional level, all productive assets were owned and managed by the central government. Because of this, there were virtually no laws governing market or commercial transactions or the rights of private property. Managers and collective members in the state-owned enterprises were well educated in a technical sense, but unaccustomed to making important business decisions. The only market relations were the illegal ones that managers were driven to use to secure essential supplies that were unavailable through official channels. This familiarized enterprise managers only with illegal transactions that had to be negotiated with side payments, generally bribes using government property. Superiors had to wink at these methods or the whole production system would have collapsed. This meant that there were virtually no institutions available to give people confidence in the orderly working of a totally unfamiliar market system. They had no basis for believing that a commercial contract could be relied upon or enforced through the courts. The entire country was desperately sick—in need of intensive care.[7]

In the midst of all these handicaps and deficiencies that were products of the Communist years, the greatest assets of the country were, in our counterintuitive view, the state enterprise organizations. People in these institutions had a long history of working together with mutual caring and trust. All participants, to the lowest level, thought of themselves as members, not hired hands, and felt a commitment to one another and to the organization as a whole. They had learned to collaborate with each other to overcome the chronic shortages of materials, the problems created by obsolete equipment and the lack of information about the ultimate consumer of their products. They had learned to stick together in coping with the often-arbitrary demands of the centralized government. The rank-and-file members looked to their chief executive for support and guidance, and the chief executive typically labored long and hard to fulfill this trust. The social capital the Soviet people had created in the process was one of the few assets available to help tackle the massive reformation challenges facing the country.

This is a sketch of the more problematic issues and the one major strength that faced the foreign experts who were brought in to advise the Russian leadership in 1991. With very limited knowledge of these baseline conditions, they moved quickly to introduce a virtually unrestricted market system by shock therapy. They gave first priority to privatizing the productive assets owned by the state on the assumption that—all by itself—private ownership would lead to economic growth. Given our four-drive diagnosis, the consequences in Russia were predictable.

Guided by their Western experts, the Russians in rapid sequence essentially dropped central planning, price controls, import controls, and most state ownership. They did this without having created the institutions and the social contracts that undergird the market economy in the West: the laws and norms governing commercial transactions and protecting private property rights, the banking and credit system, the market trading relationships and supply channels, and the cadre of market-trained managers. The experts taught the Russians how to issue bonds and sell them abroad but not how to invest the money wisely in value-producing assets. Assuming that the market would do the entire job, they had no plan for helping the newly privatized state enterprises change and learn how to succeed in the globally competitive marketplace. Without market-oriented laws, competencies, institutions, and established relationships, it was difficult for Russians not to be lawless. The result was a chaotic Hobbesian struggle, probably driven more by fear than greed, of each against all others. Historians report that the Russians' greatest fear has always been anarchy—and now their fears were being realized.

The biggest shock of the big bang fell on the newly privatized enterprises, now mostly owned by their old managers and employees. Rapid privatization doomed these firms to failure. The social capital they represented was wasted. They were totally incapable of coping with the sudden onslaught of competition from foreign imports. They started off in debt and quickly became hopelessly in debt—to their suppliers, their employees, and the government for any loans they successfully secured as their share of money borrowed from abroad. They were bankrupt without any relevant bankruptcy laws.

The ex-state enterprises responded to the shock by going on the defensive (D4), freezing in place without knowing what to do. To the great surprise of the outside experts they did not lay off employees. In spite of plummeting production rates and sales revenue, they retained the members of their workers' collectives to honor their moral obligations. Of course, some of the owner-managers, faced with no hope of making a profit, followed the example of those government officials who were acting as they believed any capitalist would, lining their own pockets with any liquid assets they could salvage from the wreckage. By so doing these managers broke their commitments to their workers and the social contract was destroyed. But many other managers elected to stick by their commitments and struggle, usually in vain, to save their enterprises.

Meanwhile, at the individual level, people who were starved for acquisitions turned totally opportunistic in grabbing for any available goods. People who had been powerful strove to defend their power. People who were told to start market trading undertook it with the bribery with which they were familiar. The criminal syndicate known as the Russian Mafia, which emerged in the early 1990s, was about the only institution that emerged quickly as a result of the shock. An important part of the Russian Mafia were the hastily formed private banks that were later implicated in the corrupt misuse of the funds flowing in from international agencies. A very, very few profited greatly from the turmoil. All others found their belief system in shreds, their livelihood severely curtailed, their social bonds in tatters, and themselves in as much fear as many had experienced under the Communists. Life expectancy fell dramatically. Crime rates soared. All four basic drives were threatened. Tragically, the downward spiral of the economy has not yet stopped. In 2000, Russia's GNP was about half of its 1989 level. The waste of capital—physical, social, and human—has been immense.[8] The disruption has been nearly total.

The four-drive model highlights the absolutely fundamental, massive change that was required in Russia. At the individual level, a change was required that could open up the blockages to fulfillment of their frustrated D1 and D3 drives without creating chaos. A change was required that would shift people from a heavy reliance on social relations by authority ranking (AR) with a backup of communal sharing (CS) to a primary reliance on long-term reciprocity (EM) with a backup of market pricing (MP). It required the development of an entirely unfamiliar ideology based on belief in a balanced socioeconomic system unified by a modern social contract between the people and their government. The overall conclusion would have to be that such a set of changes would at best take many, many years. People would need to be given time to learn their new roles in a totally new system. Any rational approach to such a change would have to be taken one step at a time with a carefully planned sequence and timetable.

For example, import barriers would need to be lowered slowly to give restructured local enterprises some time to get up to speed with external competition. Central planning and price controls would have to be removed slowly, one industry at a time, as each came up with a set of market-based business plans that had been at least partially implemented. This transformation effort would probably best be started in the banking and financial services sector. First, modern bank regulations would have to be enacted and a cadre of bank examiners trained to coach the banks on how to do their jobs properly, free of corruption. All these steps would be simply a buildup to the central issue of restructuring the state enterprises so as to utilize their social capital rather than destroy it. Perhaps the best way to achieve this would be to urge these large mother firms to spin off parts, by means of stock splits, that could evolve into freestanding, market-oriented businesses. Each such new firm would be designed around a promising product line. It would be staffed afresh with qualified applicants from the mother firm. It would develop a complete business plan with production, market, and finance segments. With such a plan and staff, it would be eligible for foreign and domestic credit, and perhaps for a foreign joint venture partner and coach from the same product sector. This approach could build on the strength of the bonds of the mother firm while avoiding its bureaucratic entanglements and impossible debt load. Healthy, competitive enterprises could have been created, one at a time. This general approach could, we believe, have gotten the reform effort in Russia on to a much stronger track. While clearly extremely difficult to follow, it would still have been the more promising path.

## Ireland's Achievement

During the same last decade of the twentieth century, an example of a course very like the one prescribed for Russia was unfolding in Ireland. Ireland's reform efforts were much more consistent with the precepts of four-drive theory and achieved dramatically better results.

The story of Ireland's economic and social success during the years between 1987 and 1999 has become a focus of great attention in Europe. And well it might. The basic numbers are little short of miraculous—the highest and longest rate of economic growth of any nation in postwar Europe. Here are some of the highlights:[9]

- Growth in GDP averaged over 9 percent per year from 1994 through 1998.
- In 1987 Irish income per person was two-thirds of the EU average; by 1998 this income gap was virtually closed.
- In 1987, 17 percent of the labor force was jobless; in 1999, just 6.4 percent.
- Industrial disputes decreased from more than one million days lost in 1979 to less than forty thousand in 1998.
- Employment has risen by more than a third since 1987.
- Between 1987 and 1999 the average worker's earnings after inflation increased by 58 percent.
- Immigrants outnumber emigrants for the first time in over 150 years.
- The government's annual budget went from a deficit equal to 8.6 percent of GDP in 1987 to a surplus in 1998 equal to 2.1 percent of GDP.
- Inflation averaged 2.5 percent per year from 1987 to 1998.
- With only 1 percent of the EU population, Ireland has attracted over 20 percent of its foreign direct investment capital.

How can this have happened? Ireland has been a poor performer economically as far back as records go. What has happened is nothing less than a story of the four drives at work within a renewed social contract. The immediate causes of the Irish success story turn out to be fairly obvious and simple. The mystery arises from how the Irish so consistently applied the formula. The principal ingredients of the three-year plan that was put in place in 1987 were as follows:

- Government promised to move from deficit to surplus in national budgets and to gradually reduce taxes.
- Business promised to make investments in creating new jobs.
- Unions promised to moderate wage demands and to minimize strikes.

Starting in 1987 these three simple policies were consistently pursued. At first, economic gains came slowly, but by 1993 the pace quickened. For the following five years the annual gain in GDP averaged 9 percent.

Of course, the story did not start abruptly in 1987. The foundation for economic growth was already in place. Two kinds of long-term investments had been made over a number of years by the Irish government: economic infrastructure—road and rail improvements, communication facilities, and power and water supplies—and in education.

The investment in education proved most important. In 1965 an OECD-sponsored study highlighted major shortcomings in the educational system. The report revealed serious inequalities of opportunity for children from poorer backgrounds: too few moved from primary to secondary schooling and fewer still entered higher education. Mac Sharry and White pick up the story: "So in the late sixties a long overdue reform in education began. . . . Increased public spending on education became an investment in learning and the creation of human capital. . . . Over the past three decades the continuing investment in education made by successive governments has laid the long-term foundation for part of the economic success we now enjoy."[10]

An additional critical step during the buildup to the 1987 takeoff was Ireland's decision to join the European Economic Community in 1973. EEC membership made it easier for Ireland to attract foreign direct investment as multinational firms, primarily American, could use the country as a platform for exports to the European market of 250 million people. EEC membership also made Ireland eligible for financial assistance for infrastructure improvements and also for farm price supports. The government's consistent effort to attract foreign direct investments also helped create a foundation for the takeoff. The vehicle for this purpose was the Industrial Development Authority (IDA), started in 1956. The initial inducement offered to multinationals was a period of zero taxes on profits. As time went on, the emphasis shifted to the promise of well-trained and hard-working employees, attractive building sites, a strong infrastructure, and the full support of government at all levels. Over the years, the IDA focused increasingly on high-tech firms that would commit to place more than just semiskilled assembly operations in Ireland. The target was to create skilled jobs in marketing and R&D as well. This effort has been successful, especially since the takeoff of 1987.

A final element that was essential for the takeoff was the formation, through a multiyear process, of a social partnership among the leaders of the employer associations, major unions, farmers' associations, and top government officials. During the 1970s and into the 1980s, this group held extensive meetings and, in fact, developed national wage agreements. The parties were not entirely satisfied with the results but they did develop mutual trust. A diverse group of experts reviewed the experience and recommended two important changes. First, the agreements should cover four to five years, rather than the shorter periods of earlier agreements. Second, the government should take a more assertive role in the negotiations in its dual capacity as public sector employer and as manager of the national economy. These recommendations were accepted and the Social Partners, as they became known, convened in 1986 to develop a multiyear plan.

At the time the evidence of an economic crisis was clear. Despite the benefits flowing from EEC membership, unemployment was at an all-time high of 17 percent, and employment had fallen by seventy thousand jobs in five years. At the heart of the crisis were a huge budget deficit and growing national debt. This understanding was acted on in specific detail in 1987 with the tripartite social contract listed earlier. This was the rock upon which subsequent economic growth was built. The partners stuck to their promises and conditions began to turn around. The amazing economic and social achievements of Ireland from 1987 to 1999 have been explained.

In four-drive terms, the 1987 agreement first and foremost represented a fresh bonding between Irish citizens and their national government. It was a social contract that committed all parties to cooperate for the common good. The agreement promised, if all parties cooperated, to improve the well-being of all. Business leaders agreed to invest in new job creation and to compete vigorously with one another within the framework of governmental ground rules. Unions agreed to cooperate with business within the wage and tax ground rules. Government, for its part, agreed to balance the budget and to support business development and educational opportunities for all citizens. All these pieces were carefully fitted together in a way that offered hope for the fulfillment of all four drives for Irish citizens. And it worked.

The drive to learn was explicitly addressed in the commitment to provide technically sophisticated education for all citizens and to support foreign direct investments that created jobs that called on the intellectual talents of employees. The drive to bond was implicit in the involvement of all citizens through their chosen representatives, the Social Partners, who hammered out the contract and made the binding commitments to fulfill each of their ends of the bargain. The people who prepared the plan were not explicitly guided by four-drive theory, but they acted implicitly as if they were.

## Does the Theory Promote Consilience?

One of the advantages we see in moving to the four-drive theory is the connection it forges between the social sciences and the field of biology. Starting with the four-drive building blocks enables the theory to cut across disciplinary and cultural lines. It supports multilevel analysis. It helps everyone recognize the relevance of both emotion and cognition. In this regard we would comment on the distinction some scholars make that rational behavior is only reflected in humans' efforts to meet their economic needs and that other behaviors are nonrational or even irrational. With four-drive theory this issue is made moot, since humans can accurately be described as employing their rational thinking powers to meet their drives for social bonds and for learning, as well as for acquiring and defending desired objects and experiences.

Linking to biology also helps legitimate the methods that have been fruitful in the development of biological knowledge, ones that are often different from those that have been fruitful in the physical, inorganic sciences. In developing our thinking in this regard we drew primarily on the work of Ernst Mayr.[11] For example, biologists understand at a fundamental level that they are studying emergent phenomena. Because of this, systematic historical narrative is a key scientific method for them—the basic way they have come to understand evolution and coevolution, which, of course, are at the center of our biological theories. Historical narratives are developed by fieldwork, archival work, and, recently, computer simulation.

Another example of the advantage of the strong linkage with biology comes from thinking of human development as an extension of the development of all life. If you think of the drive to acquire more broadly, as natural selection for a brain that enhances success in securing life-required resources, it is clear that humans share this drive with all forms of life that have any kind of central nervous system. If you think of the drive to bond more broadly, it is clear that humans share it with all animals that live and work in groups, even though in other mammals the bonding drive seems derivative, not independent and extended as it is in humans. If you think of the drive to learn more broadly, it does look like a drive that has more exclusively human features. It is not that other animals are incapable of learning, but it seems clear that no other animal has a brain with anything like the human representational capacity to visualize the past, present, and future; to work at multiple levels of abstract symbolization; or to exercise significant freedom of choice. When this is combined with a brain with a strong drive for bonding and related moral skills, it is fair to say that humans have truly been transformed from their primate ancestors. This is, of course, a doctrine of all major religions. This provides a scientific basis for the belief that human life is uniquely precious.

If the scientific community is to build toward the goal of the unity of all knowledge of human behavior, there will need to be movement beyond the narrow specializations of the sciences as presently constituted. All of them will need to study each other's fields to a point that will enable respectful dialogue, even as they continue to pursue knowledge in their own specialization. Each of the major disciplines seems to have a characteristic bias that will need to be adjusted in some way if they are to deliver their potential contribution toward consilience. Biologists seem to have a bias toward understating the significant differences between humans and other primates, such as in sexual and family behavior. This bias probably stems from their desire to overcome the continuing doubt among the public about the evolution of humans from primates. For their part, the inorganic sciences of physics and chemistry might need to stretch their thinking to come to respect the social sciences precisely because, in these fields, truth-seeking leads to the recognition of the limits of predictability. Sociologists seem to have an aversion to "reductionism," to working their analysis back and forth between the societal and the individual levels, and also to "functionalism," to addressing what contribution an item of social behavior might make to the survival and success of humans. These aversions could make it difficult for them to enter fully into the exploration of the biological nature of humans. Psychologists have a strong attraction to controlled laboratory experiments that are not always the most useful method for testing developmental, path-dependent theories. Anthropologists are heavily committed to an exclusively culture-driven theory of human behavior that will need to be broadened.

Perhaps economists will need to make the largest adjustments in their dominant paradigm. Modern economics is based on a largely axiomatic theory that builds off the untested assumption that all human behaviors can be explained as the sum of rational choices to maximize individual self-interest. Clearly, this axiom will need to change if economists are to move toward consilience with biology and with the other social sciences. Economists have a big investment in their present belief system, and a change of this magnitude will be difficult for them. Moreover, they have a penchant for elegant, deductive mathematical models that may be difficult to create around a multi-drive, emergent model of human behavior—and their current status as the most dominant and influential social science will not make the adjustment easier. But we are optimistic that, if the model of human nature that we have hypothesized is supported by further research, the changes will come. Certainly, if it becomes clear to economists that prescribing the limited theory of neoclassical economics to large numbers of people can at times contribute to the painful, unintended side effects seen in Russia, few will want to proceed further down that road. But we primarily believe they will join in the effort because every one of the social disciplines is essential to the creation and testing of a more complete and accurate theory of human behavior—and this, we believe, is a goal of all humans, especially social scientists.

As we said in Chapter One, for well over a century the social sciences have almost entirely neglected the question of the universal nature of the human species. The various arts have probably added more to the knowledge and understanding of human nature over this period than have any of the social sciences. Each branch of the social sciences has focused on a limited part of the puzzle, talking only among professional colleagues, the members of its own in-group. Each has treated the others more as competitors than as collaborators. This has served to stimulate a great deal of creative effort but at the cost of an unacceptable risk. The risk is of the unintended negative side effects of seriously applying any one of the incomplete theories that have been generated. Scientific ideas, like related ideological fashions, are no longer a local phenomenon. They tend to go global very quickly. The tests of these ideas occur on too large a scale to tolerate many errors. The record of the twentieth century is one of lurching from one dangerous ideological extreme to another. The record of the social sciences is not, unfortunately, all that different. For the safety of the species all practitioners need to adopt the medical dictum of "least harm" and subject social theories to a slow and painstaking process of testing before permitting their general use.

In the face of the great unknown, social scientists need to cultivate humility, avoid hubris, and strive for the consilience of knowledge. In this regard Darwin is a wonderful role model and the record of the past decade is encouraging. This book cites the work of scientists from all the major relevant disciplines who are striving toward consilience in understanding human behavior. They represent the best tradition of multidisciplinary work. Or perhaps they are the pioneers in an emerging interdisciplinary science of *human* behavior, with no modifiers. We hope our work will serve to enhance this trend.

The rule of caution should be applied as much to the four-drive theory as to any other, especially because our theory claims to be more general and more complete than others. We are very much aware that it is, inevitably, still incomplete. At its best, it shares with all human theories the hard fact that, as a mental representation (or social construction, if you will), it can only be an approximation of reality. The relevant test is not the unattainable goal of perfect accuracy but the goal of relative accuracy in comparison with other choices. But have no doubt the reality is out there, waiting to supply the ultimate test of any theory. As Winston Churchill is credited with saying, in answer to the familiar philosophic question about whether there is any reality beyond perception: "I can't answer the philosophic question but I do know for sure that, whether you perceive the sun or do not, if you fly too close to it, you will be burned to a crisp." It is much more important that our work stimulate a renewed effort by many scholars to address once again the big question of the universals of human nature than that our particular theory be accepted as the currently most useful approximation of the truth.

## Consilience Between
## the Arts and the Sciences

One of the criticisms about biological or evolutionary theories of human nature is that they are seen as inimical to the human pursuit of the arts and religion. One of the cutting-edge signs of important progress in modern times is the beginning of a convergence between science and the arts. It is of note that this developing convergence can be tied to four-drive theory. Since the time of the Great Leap, humans across all cultures have displayed a universal tendency to create and enjoy artistic works. This universality of the arts strongly suggests that artistic expression and consumption reflect latent skill sets of innate human nature. E. O. Wilson suggests that the arts derived primarily from the drive to learn.

> The dominating influence that spawned the arts was the need to impose order on the confusion caused by intelligence. . . . Because of the slowness of natural selection, there was not enough time for human heredity to cope with the vastness of new contingent possibilities revealed by high intelligence. . . . The arts filled the gap. Early humans invented them in an attempt to express and control through magic the abundance of the environment, the power of solidarity, and other forces in their lives that mattered most to survival and reproduction. The arts were the means by which these forces could be ritualized and expressed in a new, simulated reality.[12]

Consider for example some of the common themes in paintings found both in prehistoric caves and in modern museums. Artists have always chosen themes that reflect the four drives. The drive to acquire is portrayed in hunting scenes from all ages. The drive to bond is portrayed in the countless renderings of the relationship between mother and child. The drive to learn and to imagine new possibilities is always being expressed in new forms of art. And the drive to defend is plainly evident in the countless paintings of battle scenes. These images appeal to people of all backgrounds because they tap into the basic drives and the emotions they generate.

The linkage between the evolving understanding of the human brain and the arts has also begun to be explored in the arts themselves. The views of Cynthia Freeland, a professor of philosophy, are representative of this emerging consilience. "Many scholars in aesthetics agree that the 'cognitive revolution' has great consequences for our understanding of the creation, interpretation, and appreciation of artworks in all mediums. New studies of the mind, perception, emotion, and imagination will have an impact on many aspects of the investigation of art and aesthetics. And reciprocally, the experiences intrinsic to artistic creation and experience warrant serious attention from all who propose to investigate and explain the human mind."[13] To advance this dialogue, Freeland has created a center at the University of Houston devoted to cognitive science and the arts. Here are some of the research questions that this initiative hopes to tackle: Is the ability to imagine (to put oneself in the shoes of someone else) hardwired—and can this explain why autistic children have such a hard time empathizing with the experience of others? Are the emotions people experience in response to works of art evidence that humans can adapt to others in ways that add to the survival potential of the species? What cognitive, perceptual, and other skill sets are used in interpreting works of art? This field of inquiry is still in its infancy. Many more research questions will need to be posed and answered. One question that we would add is: How do the four drives influence the creation and appreciation of different forms of art? Our conjecture is that such a link exists and needs to be better understood.

## THE ROAD FORWARD

In spite of the record of human progress, in spite of the possibilities of further progress we have been exploring, the hazards from the dark side of human nature are massive and real. We cannot afford to depend on luck—or business as usual—to surmount them. It will take our very best thinking and our best concerted effort to avoid them. And we must conquer these hazards if we are to keep the door open to human progress for future generations. Our genetic heritage has given us the responsibility to choose our course in the universe. Free will is real; it is built into every individual. The challenge is to find a course forward that fulfills all of our basic drives in some creative, balanced way. It is not an answer to deny or frustrate the reality of any of the four drives. The way forward must be to use the best side of each drive to check the dark, excessive potential of human nature. Like the U.S. Constitution, we are built with checks and balances inside us. Each drive puts a sensible constraint on the others. We can use any means to fulfill our desire to acquire—as long as we do not harm others. We can go all out to help others—as long as we do justice to our own survival requirements. We can explore the unknown—as long as we respect our own safety requirements and those of others. There is no overwhelming reason why we should not be wise enough to see the way forward that leads to real progress even though the best course to follow will never be obvious.

The search for better answers needs to go on at all levels— societal, organizational, family, local community, and individual— as people struggle with the difficult choices in their lives. We are all fated by our genetic makeup to have to choose and to assume responsibility for the consequences of our choices. Even a strict authority ranking system such as a military organization does not remove the responsibility of choice from its individual members. There is no escape. At the same time, we should remind ourselves to savor the joys of our achievements in regard to all four drives. This is essentially, we believe, what Socrates was teaching when he advised that true humans should attend to the well-being of their souls. This can help everyone avoid the excessive pursuit of any one drive. And we especially need to find better ways to nurture all our children, helping them discover their unique gifts and skills that they can develop further with our help.

~

We have many reasons to be grateful that we, as members of the human species, come well equipped for these challenges. We are truly marvelous, adaptable creatures, products of an exciting and inspiring—even though often dangerous—evolutionary story, a story to be celebrated with conviction and enthusiasm even as we move on to new challenges. All four of the drives of our human nature at work in our everyday lives can, when in balance, help us find the right road forward. And finding the right road must be at the heart of the meaning, the purpose of human life. It is our destiny, based on our human nature, to *forever* seek to create, as best we can, heaven on earth and beyond. Rest assured, however, that humans will always be contentious and will never reach the boredom of complete agreement on the nature of that heaven.

# AFTERWORD
## FUTURE RESEARCH PROPOSALS

*The grand aim of all science is to cover the greatest number of*
*empirical facts by logical deduction from the smallest number*
*of hypotheses or axioms.*

—ALBERT EINSTEIN

Throughout this book, we have drawn on prior research wherever feasible to provide empirical support for our ideas. We have also used case studies, such as the extended analyses of General Motors and Hewlett-Packard or Russia and Ireland, to show how our ideas apply in specific situations. What we have not yet done is test our ideas in large-sample empirical studies. This section outlines research proposals for several such studies at various levels of analysis, to provide a starting point for future empirical research—by us and by others—that will help validate or falsify four-drive theory.

## TESTING FOUR-DRIVE THEORY AT THE INDIVIDUAL LEVEL OF ANALYSIS

We could test four-drive theory at the individual unit of analysis by studying the adaptive well-being of a panel of individuals over time. We might focus, for instance, on their mortality or morbidity rates. In this regard four-drive theory would predict that individuals who found ways of fulfilling (at least in some reasonable measure) all four of their drives would do better than those that had managed to fulfill only one or two, even to abundance. Take, for example, the Whitehall studies discussed in Chapter Four. In this study Michael Marmot and his colleagues examined the well-being of British civil servants and found that those that reached higher positions in the bureaucracy lived longer and were less likely to die of certain ailments. It would be useful to obtain data on the extent to which these individuals had formed close bonded relationships with family, friends, and others in the community (D2), had found ways to express their desire to learn through on-the-job activity, through additional reading, or through participation in the arts (D3), and had been able to defend themselves if needed through such means as the level of insurance they carried to protect themselves from various contingencies (D4). If such data could be found for the group of individuals included in the Whitehall studies or in any other longitudinal panel of individuals, we could test how well four-drive theory works at the individual level of analysis.

## TESTING FOUR-DRIVE THEORY AT THE ORGANIZATIONAL LEVEL OF ANALYSIS

A study designed to test four-drive theory at the organizational level of analysis might focus on a sample of firms drawn from a single industry or from across multiple industries. The study could be cross-sectional or longitudinal. We would use the relative profitability of firms (compared to peers in the same niche) as a measure of adaptability. This would be the dependent variable. If the study were cross-sectional, it would be important to look at average performance over a reasonable period of time (say, five years), since adaptability is inherently a dynamic construct.

The primary independent variables would be indices that captured the extent to which the firm was able to fulfill the four drives of its various constituencies. We might, for instance, use measures of wage inequality, hierarchical levels, and rates of employee mobility through these levels as measures in an index that captures the firm's ability to meet the drive to acquire. Similarly, we might use the overall intrafirm density of social ties, membership of individuals in small groups, participation of the firm in local community activities, the inverse of the average number of suppliers for any given part, and customer loyalty (repeat business) to construct an index of the firm's ability to meet the drive to bond. An index of the drive to learn could be constructed using measures such as the firm's investment in R&D, the extent to which its employees felt they had the slack to pursue their own ideas, and the number of intellectual partnerships the firm had forged with competitors, suppliers, customers, and other institutions such as universities. Finally, we could use measures of the extent to which the firm was willing to litigate to defend its interests, to delay laying off employees, to protect intellectual property, or embrace anti-takeover protections as indicators of an index of the drive to defend.

Our prediction would be that in comparable conditions each of these four indices—capturing the extent to which the firm was designed to meet each of the four basic drives—would be significant in a multiple regression model in which firm adaptability was the dependent variable. Firms that scored higher on all these indices would be more adaptive (both cross-sectionally and over time) than firms that did well on only a subset.

## TESTING FOUR-DRIVE THEORY AT THE COMMUNITY LEVEL OF ANALYSIS

In *Bowling Alone: The Collapse and Renewal of American Community*, Robert Putnam proposes a measure for the amount of social capital any given community has at a point in time.[1] Using this measure, he has calculated a Social Capital Index for each of the forty-eight U.S. continental states. In four-drive terms, Putnam's index is measuring the extent and strength of the social bonds in any community.

Using this Social Capital Index, Putnam presents the clearest, best-documented evidence of the consequences of the decline in social capital in American communities. He shows how the Social Capital Index of each state in the continental United States is correlated with general indicators of social well-being—child welfare, educational performance, violent crime, economic prosperity, general health, and the mortality rate.[2]

As impressive as Putnam's findings are, we believe four-drive theory would offer an even better explanation of a community's adaptive fitness. We could use Putnam's comprehensive index of health as an indicator of a community's adaptive fitness. We could also use other measures such as Peter Blau and Otis M. Duncan's measure of intergenerational mobility or net immigration as measures of a community's adaptability.[3] In addition to Putnam's Social Capital Index (which in our four-drive theory measures the extent to which the drive to bond is being fulfilled), we would have to develop indicators that captured a community's capacity to fulfill the drives to acquire, learn, and defend. For instance, we might use measures of income inequality, the rates of new business creation and bankruptcy, and the share of imports and exports in gross domestic product as indicators of a community's acquisition index. We could use per capita investment in education, and per capita use of public libraries, museums, and theaters as some indicators of a community's learning index. Similarly, we might use investment in policing and public safety, percentage of cases filed by public prosecutors that were successful, and rate of turnover in elected officials as indicators of a community's defense index. Our four-drive theory would predict that all four of these indices would have a significant influence on a community's adaptive fitness, and that each would enhance the model's explanatory power relative to using the Social Capital Index alone.

Though it would take some careful empirical work and probably some additional thinking to develop reliable indices for all four drives, our hypothesis is readily testable. Such a study would provide a clear way of validating four-drive theory at the community level of analysis. Notice that Putnam's measures of social capital, as well as the ones we have outlined as indices for the four drives, could easily be extended upward to nation states as the unit of analysis, or downward to cities, towns, and neighborhoods.

# Notes

## CHAPTER 1

1. Groopman, 1998.
2. Rousseau, [1762] 1987.
3. Lawrence and Vlachoutsicos, 1990.
4. See Cohen, Schwartz, and Zysmen, 1998. Also see Gray, 1998, and Puffer, McCarthy, and Naumov, 2000.
5. This criterion suggests reductionism to sociologists. We would agree that abrupt and reckless reductionism needs to be avoided, but we aspire to a careful, one-step-at-a-time reductionism that we argue is essential to building more complete explanations.
6. Consistent with biological usage, we will refer to the contemporary form of *Homo sapiens* as *modern,* as distinct from the prior variety known as *archaic.*
7. MacKinnon (1958), Dawkins (1989), and Wrangham and Peterson (1996).
8. Wilson, 1998, p. 66.

## CHAPTER 2

1. See Mayr, 1997.
2. Weiner, 1995.
3. Pinker, 1997, p. 83.
4. Weiner, 1999.
5. This example is drawn from one of the leaders of this research. See Edelman, 1992.

6. Ridley, 1993, p. 324.
7. Pinker, 1997, pp. 202–203.
8. Wilson, E. O., 1998, p. 48.
9. Damasio, 1994, p. 10.
10. Donald, 1991.
11. For a more contemporary description of how human memory works, see Schacter, 1996.
12. Diamond, 1992.
13. Deacon, 1997.

## CHAPTER 3

1. Pinker, 1997.
2. Pinker, 1997, adapted from exhibit on p. 420.
3. Marcus, Vijkayan, Bandi Rao, and Vishton, 1999.
4. Baldwin, 1902.
5. Pinker, 1997, p. 301.
6. Pinker, 1997, p. 302
7. Buss, 1999.
8. Mithen, 1996.
9. Carter, 1998, p. 182.
10. Carter, 1998, p. 182.
11. Damasio, 1994, pp. xi–xii.
12. Principally the hippocampus, the thalamus, the amygdala, and the caudate nucleus.
13. Damasio, 1994, pp. 200, 245.
14. Barkow, Cosmides, and Tooby, 1992.
15. Durham, 1991.
16. Lumsden and Wilson, 1981.
17. E. O. Wilson, 1998, p. 113.
18. Pinker, 1997, pp. 372–373.

19. Waldrop, 1993.

**CHAPTER 4**

1. The studies were conducted by Michael Marmot, an epidemiologist, along with several collaborators, in the late 1960s and the late 1980s. See Marmot, Rose, Shipley, and Hamilton, 1978, and Marmot, Davey-Smith, Stanfield, and others, 1991.

2. Frank, 1999, p. 144

3. We are grateful to one of our reviewers for highlighting this distinction.

4. Veblen, 1953 [1899].

5. Mann, 1994 [1900].

6. Freud, 1960 [1901].

7. E. O. Wilson, 1978, p. 121.

8. E. O. Wilson, 1978, p. 141.

9. Frank, 1988. Also see Elster, 1999a.

10. Frank, 1999, p. 124.

11. Frank, 1999, p. 125.

12. Frank, 1999, p. 125.

13. Elster, 1999b.

14. Beer and Nohria, 2000.

15. Kahneman, Diener, and Schwarz, 1999.

16. Burnham and Phelan, 2000, p. 118.

17. Frank, 1999.

18. Elster, 1999b, p. 74

19. Elster, 1999b, p. 12.

20. Sen, 1904.

21. Frank, 1999, p. 135.

22. Frank, 1999, p. 135.

23. Frank, 1999, p. 140.

24. Champy and Nohria, 1999. Also see Moldoveanu and Nohria, in press.

25. Ridley, 1998.

26. See E. O. Wilson, 1978, pp. 99–120.

27. Ridley, 1998, p. 46.

28. Frank, 1988, pp. 2–3.

29. Becker, 1976.

30. Marshall, 1956 [1890], p. 8.

**CHAPTER 5**

1. Bombardieri, 2000.

2. Smith, 1759, p. 47.

3. Hirschman, 1997.

4. Bateson, 1988, p. 14.

5. Baumeister and Leary, 1995.

6. Baumeister and Leary, 1995, p. 497.

7. Baumeister and Leary, 1995, p. 522.

8. Darwin, 1998 [1871], p. 111.

9. Darwin, 1998 [1871], p. 108.

10. Darwin, 1998 [1871], p. 108.

11. Bateson, 1988, pp. 14–15.

12. deWaal, 1996, p. 170.

13. Sober and Wilson, 1998.

14. Trivers, 1992, pp. 35–57.

15. Sober and Wilson, 1998, p. 171.

16. Miller, 1992.

17. This aspect of the argument has been most clearly advanced by Robert Frank (1988).

18. Hays, 1985.

19. Frank, 1999, p. 116.

20. Putnam, 1993.

21. For a complete review of this institutional process see Scott, 1995.

22. Berlin, 1990.

23. Cory, 1999.

24. See Gabarro, 1997.

25. Wright, 1994.

26. E. O. Wilson, 1998, p. 153.

27. Brown, 1991, p. 136

28. J. Q. Wilson, 1993, p. 70.

29. Kohlberg, 1981.

30. deWaal, 1996, p. 87.

31. E. O. Wilson, 1998, p. 179.

32. McGinn, 1993.

33. Wright, 1994.
34. Darwin, 1998 [1871], p. 101.
35. Searle, 1997.
36. Simon, 1991.
37. Diamond, 1992, pp. 285–286.
38. E. O. Wilson, 1998, p. 153.

## CHAPTER 6

1. Wynn, 1990.
2. See Weick (1995) for a detailed discussion of this process in organizational life.
3. See Gribbin and Gribbin, 1995.
4. Damasio, 1994, p. 245.
5. Loewenstein, 1994, p. 76.
6. Loewenstein, 1994, p. 76.
7. Loewenstein, 1994, p. 76.
8. Loewenstein, 1994, p. 77.
9. Loewenstein, 1994, p. 77.
10. Loewenstein, 1994, p. 87.
11. Festinger, 1957.
12. Deacon, 1997, p. 421.
13. Dennett, 1995; Durham, 1991.
14. Hannan and Freeman, 1977.
15. Darwin, 1998 [1871], p. 97.
16. See, for example, Miller, 1999; Hawking, 1988; and Jastrow, 1978.
17. Stevenson, 1998.
18. See Argyris and Schön (1978) and Senge (1990).
19. Lodge, 1987.
20. Plotkin, 1997.
21. Loewenstein, 1994, p. 74.
22. Loewenstein, 1994, p. 94.
23. Deacon, 1997.
24. White, 1967; Maslow, 1954; McClelland, 1961; Deci, 1980; Amabile, 1983; Bandura, 1997.
25. Rogers, 1961.
26. Hertzberg, Mausner, and Snyderman, 1959.
27. Roberti, 2001.
28. Joy, 2000.

## CHAPTER 7

1. Cosmides, 1985.
2. See Freeman, 1996.
3. One such comprehensive article appeared in the *New York Times Magazine*—see Hall, 1999. We will avail ourselves of some of his coverage.
4. LeDoux, 1991.
5. For more detail on the working of the pain avoidance reflex, see Goleman, 1995. We have also found useful insights in Michael Jensen's unpublished paper, "Nonrational Behavior, Agency Costs, and Organizations," 1995.
6. Goleman, 1995.
7. These are also the learning feedback loops described by Argyris and Schön, 1978.
8. Damasio, 1999.

## CHAPTER 8

1. For an insightful analysis of the design process, see Baldwin and Clark, 2000.
2. Kidder, 1940.
3. Darwin, 1965 [1872].
4. Plutchik, 1980.
5. Deci, 1980.
6. Deci, 1980, p. 23.
7. Deci, 1980, p. 54.
8. Deci, 1980, p. 48.
9. Gardner, 1983, p. 275.
10. Gardner, 1983, p. 102.
11. Chernow, 1998.
12. Peterson, 1999.
13. Peterson, 1999, p. 19.
14. Fiske, 1991.
15. Fiske, 1991, p. 408.
16. Murdock, 1945; Brown, 1991.
17. Malinowski, 1966 [1922].

## CHAPTER 9

1. See Gould, 1989.
2. Tattersall, 1998.
3. See Weiner, 1999.
4. Buss, 1989, p. 100.
5. Buss, 1989, p. 128.
6. Buss, 1989, p. 129.
7. Buss, 1989, p. 121.
8. Hrdy, 1981, 1999.
9. Harrell, 1997, pp. 26–30.
10. Kuper, 1994, p. 174.
11. Sober and Wilson, 1998.
12. Darwin, 1998 [1871], pp. 619–620.
13. Darwin, 1998 [1871], pp. 619–621.
14. Darwin, 1998 [1871], p. 621.
15. Deacon, 1997, p. 417
16. Deacon, 1997, p. 416.
17. The hypothesis concerning a single original human language has been proposed by several scientists but the leading linguist whose work supports the idea is Joseph Greenberg of Stanford. See Wade, 2000.

## CHAPTER 10

1. Diamond, 1992.
2. Diamond, 1992, pp. 235–236.
3. Diamond, 1992, p. 238.
4. Diamond, 1992, p. 244.
5. Diamond, 1992, p. 237.
6. Ridley, 1993.
7. Jablonski and Chaplin, 2000.
8. Boehm, 1993.
9. Lacey and Danziger, 1999, pp. 89–90.
10. Putnam, 1993.
11. Some of the most comprehensive studies on twins have been conducted at the University of Min-

nesota's Psychology Department, see http://www.cla.umn.edu/psych/psy-labs/mtfs/mtfsspec.htm. An accessible summary of the research on twins can be found in Wright, 1997.

## CHAPTER 11

1. Janis, 1982.
2. Many of the facts about the automobile industry are drawn from the chapter on the subject in Lawrence and Dyer, 1983.
3. Lawrence and Dyer, 1983, p. 56.
4. The negative reaction of assembly-line workers to their jobs is well documented. See especially Walker and Guest, 1952. Also see Turner and Lawrence, 1965.
5. Chandler, 1962.
6. Fujimoto, 2000.
7. See Lawrence and Lorsch, 1967.
8. Fukuyama, 1995.
9. Reich, 2001.
10. Beer and Rogers, 1995a, 1995b.
11. Beer and Rogers, 1995a, p. 2.
12. Beer and Rogers, 1995a, p. 6
13. Beer and Rogers, 1995a, p. 6.
14. Beer and Rogers, 1995a, p. 2.
15. Beer and Rogers, 1995a, p. 10.
16. Beer and Rogers, 1995a, p. 7.
17. Beer and Rogers, 1995a, pp. 7–8.
18. Beer and Rogers, 1995a, p. 9.
19. Beer and Rogers, 1995a, p. 7.
20. Beer and Rogers, 1995a, p. 5.
21. Beer and Rogers, 1995a, p. 9.
22. Beer and Rogers, 1995a, p. 4.
23. Beer and Rogers, 1995a, pp. 8–9.
24. Beer and Rogers, 1995a, p. 5.
25. Beer and Rogers, 1995a, p. 5.
26. Beer and Rogers, 1995b, pp. 1–2.

27. Beer and Rogers, 1995b, p. 2.

28. Beer and Rogers, 1995b, p. 2.

29. Beer and Rogers, 1995b, p. 3.

30. Beer and Rogers, 1995b, pp. 3–4.

31. Beer and Rogers, 1995b, p. 4.

32. This idea has been discussed by such scholars as Barnard, who placed the clarification of purpose as the primary function of the executive. See Barnard, 1938.

33. Donaldson and Dunfee, 1999. See also Frederick, 1995.

## CHAPTER 12

1. Michels, 1949 [1915].

2. Putnam, 1993.

3. Levi-Strauss, 1966.

4. E. O. Wilson, 1978.

5. Friedman, 1966.

6. Such studies might be pursued, for example, by the Laboratory for Affective Neuroscience at the University of Wisconsin, which for years has been studying the circuitry in the brain that gives rise to emotional states.

7. Comments on Russia are drawn primarily from Lawrence and Vlachoutsicos, 1990. Comments on more recent events are drawn primarily from Vlachoutsicos (in press), Gray (1998), and Puffer, McCarthy, and Naumov, 2000.

8. Cohen, Schwartz, and Zysmen, 1998.

9. The facts in this account are drawn primarily from Mac Sharry and White, 2000, whose authors were respectively minister of finance in the critical years 1987–1988 and managing director of the Industrial Development Authority of Ireland from 1981 to 1990. Additional information is from Sweeney, 1997.

10. Mac Sharry and White, 2000, p. 26.

11. Mayr, 1997.

12. E. O. Wilson, 1998, p. 225.

13. See Freeland's Web site at http://www.uh.edu/~cfreelan/ and the Web site for the Center for Cognitive Science, Humanities, and the Arts at http://www.hfac.uh.edu/cogsci/index.html.

## AFTERWORD

1. Putnam, 2000.

2. Putnam, 2000, p. 328.

3. Blau and Duncan, 1967.

# BIBLIOGRAPHY

Amabile, T. *The Social Psychology of Creativity.* New York: Springer-Verlag, 1983.

Argyris, C., and Schön, D. A. *Organizational Learning.* Reading, Mass.: Addison-Wesley, 1978.

Baldwin, C., and Clark, K. *Design Rules: The Power of Modularity.* Cambridge, Mass: MIT Press, 2000.

Baldwin, J. M. *Development and Evolution.* New York: Macmillan, 1902.

Bandura, A. *Self-Efficacy: The Exercise of Control.* New York: Freeman, 1997.

Barkow, J. H., Cosmides, L., and Tooby, J. *The Adapted Mind: Evolutionary Psychology and the Generation of Culture.* Oxford, England: Oxford University Press, 1992.

Barnard, C. L. *The Functions of the Executive.* Cambridge, Mass.: Harvard University Press, 1938.

Bateson, P. "The Biological Evolution of Cooperation and Trust." In D. Gambetta (ed.), *Trust.* Oxford, England: Blackwell, 1988.

Baumeister, R. F., and Leary, M. R. "The Need to Belong: Desire for Interpersonal Attachments as a Fundamental Human Motivation." *Psychological Bulletin,* 1995, *117*(3), 497–529.

Becker, G. S. *The Economic Approach to Human Behavior.* Chicago: University of Chicago Press, 1976.

Beer, M., and Nohria, N. (eds.). *Breaking the Code of Change.* Boston: Harvard Business School Press, 2000.

Beer, M., and Rogers, G. *Human Resources at Hewlett-Packard (A).* Boston: Harvard Business School Press, 1995a.

Beer, M., and Rogers, G. *Human Resources at Hewlett-Packard (B).* Boston: Harvard Business School Press, 1995b.

Bell, D. *The End of Ideology.* New York: Free Press, 1960.

Bellah, R. N., Madsen, R., Sullivan, W., Swider, A., and Tipton, S. *Habits of the Heart: Individualism and Commitment in American Life.* New York: HarperCollins, 1985.

Berlin, I. *Four Essays on Liberty.* Oxford, England: Oxford University Press, 1990.

Blau, P. M, and Duncan, O. D. *The American Occupational Structure.* New York: Wiley, 1967.

Boehm, C. "Egalitarian Society and Reverse Dominance Hierarchy." *Current Anthropology,* 1993, *34,* 227–254.

Bombardieri, M. "Diverse Parish Looks in Mirror, and Learns." *Boston Globe,* Feb. 9, 2000, p. 1.

Brown, D. E. *Human Universals.* New York: McGraw-Hill, 1991.

Burnham, T., and Phelan, J. *Mean Genes.* Cambridge, Mass.: Perseus, 2000.

Buss, D. "Sex Differences in Human Mate Preferences: Evolutionary Hypotheses Tested in 37 Cultures." *Behavioral and Brain Sciences,* 1989, *12,* 1–49.

Buss, D. "Mate Preference Mechanisms: Consequences for Partner Choice and Intrasexual Competition." In J. H. Barkow, L. Cosmides, and J. Tooby (eds.), *The Adapted Mind: Evolutionary Psychology and the Generation of Culture.* New York: Oxford University Press, 1992.

Buss, D. *Evolutionary Psychology: The New Science of the Mind.* Boston: Allyn & Bacon, 1999.

Carter, R. *Mapping the Mind.* Berkeley: University of California Press, 1998.

Champy, J., and Nohria, N. *The Arc of Ambition: Defining the Leadership Journey.* Cambridge, Mass.: Perseus, 1999.

Chandler, A. D., Jr. *Strategy and Structure.* Cambridge, Mass.: MIT Press, 1962.

Chernow, R. *Titan: The Life of John D. Rockefeller, Sr.* New York: Random House, 1998.

Cohen, S., Schwartz, A., and Zysmen, J. (eds.). *The Tunnel at the End of the Light: Privatization, Business Networks, and Economic Transformation in Russia.* Berkeley: University of California Press, 1998.

Coleman, J. *Foundations of Social Theory.* Cambridge, Mass.: Harvard University Press, 1990.

Cory, G. A., Jr. *The Reciprocal Modular Brain in Economics and Politics.* Norwell, Mass.: Kluwer, 1999.

Cosmides, L. "Deduction or Darwinian Algorithms? An Explanation of the 'Elusive' Content Effect on the Wason Selection Task." Unpublished Ph.D. dissertation, Department of Psychology, Harvard University, 1985.

Damasio, A. *Descartes' Error: Emotion, Reason, and the Human Brain.* New York: Putnam, 1994.

Damasio, A. *The Feeling of What Happens: Body and Emotion in the Making of Consciousness.* New York: Harcourt Brace, 1999.

Darwin, C. *The Expression of the Emotions in Man and Animals.* Chicago: University of Chicago Press, 1965. (Originally published 1872.)

Darwin, C. *The Descent of Man.* Amherst, New York: Prometheus Books, 1998. (Originally published 1871.)

Dawkins, R. *The Selfish Gene.* (new ed.) New York: Oxford University Press, 1989.

Deacon, T. W. *The Symbolic Species: The Co-evolution of Language and the Brain.* New York: Norton, 1997.

Deci, E. *The Psychology of Self-Determination.* Lexington, Mass.: Lexington Press, 1980.

Dennett, D. C. *Darwin's Dangerous Idea: Evolution and the Meanings of Life.* New York: Simon & Schuster, 1995.

deWaal, F. *Good Natured: The Origin of Right and Wrong in Humans and Other Animals.* Cambridge, Mass.: Harvard University Press, 1996.

Diamond, J. *The Third Chimpanzee: The Evolution and Future of the Human Animal.* New York: HarperCollins, 1992.

Diamond, J. *Guns, Germs, and Steel.* New York: Random House, 1997.

Dimaggio, P. J., and Powell, W. W. "The Iron Cage Revisited; Institutional Isomorphism and Collective Rationality in Organization Fields." *American Sociological Review,* 1983, *46,* 147–160.

Donald, M. *Origins of the Modern Mind.* Cambridge, Mass.: Harvard University Press, 1991.

Donaldson, L. *The Contingency Theory of Organizations.* Thousand Oaks, Calif.: Sage, 1999.

Donaldson, T., and Dunfee, T. *The Ties That Bind: A Social Contracts Approach to Business Ethics.* Boston: Harvard Business School Press, 1999.

Durham, W. H. *Genes, Culture, and Human Diversity.* Stanford, Calif.: Stanford University Press, 1991.

Edelman, G. M. *Bright Air, Brilliant Fire: On the Matter of the Mind.* New York: Basic Books, 1992.

Ellison, P. *On Fertile Ground: A Natural History of Human Reproduction.* Cambridge, Mass.: Harvard University Press, 2001.

Elster, J. *Alchemies of the Mind: Rationality and the Emotions.* Cambridge, England: Cambridge University Press, 1999a.

Elster, J. *Strong Feelings: Emotion, Addiction, and Human Behavior.* Cambridge, Mass.: MIT Press, 1999b.

Etzioni, A. *The Moral Dimension: Toward a New Economics.* New York: Free Press, 1988.

Etzioni, A. *The Spirit of Community.* New York: Simon & Schuster, 1993.

Festinger, L. *The Theory of Cognitive Dissonance.* Stanford, Calif.: Stanford University Press, 1957.

Fiske, A. *Structures of Social Life: The Four Elementary Forms of Human Relations.* New York: Free Press, 1991.

Frank, R. H. *Passions Within Reason.* New York: Norton, 1988.

Frank, R. H. *Luxury Fever: Why Money Fails to Satisfy in an Era of Excess.* New York: Free Press, 1999.

Frederick, W. *Values, Nature and Culture in the American Corporation.* New York: Oxford University Press, 1995.

Freeman, S. "Organizational Loss." In B. Keys and L. Dosier (eds.), *Academy of Management Best Papers Proceedings.* Madison, Wis.: Omnipress, 1996.

Friedman, M. *Essays in Positive Economics.* Chicago: University of Chicago Press, 1953.

Freud, S. *The Psychopathology of Everyday Life.* London: Hogarth, 1960. (Originally published 1901.)

Fujimoto, T. *The Evolution of a Manufacturing System.* Oxford, England: Oxford University Press, 2000.

Fukuyama, F. *Trust: The Social Virtues and the Creation of Prosperity.* New York: Free Press, 1995.

Gabarro, J. J. "The Development of Working Relationships." In J. Lorsch (ed.), *Handbook of Organizational Behavior.* Englewood Cliffs, N.J.: Prentice Hall, 1997.

Gadagkar, R., *Survival Strategies: Cooperation and Conflict in Animal Societies.* Cambridge, Mass.: Harvard University Press, 1997.

Gardner, H. *Frames of Mind: The Theory of Multiple Intelligences.* New York: Basic Books, 1983.

Goleman, D. *Emotional Intelligence.* New York: Bantam, 1995.

Gould, S. J. *Wonderful Life.* New York: Norton, 1989.

Granovetter, M. "Economic Action and Social Structure: A Theory of Embeddedness." *American Journal of Sociology,* 1985, *91,* 481–510.

Gray, J. *False Dawn.* New York: New Press, 1998.

Gribbin, M., and Gribbin, J. *On Being Human.* London: Orion, 1995.

Groopman, J. *The Measure of Our Days: A Spiritual Exploration of Illness.* New York: Penguin, 1998.

Hackman, J. R., and Oldham, G. R. *Work Redesign.* Reading, Mass.: Addison-Wesley, 1980.

Hackman, J. R. "The Design of Work Teams." In J. Lorsch (ed.), *Handbook of Organizational Behavior.* Englewood Cliffs, N.J.: Prentice Hall, 1987.

Hall, S. "Fear Itself." *New York Times Magazine,* Feb. 28, 1999, p. 42.

Hannan, M. T., and Freeman, O. H. "The Population Ecology of Organizations." *American Journal of Sociology,* 1977, *82,* 929–964.

Harrell, S. *Human Families.* Boulder, Colo.: Westview, 1997.

Hauser, M. D. *The Evolution of Communication.* Cambridge, Mass.: MIT Press, 1997.

Hawking, S. *A Brief History of Time.* New York: Bantam Books, 1988.

Hays, R. B. "A Longitudinal Study of Friendship Development." *Journal of Personality and Social Psychology,* 1985, *48*(4), 909–924.

Hertzberg, F., Mausner, B., and Snyderman, B. *The Motivation to Work.* New York: Wiley, 1959.

Hirschman, A. *Passions and the Interests.* Princeton, N.J.: Princeton University Press, 1997.

Homans, G. *The Human Group.* New York: Harcourt, Brace, 1950.

Hrdy, S. B. *The Woman That Never Evolved.* Cambridge, Mass.: Harvard University Press, 1981.

Hrdy, S. B. *Mother Nature: A History of Mothers, Infants, and Natural Selection.* New York: Pantheon Books, 1999.

Jablonski, N., and Chaplin, G. "The Evolution of Human Skin Coloration." *Journal of Human Evolution,* July 2000, pp. 57–106.

Janis, I. *Group Think.* Boston: Houghton Mifflin, 1982.

Jastrow, R. *God and the Astronomers.* New York: Norton, 1978.

Jolly, A. *Lucy's Legacy: Sex and Intelligence in Human Evolution.* Cambridge, Mass.: Harvard University Press, 1999.

Joy, B. "Why the Future Doesn't Need Us," *Wired Magazine,* April 2000.

Kahneman D., Diener, E., and Schwarz, N. (eds.). *Well-Being: The Foundations of Hedonic Psychology.* New York: Russell Sage Foundation, 1999.

Katz, D., and Kahn, R. L. *The Social Psychology of Organizations.* (2nd ed.) New York: Wiley, 1978.

Kidder, A. V. "Looking Backward." *Proceedings of the American Philosophical Society,* 1940, *83*, 527–37.

Kohlberg, L. *The Philosophy of Moral Development.* San Francisco: Harper-Collins, 1981.

Kuper, A. *The Chosen Primate: Human Nature and Cultural Diversity.* Cambridge, Mass.: Harvard University Press, 1994.

Lacey, R., and Danziger, D. *The Year 1000.* Boston: Little Brown, 1999.

Langer, E. J. *Mindfulness.* Reading, Mass.: Addison-Wesley, 1989.

Lawrence, P. R. *The Changing of Organizational Behavior Patterns.* Boston: Division of Research, Harvard Business School, 1958.

Lawrence, P. R., and Dyer, D. *Renewing American Industry.* New York: Free Press, 1983.

Lawrence, P. R., and Lorsch, J. *Organization and Environment: Managing Differentiation and Integration.* Boston: Harvard Business School Press, 1967.

Lawrence, P. R., and Vlachoutsicos, C. (eds.). *Behind the Factory Walls: Decision-Making in Soviet and American Enterprises.* Boston: Harvard Business School Press, 1990.

LeDoux, J. *The Emotional Brain.* New York: Simon & Schuster, 1991.

Levi-Strauss, C. *The Savage Mind.* Chicago: University of Chicago Press, 1966.

Lodge, G. *Ideology and National Competitiveness.* Boston: Harvard Business School Press, 1987.

Loewenstein, G. "The Psychology of Curiosity: A Review and Reinterpretation." *Psychological Bulletin,* 1994, *116*(1), 75–98.

Lombard, G.F.F. *Behavior in a Selling Group.* Boston: Division of Research, Harvard Business School, 1955.

Lumsden, C. J., and Wilson, E. O. *Genes, Mind, and Culture: The Coevolutionary Process.* Cambridge, Mass.: Harvard University Press, 1981.

MacKinnon, J. *The Ape Within Us.* New York: Holt, Rinehart & Winston, 1958.

Mac Sharry, R., and White, P. *The Making of the Celtic Tiger: The Inside Story of Ireland's Boom Economy.* Cork, Ireland: Mercier Press, 2000.

Malinowski, B. *Argonauts of the Western Pacific.* New York: Dutton, 1966. (Originally published 1922.)

Mann, T. *Buddenbrooks: The Decline of a Family* (John E. Woods, trans.). New York: Vintage International, 1994. (German edition originally published 1900.)

Marcus, G., Vijkayan, S., Bandi Rao, S., and Vishton, P. "Rule Learning by Seven-Month-Old Infants." *Science,* 1999, *283,* 77–80.

Marmot, M., Rose, G., Shipley, M., and Hamilton, P.T.S. "Employment Grade and Coronary Heart Disease." *British Medical Journal,* 1978, *2,* 1109–1112.

Marmot, M., Davey-Smith, G., Stanfield, S., and others. "Health Inequalities Among British Civil Servants: The Whitehall II Studies." *Lancet,* 1991, *337,* 1387–1393.

Marshall, A. *Principles of Economics.* London: Macmillan, 1956. (Originally published 1890.)

Maslow, A. H. *Motivation and Personality.* New York: HarperCollins, 1954.

Mayo, E. *The Human Problems of an Industrial Civilization.* New York: Macmillan, 1933.

Mayo, E. *The Social Problems of an Industrial Civilization.* Boston: Division of Research, Harvard Business School, 1945.

Mayo, E. *The Political Problems of an Industrial Civilization.* Boston: Division of Research, Harvard Business School, 1946.

Mayr, E. *This Is Biology.* Cambridge, Mass.: Harvard University Press, 1997.

McClelland, D. C. *The Achieving Society.* Princeton, N.J.: Van Nostrand, 1961.

McGinn, C. "In and Out of the Mind" (review of Hilary Putnam, *Renewing Philosophy*). *London Review of Books,* Dec. 2, 1993, pp. 339–402.

Michels, R. *Political Parties: A Sociological Study of the Oligarchical Tendencies of Modern Democracy.* New York: Free Press, 1949. (Originally published 1915.)

Miller, G. F. "Sexual Selection for Protean Expressiveness: A New Model of Hominid Encephalization." Paper delivered to the Human Behavior and Evolution Society, Albuquerque, New Mexico, July 22–26, 1992.

Miller, K. *Finding Darwin's God.* New York: HarperCollins, 1999.

Mintzberg, H. *The Structuring of Organizations.* Englewood Cliffs, N.J.: Prentice Hall, 1979.

Mithen, S. *The Prehistory of the Mind: The Cognitive Origins of Art, Religion, and Science.* London: Thames & Hudson, 1996.

Moldoveanu, M., and Nohria, N. *The Master Passions.* Cambridge, Mass.: MIT Press, in press.

Moss, C. *Elephant Memories.* New York: Morrow, 1988.

Murdock, G. P. "The Common Denominator of Cultures." In R. Linton (ed.), *The Science of Man in the World Crisis.* New York: Columbia University Press, 1945.

Nohria, N., and Ghoshal, S. *The Differentiated Network: Organizing Multinational Corporations for Value Creation.* Boston: Harvard Business School Press, 1997.

Peterson, J. B. *Maps of Meaning: The Architecture of Belief.* New York: Routledge, 1999.

Pfeffer, J. *The Human Equation: Building Profits by Putting People First.* Boston, Harvard Business School Press, 1998.

Pfeffer, J., and Salancik, G. R. *The External Control of Organizations.* New York: HarperCollins, 1978.

Pinker, S. *The Language Instinct: How the Mind Creates Language.* New York: HarperCollins, 1994.

Pinker, S. *How the Mind Works.* New York: Norton, 1997.

Plotkin, H. *Darwin Machines and the Nature of Knowledge.* Cambridge, Mass.: Harvard University Press, 1997.

Plutchik R. *Emotion: A Psycho-Evolutionary Synthesis.* New York: Harper-Collins, 1980.

Puffer, S., McCarthy, D. J., and Naumov, A. *The Russian Capitalist Experiment: From State-Owned Organizations to Entrepreneurships.* Cheltenham, England: Elgar, 2000.

Putnam, R. K. *Making Democracy Work: Civic Traditions in Modern Italy.* Princeton, N.J.: Princeton University Press, 1993.

Putnam, R. *Bowling Alone: The Collapse and Renewal of American Community.* New York: Simon & Schuster, 2000.

Reich, R. *The Future of Success.* New York: Knopf, 2001.

Ridley, M. *The Red Queen: Sex and the Evolution of Human Nature.* New York: Penguin Books, 1993.

Ridley, M. *The Origins of Virtue: Human Instincts and the Evolution of Cooperation.* New York: Penguin Books, 1998.

Roberti, M. "General Electric's Spin Machine," *Industry Standard,* Jan. 22–29, 2001.

Roethlisberger, F. J., and Dickson, W. J. *Management and the Worker.* Cambridge, Mass.: Harvard University Press, 1939.

Rogers, C. *Becoming a Person.* Boston: Houghton Mifflin, 1961.

Ronken, H., and Lawrence, P. *Administering Changes.* Boston: Division of Research, Harvard Business School, 1952.

Rousseau, J-J. *The Social Contract.* New York: Penguin Classics, 1987. (Originally published 1762.)

Schacter, D. L. *Searching for Memory.* New York: Basic Books, 1996.

Scott, R. *Institutions and Organizations.* London: Sage, 1995.

Searle, J. R. *The Construction of Social Reality.* New York: Free Press, 1997.

Sen, A. *Poverty and Famines: An Essay on Entitlement and Deprivation.* London: Oxford University Press, 1904.

Senge, P. M. *The Fifth Discipline: The Art and Practice of the Learning Organization.* New York: Doubleday, 1990.

Simon, H. "Organizations and Markets." *Journal of Economic Perspectives,* 1991, *5*(2), 34–38.

Smith, A. *The Theory of Moral Sentiments.* London: Millar, Kincaid & Bell, 1759.

Sober, E., and Wilson, D. S. *Unto Others: The Evolution and Psychology of Unselfish Behavior.* Cambridge, Mass.: Harvard University Press, 1998.

Stevenson, H. *Do Lunch or Be Lunch.* Boston: Harvard Business School Press, 1998.

Sweeney, P. *The Celtic Tiger: Ireland's Economic Miracle Explained.* Dublin: Oaktree Press, 1997.

Tattersall, I. *Becoming Human: Evolution and Human Uniqueness.* New York: Harcourt Brace, 1998.

Thompson, J. D. *Organizations in Action.* New York: Free Press, 1967.

Trivers, E. "The Evolution of Reciprocal Altruism," *Quarterly Review of Biology,* 1992, *46,* 35–57.

Turner, A., and Lawrence, P. *Industrial Jobs and the Worker: An Investigation of Response to Task Attributes.* Boston: Division of Research, Harvard Business School, 1965.

Veblen, T. *The Theory of the Leisure Class.* New York: Mentor, 1953. (Originally published 1899.)

Vlachoutsicos, C. "Russian Communitarianism: An Invisible Fist in the Transformation Process." Ann Arbor, Mich.: Davidson Institute, in press.

Wade, N. "Scientist at Work: Joseph H. Greenberg; What We All Spoke When the World Was Young," *New York Times,* Feb. 1, 2000, p. D1.

Waldrop, M. *Complexity: The Emerging Science at the Edge of Order and Chaos.* New York: Simon & Schuster, 1993.

Walker, C. R., and Guest, R. H. *The Man of the Assembly Line.* Cambridge, Mass.: Harvard University Press, 1952.

Weick, K. *Sense-Making in Organizations.* Thousand Oaks, Calif.: Sage, 1995.

Weiner, J. *The Beak of the Finch: A Story of Evolution in Our Time.* New York: Random House, 1995.

Weiner, J. *Time, Love, Memory: A Great Biologist and His Quest for the Origin of Behavior.* New York: Knopf, 1999.

White, R. W. "Competence and the Growth of Personality," *Science and Psychoanalysis,* 1967, *11,* 42–58.

Williamson, O. *Markets and Hierarchies.* New York: Free Press, 1975.

Wilson, E. O. *On Human Nature.* Cambridge, Mass.: Harvard University Press, 1978.

Wilson, E. O. *In Search of Nature.* Washington, D.C.: Island Press, 1996.

Wilson, E. O. *Consilience: The Unity of Knowledge.* New York: Knopf, 1998.

Wilson, J. Q. *The Moral Sense.* New York: Free Press, 1993.

Wilson, M., and Daly, M. "The Man Who Mistook His Wife for a Chattel." In J. H. Barkow, L. Cosmides, and J. Tooby, *The Adapted Mind: Evolutionary Psychology and the Generation of Culture.* Oxford, England: Oxford University Press, 1992.

Wrangham, R., and Peterson, D. *Demonic Males: Apes and the Origins of Human Violence.* Boston: Houghton Mifflin, 1996.

Wrangham, R., McGrew, W., deWaal, F., and Heltne, P. (eds.). *Chimpanzee Cultures.* Cambridge Mass.: Harvard University Press, 1994.

Wright, L. *Twins: And What They Tell Us About Who We Are.* New York, Wiley, 1997.

Wright, R. *The Moral Animal: The Way We Are.* New York: Vintage Books, 1994.

Wynn, K. "Children's Understanding of Counting." *Cognition,* 1990, *36,* 155–193.

# INDEX